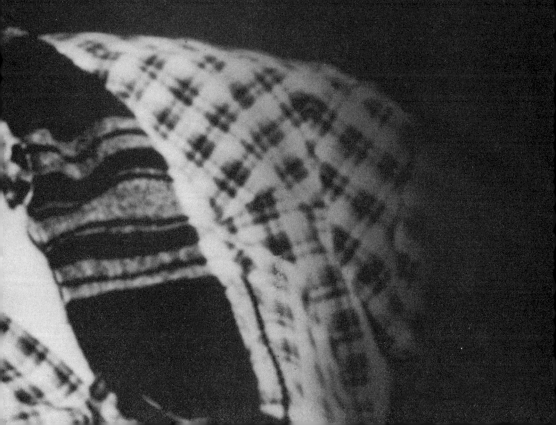

LOVE
IS COLDER
THAN
DEATH

LOVE
IS COLDER
THAN
DEATH

THE LIFE AND TIMES OF

RAINER
WERNER
FASSBINDER

ROBERT KATZ

RANDOM HOUSE ▫ NEW YORK

Library of Congress Cataloging-in-Publication Data

Katz, Robert, 1933–
Love is colder than death.

1. Fassbinder, Rainer Werner, 1946–
2. Moving-picture producers and directors—Germany
(West)—Biography. I. Title.
PN1998.A3F27445   1986   791.43'0233'0924   [B]
86-11896
ISBN 0-394-53456-5

Manufactured in the United States of America
24689753

First Edition

Typography and Binding Design
By Barbara M. Bachman

TO
THE
MEMORY
OF
PETER
CHATEL

CONTENTS

AUTHOR'S NOTE

LOVE IS COLDER THAN DEATH is an exemplar of those books which could not have been written without the collaboration of another person. Peter Berling is the man who personally introduced me to Rainer Werner Fassbinder and his world. Elsewhere (beginning with p. xviii), I present Berling's credentials as a supremely authoritative Fassbinder-watcher—at just enough distance to lend a true-blue perspective to his observations—but here, at the very outset, I would like to emphasize his contribution to the work as a whole.

When, three or four months after Fassbinder's death, I began to pursue the rather wild-eyed idea of tackling this subject and just as quickly lost my way in a Schwarzwald whose trails I knew only naïvely, Berling came to the kind of rescue you start praying for as the wolves come out of their den. Not only did he guide me around in that dark forest, but he provided a rich lode of firsthand information that covered the entire span of Fassbinder's career. An inveterate archivist by nature, he has a file on the Fassbinder years that ranges from taxi receipts and restaurant menus (including what everyone ate) dating back to 1965 to diaries and memoirs bristling with both insight and minutiae. I owe him much. On the other hand, I alone am responsible for the story as finally told here, so if I've got something wrong or wrong-headed—and experience tells me you can't ever get home free—I, neither Berling nor anyone else, am the one to blame.

FOREWORD

I WANTED TO MAKE
THEM ANGRY, AS
ANGRY AS I WAS.
—R W F

'D taken a red-eye express train to arrive not too late for a brunch given by the German film industry at the Majestic, a money-man's hotel across the street from the old casino. I was on a mission for some high-rolling producers who had been talking eight figures—and for myself: to persuade Fassbinder to let me write *Rosa L.,* his "biggest, most important film," which was how it was being sold at Cannes. I'd worked with him the year before, and the high-rollers thought it would be good business to get us together again. Me too. It was champagne and caviar for starters, and the party, if not officially in Fassbinder's honor, was certainly in what I'd learned was his style; he was the main attraction, surrounded.

A cigarette dangled from his lips. Smoke smarted his eyes. He was holding a mug of beer. He was wearing his usual summer outfit—leather vest and loose-fitting cottons—and, as usual, he looked as if he'd slept in it, which he probably had. He seemed terribly annoyed. He was flicking his free hand at the wrist, the way you'd shake muck from your fingers, complaining to anyone around him who'd listen, and everyone around him listened. This, aside from some moments of genius in his films, was becoming the predominant image I had of him: a man surrounded, irascible, whining, enveloped in smoke and the smell of beer.

"Herr Katz," he said when he saw me, "you must speak to me in

xiii

German," though he knew English well and I had told him I was a *Dummkopf* in German (he was convinced that I had always lied about this). He offered me a seat at his table. It was almost a good beginning.

I was at his table for the next two days, getting nowhere: his table on the Carlton terrace, his table at the Martinez beach club, his table at the great fish place La Coquille, his table at the Petite Carlton Bar, which was not a table but half the bar. We were hardly ever fewer than a rambunctious crowd of actors, producers, critics, writers, held together by a seductive aura—expensive wine, and the comings and goings of professional sexual objects. There was something for everyone.

I doubt whether any of us remembers much of what we talked about—certainly there was not a word about my working on *Rosa*. All I retain are scatterings of loose conversation, a dark feeling that lives we touched were in some way scuffed, and an indelible impression of Fassbinder going on thrity-seven, with a fire under his skin, on top of the film world and no place to go but higher. He'd just finished *Querelle,* his forty-third film, one motion picture every hundred days for the past thirteen years. That's an industry unto itself, and it wasn't the half of it. He'd produced, written, and cut almost all of his films, and he had acted in and done the camerawork for many. That's prodigious efficiency. He'd made a lot of money for a lot of people, including himself. He had also created art. There was much to celebrate, though he continued to behave as though the world had done him wrong.

"Und *Rosa L.* mach' ich mit der Jane Fonda," he said in a light moment. His eyes beamed. "Jawohl, Jane ist richtig für die *Rosa L.,* das gefällt mir gut!" He was going to get Jane Fonda to play Rosa (no one doubted that he could) and I was *not* going to write it! Later, Fonda called from Los Angeles. One of the producers had arranged it. Fassbinder had never met her, and vice versa. To *her,* he spoke English. Mostly, he listened. Everyone strained an ear. "Jane, we love you," he said. He hung up. What'd she say, Rainer? He looked very taken. "She said, 'This is Jane Fonda herself.' " The next day, whoever got Rainer on the phone heard him answer, "This is Fassbinder himself." In English.

That was about the only talk of *Rosa L.* I was not going to win him over and I grew less sure by the hour that I wanted to. I couldn't keep pace with the group, with the sleepless, orgiastic abuses of the body, Fassbinder the most profligate of all. I knew he was going to die young and I told him so. "I've got five years," he said, as though five years was forever. "Most people are already dead."

Cannes, as always, was in May, and by June I'd given up on the project. But on Friday the fourth of June I got a call from Germany at my home in Tuscany. Fassbinder wanted me to write his next film. Shooting would start in October. A remake of Joan Crawford's *Possessed*. Could we meet in Munich on Monday?

"Whatever happened to *Rosa*?"

"That's February. You want to do *Possessed*?"

"Let's talk in Munich."

I couldn't book a flight for Monday. Holiday weekend and all that. I could do no better than Thursday. Fassbinder never woke up on Thursday. I went to his funeral instead.

It was the damnedest funeral you ever saw—no priests, no eulogies, and, secretly, no corpse in the coffin (the authorities were still working over the body, looking for drugs, even inside his skull; needless to say, they found plenty). Just the group, from the inner to the outer circles, about a hundred Fassbinder people, as they were called derisively by the press, with the connotation that they were all perennially stoned. Some were, gathered with the rest of us around the empty coffin to make it look good on-camera, which was rather impossible, given the departed's public image. His notorious life-style had grated on West German sensibilities for a decade, and his death seemed the wages of sin. We stood. We listened to a solid ninety minutes of Fassbinder movie music: Vangelis, Leonard Cohen, Elvis, The Platters, some hard rock, and the theme from *Lili Marleen*. It was tough on the feet, and after Hanna Schygulla read a poem, attendance began to fall off. We ended up at the Deutsche Eiche, his place, a gay bar. We were served beer and Weisswürstchen, a Bavarian breakfast sausage made of veal. There was no champagne and beluga; Fassbinder would have turned over in his grave if he'd had one.

The most beautiful people of the New German Cinema lit up the room—the mood was never somber, and by noon it was suddenly one helluva party. It was packed, smoky. The waiters, squeezing through, spilled beer on your shoulders. The producers, irresistibly, began wheeling and dealing. The stars struck poses for the picture magazines. Irreverent, of course, but somehow apropos. I thought of the first time I'd met him, after the world premiere of *Lola*. He'd thrown the most lavish party I'd ever been to, Hollywood A parties included. Now, even with only hot dogs and brew, he was going out in a celebration of his own style. In the meantime, his body had been released from the morgue, and Rainer Werner Fassbinder was burning. What kind of a star was this, I thought, that had burned out so young and so incandescently?

Later that summer the woman who may or may not be Fassbinder's widow came to visit with me for a while. Tall and severe, Juliane Lorenz had lived with him in the later years in his spacious apartment in the Clemensstrasse in Munich. She had cut all his films since *The Marriage of Maria Braun* and had played small parts in some of them. She had also made his appointments, cooked for him, dressed him, and discovered his corpse with a cigarette butt in his right hand. Once, she says, in Florida Rainer and she decided to marry on a whim. They went to a justice of the peace, the way it was done in an American movie, and, after haggling about their passports and a blood test, he pronounced them man and wife, but all too soon it was a whim forgotten, at least by the groom, and the bride knew better than to remind him. Fassbinder, though he already had an ex-wife, was not the marrying kind.

I really didn't know Juliane very well. She'd always been a buffer between Fassbinder and me, but I was quite pleased to receive her. She had come down to my place in the country from the Venice Film Festival. She was tired, cross, and tense. Venice had been heavily weighted that year to render homage to Fassbinder, but things had not gone well. *Querelle* had been selected for the main competition, and the film I'd written for him, *Kamikaze '89*, was shown but was not in the running. Insiders had predicted that *Querelle* would win the Gold Lion handily; instead it caused a row and an unmendable split in the jury and it didn't take the prize. Two documentaries had also been presented, about the making of both films, and Juliane had tried and failed to get a court order to prevent the showing of one of them. It contained a long interview with Fassbinder, filmed in his Munich apartment a few hours before his death, and he appeared on the screen unnaturally subdued and spent.

"He'd never have let them show it, and they wouldn't have dared disobey him," said Juliane as I poured her a glass of chilled wine, hoping it might relax her. To make matters worse, she told me, an "unauthorized" death mask of Fassbinder had been circulating clandestinely at Venice, making the rounds of cafés and hotel lobbies in a plastic shopping bag. By a curious coincidence, she explained, Fassbinder had had an appointment on the day of his death to sit for a portrait by Karin Mai, a German sculptress known for her busts of celebrities. When she arrived with her clay in a bucket at the Clemensstrasse, her subject was on the way to the morgue, but she was commissioned to do a death mask. It had been Juliane's own idea, her intentions having been as noble as those that accompanied the making of Goethe's mask, which was why the "ghouls of Venice," as she called them, had so upset her. She had even tried to burglarize the $300-a-day suite at the Lido where she thought the pirated copy was being kept at night, but after she'd broken in, she couldn't find it.

"He was so good," she said when the wine and the sun had finally warmed her. "No one but me knows how good he was."

Apart from the rave reviews of his films, I realized, I'd never before heard anyone say something unqualifiedly nice about Fassbinder. I knew he had been loved and even worshiped by men and women, but every love had ended badly. Juliane began to recall some of those very episodes, but she was speaking of a saint, not the monster some said he had become in the end.

"They're all betraying him now," said Juliane, "now that he can't get them work. All his 'friends,' telling lies and gossip to the highest bidder." I knew she was referring to the books being written and the interviews being given by Fassbinder's ex-lovers. "You should write a book," she said more or less out of the blue. "You didn't know him enough to hate him, certainly not enough to love him." She eased back in her deck chair and closed her eyes. She ran the rim of her wine glass along her forehead. A smile crossed her lips.

xvii

. . .

Over the next few years, our house in the country became somewhat of a wayside place where a Fassbinder person on the road
would stop for a while for refreshment and perhaps to reminisce. I
was struck not only by their frequently disarming candor (only
Hanna Schygulla, true to form, remained aloof), but, at a certain
point, by the realization that they had undoubtedly inherited this
quality from Rainer, who would reveal any intimacy he knew, the
darker the better.

Peter Berling cannot himself be called a Fassbinder person, though
he knew him longer and in many ways more intimately than any of
the most confirmed FP's. One balmy evening, after a bountiful grill
and enough red wine to add five pounds to his three hundred, he told
the story of his first meeting with Fassbinder:

"In those days [1966], I was the king of short movies in Germany.
I'd produced over fifty premiered short movies, and all the young
directors worked with me. One day, this girl walked into my office
and said, 'I'm an agent. I represent young, talented people, un-
knowns but big talents. You must help them.' She showed me some
photos and someone stood out because he was so ugly and pockmarked, a pickle face, as we say in Germany. So I said, 'Who is this
ugly guy?' 'This is Rainer Werner Fassbinder,' she said with some
reverence. 'Never heard of him,' said I, 'and I don't want to make
movies with him.' I sent her away, but she came again and again, and
we struck up a kind of friendship. It was the kind in which she always
asked me to give some money, which I didn't, to finish two short
movies he'd started but couldn't complete.

"Then, one night, I was drunk in a bar and I was thinking I wanted
company, so I dragged out my little telephone book and I literally
fell on her name. I called her and said, 'Okay, I'll come by and see
you.' She said, 'Oh, yes, please come.' So I staggered over there and
the next thing I knew it was morning, around eightish, and she was
leaving, telling me to slam the door on the way out. I slept for a while
longer and woke suddenly to the sound of a key in the lock, and there
was this pickle face I'd seen in the photo. I said, 'Hello,' and he said,
'Hello,' very shyly, and I said, 'I can't get up to greet you because
I'm naked, so I prefer to stay under the covers.' 'Think nothing of

it,' said he. 'I just want to get a pair of pants out of my fiancée's closet.' So he did, and he left.

"We never spoke of it until much later. Funny, not until this year at Cannes. 'Oh, yeah,' Rainer said, barely remembering. 'I slapped her around for that one.' "

Everyone at the table laughed; looking back, though, it struck me that that was the first time I heard mention of violence. Violence and sex, some of it truly perverse, were often the leitmotifs of Fassbinder table talk and somehow, I began to discern, were always related to Fassbinder's psychic and creative powers.

"The most important thing for Rainer," Peter Berling told me, "was to surround himself with people who needed him for their own survival. He disliked anyone who, after the day's work was done, went home to a private life. From the very beginning he wanted to create a 'family,' something he himself never had. He had to be master of all living things in his reach, and the set, the film set, gave him the possibility. Making one film after another was the method. Everybody knew that if he pleased Rainer he would be in the next movie, and the start of the next movie was only a few weeks away. If his films had been spaced a year or a year and a half apart, which is normal, he could never have exercised the same power over people, and when there were periods when his pace slowed—and there were a few—people began to drift away and he became desperate, lavishing favors for their company only to seek revenge in return."

Daniel Schmid, a film director known as "the Aunt" in the Fassbinder crowd, had quite a different analysis. He said, "Rainer Werner Fassbinder wanted to be Marilyn Monroe. No one else. He wanted to walk down a staircase wearing feathers and a gown. He died the same age as she did, the same way as she."

I came away from these and other encounters with a vivid but incomplete picture of Rainer Werner Fassbinder. It hung in a gallery of my mind along with impressionistic images of other famous over-achievers of fact and fiction. There was an obvious common denominator looking back at me, but with a difference that set Fassbinder apart from a lot of the others: he had used the gift—the ability to harness the inchoate energy of one's place and time—to create beauty. The how and the why of it all seemed worthy of further pursuit.

xix

In the process, the shadows that lay across my Fassbinder picture began to lighten and facets of his persona hitherto obscured came into relief. They filled in part of what I'd set out to look for, but not all. On the other hand, I suddenly had rather more than I'd bargained for. Thus what follows is as much a story of one man's life making movies as it is a picture of a few very lively members of the first homegrown generation after Hitler's war.

R. K.
Pieve a Presciano
December 1986

CAST OF MAIN CHARACTERS

(in order of their appearance in the life of RWF)

MOTHER FASSBINDER (Liselotte)

Aka Lilo Eder, Lilo Pempeit. RWF will make her an actress, a feature player in many of his films, but he will never forgive her for having "force-fed" him raw apples as a child.

FATHER FASSBINDER (Hellmuth)

Physician, illegal abortionist, poetaster, and slumlord. RWF, abandoned by Hellmuth at the age of six, will in later life refuse to return his phone calls (mostly pleas for money).

THE STEPFATHER (Wolf Eder)

Journalist and would-be novelist. RWF's Great Despiser, from the moment the younger man brought home a transvestite to the day of the older man's death.

UDO KIER

Aka Dodo. Actor. RWF's first real friend. As adolescents they are a team: Dodo a male prostitute, RWF his pimp.

MICHAEL FENGLER

RWF's mentor, business partner, enemy, in that order. Fengler will say that RWF was just "a bad, bad guy." RWF will make him rich.

CHRISTOPH ROSER

Out-of-work actor. RWF's first live-together friend. Roser has a secret bank account, and when RWF discovers it, he will make his friend a producer—of his first two films.

HANNA SCHYGULLA
"Europe's most exciting actress" (says a 1985 *Time* cover story). RWF will meet her in acting school and make her a star, because, he will say later, "you know, she has the body; it's very useful for filming."

IRM HERMANN
Secretary-turned-actress, thanks to RWF. Her love for him will transcend abysmal rejection. He will call her a "born victim" and make her jealous rages famous on and off the screen.

DANIEL SCHMID
Aka the Aunt. Director. Another victim of love at first sight, he will live in RWF's shadow and become a master of the biting mot juste.

KURT RAAB
Aka Emma Potato. Actor, production designer. "My best girl-friend," said RWF; Kurt will rise from obscurity to national prominence, only to become RWF's domestic factotum in never-ending ménages à trois.

PEER RABEN
Aka Willi. Actor, director, composer. He will be one of the "trois" for a while, then rise and fall from grace according to the whims of his master.

URSULA STRAETZ
Theater owner, actress, painter. She will give RWF his start in the theater and fall hopelessly, madly in love with him. Her countless paintings will depict one subject only: RWF.

ULLI LOMMEL
Actor, director. As a handsome, dashing young blade of Fassbinder films, he will call RWF "a bit like God the Father," though his career will recede as fast as his hairline.

PETER CHATEL

Aka La Schletelle, "my second-best girlfriend." Actor, director. A "fashion queen" who will become "the only one who didn't freak out," according to RWF.

INGRID CAVEN

Actress, chanteuse. She will marry RWF and will try to make him a heterosexual, at least until the wedding night.

HARRY BAER

Aka Ilse Lo Zott. Actor. Perennial "artistic consultant" for RWF films. He was "too beautiful" to work in an office. RWF had a part for him.

GÜNTHER KAUFMANN

Aka "my Bavarian Negro." Seaman-turned-actor. The first of RWF's three great loves. He will wreck four Lamborghinis.

EL HEDI BEN SALEM

The second great love. Prostitute-turned-actor. His passion will turn homicidal.

ARMIN MEIER

The third great love. Butcher-turned-actor. His passion will turn suicidal.

DIETER SCHIDOR

Aka Kitty Babuffke. Actor, producer. He will have the distinction of being RWF's "archenemy," later becoming one of his closest intimates.

ISOLDE BARTH

Actress. RWF will mesmerize her, give her a chance to be a producer as well as to have a nervous breakdown.

JULIANE LORENZ

Film editor. A teenager in the RWF era, she will grow up to become the second Mrs. Fassbinder, in a way.

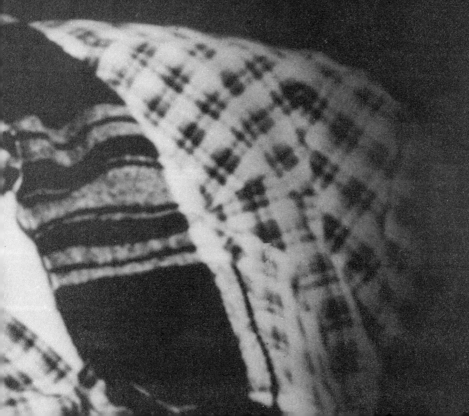

LOVE
IS COLDER
THAN
DEATH

I

THE last disappointment in the life of Rainer Werner Fassbinder occurred in New York City on April 20, 1982, seven weeks before his death. At the time it seemed more *coup de pied* than *coup de grâce,* just another blow to roll with on the championship trail. He was then at the height of his fame, with nothing to do but soar. "Now I'm really famous," he would say in good spirits a few weeks later to a friend. "Don't you think I should change my name so that I can make another name as famous as Fassbinder?" His future film projects were planned for the coming three or four years, and producers were jockeying for a chance to back them.

On the morning of that day in New York he was alone in his room on the thirty-ninth floor of the Hotel Pierre when the telephone rang. The caller was Dieter Schidor, the producer of *Querelle,* Fassbinder's forty-third and final film. Schidor, four years his junior and an actor in some of these films, was nineteen floors below him, dressed and ready to go out and conduct his business of the day. He had been hoping that Fassbinder, as was his custom, would not answer the phone. By virtue of his role as producer, he had undertaken a fearsome assignment: to convince the director to cut twenty minutes from *Querelle* to make it conform to the market demands of the American distributor, Columbia Pictures. No one, least of all Schidor ("I knew it was going to be a horror trip"), had yet found the courage to tell Fassbinder that he would have to either reduce *Querelle* to the length preferred by American exhibitors—one that allows an audience turnover every two hours—or settle for an art-house release. The difference in exposure and potential box-office receipts is enormous.

Fassbinder had completed shooting *Querelle,* one of his most expensive and most ambitious works, at the end of March, and had

3

edited it his way all along. Part of his ambition was to have it ready for the Cannes Film Festival in May. He was aiming for what he called the hat trick—one that had never been turned in cinema history. In February, he had won the Golden Bear at the Berlin Festival with *Veronika Voss,* his previous production. *Querelle,* he hoped, would win the Golden Palm at Cannes, and during the coming summer he would shoot his next film, *I'm the Happiness of this World,* which, the plan went, would take the Golden Lion at Venice in September. The larger ambition was to win the Oscar for best director in April 1983 and to make the cover of *Time.* No one had ever voiced a doubt that what he dreamed would come true.

It had been Schidor, however, with the same trepidation he felt now, who had told Fassbinder on his arrival in New York that they were not going to Cannes with *Querelle*—though it had already been invited to compete—because there was not enough time to mount the necessary promotion campaign. On hearing that, Schidor later recalled, "he didn't flip out too much." He thought it over and said, "Okay, I'll have to do my hat trick next year." But his reactions on one day were never a guide to what he might do the next, and when Fassbinder picked up the phone, Schidor's heart sank.

"What time is it?"

"Past eleven. I have to rush out, Rainer."

"Where are you going?"

"I have some business appointments."

"Come up and have breakfast with me."

"I already had breakfast. And besides, I'm late."

"Come up anyway."

Fassbinder hung up. Schidor came up anyway. The power the director, at this stage of his career, exercised over his producer—as over everyone in his circle—was just about total.

Schidor rang the bell to room 3905. Fassbinder opened the door. He was already dressed, in torn jeans, a checkered shirt, and patent-leather shoes. Everything about him was scraggly—his hair, his sparse Oriental beard, his clothes—but it was an appearance he cultivated, an image.

The room was in great disarray, rearranged haphazardly to suit his conscious and unconscious wishes. Schidor had noted that no matter where Fassbinder went, and even at home, sooner or later

4

everything plugged into a socket would be "accidentally" ripped out
—the lamps, the television set, the telephone—cutting off whatever
led to the outside world. It was the same with his body. A daily
regime of inordinate amounts of drugs, alcohol, and perhaps worst
of all, rich food had caused him to grow steadily heavier over the past
years, giving him a bloated, froglike appearance. A hundred cigarettes a day didn't help to reduce his appetite in the least. This
tendency to obesity became sharply accentuated in the last weeks of
his life. Some of his thoughts about himself during this period were
revealed and put into words by a writer of his own choosing for a
biographical documentary then being filmed.

> *Growing ugly is your way of sealing yourself off.*
> *Your stout, fat body, a monstrous bulwark against all forms*
> *of affection, which only make you skeptical. . . . The child in you*
> *screams at this bulwark, screams in your nightmares for love and*
> *harmony.*
> *Grow ugly and work. Then, and only then, let them come.*
> *. . . I want to be ugly on the cover of* Time—*it'll happen and I'm*
> *glad about it and I admit it—when ugliness has finally reclaimed*
> *all beauty. That is luxury.*

Fassbinder, sitting by a window that looked out on Central Park,
finished his breakfast. In the distance he could see the Dakota, the
apartment building where John Lennon had lived and died. That was
the only thing he liked about his room.

"Where do you have to go first, Kitty?" he asked Schidor. "I'll go
with you." Fassbinder gave female names to many of his male friends
and he often spoke of them using "she" and "her." He himself was
Mary, Bloody Mary.

Schidor tried to dissuade him from coming, hoping that he could
postpone telling him about cutting *Querelle,* but to no avail. The first
appointment on Schidor's agenda, for which he was already late, was
at the Fifty-seventh Street offices of Gaumont, the French financiers
of *Querelle.* Fassbinder put on his battered leather jacket and his
dark glasses, covering his warm, some say irresistible, eyes.

In the lobby of the Hotel Pierre, they ran into Peter Chatel, a

5

German actor and stage director, and they went outside together to wait for a taxi. A handsome, bespectacled man in his late thirties, Chatel had also appeared in many of Fassbinder's films and was as much under his sway as anyone else in the "family," although each member's relationship with the master was unique and constantly in flux. He was in New York at the express wish of Fassbinder, who was footing the expenses, including the considerable extravagance of a round-trip Concorde flight from Europe for a single night's stay in the United States. Chatel, who was in the midst of staging a play due to open shortly in Paris, had consented to fly to New York to carry a can of film needed for a private screening of *Querelle*. At the moment, he was on his way to New Jersey to visit a friend before returning to Europe. Fassbinder asked him to join them instead, and when Chatel insisted that he could not, Fassbinder tore off Chatel's glasses, dropped them, and smashed them under his heel. Then he smiled.

"Those were your sunglasses, right?"

"No, they were my regular glasses. My only pair."

"That's not true!" Fassbinder cried. "Besides, it's your fault. Why are you so stubborn?"

Fassbinder and Schidor got into a cab. "I've got to get my hands on Peter's plane ticket so that he can't fly back to Paris," Fassbinder said. "He has no money and no credit cards, and if Andreas invites us to a party with Jackie O., we won't take Peter along. That's his punishment." Andreas was Fassbinder's name for Andy Warhol. Jackie O. was Mrs. Onassis, who apparently was eager to meet the director.

Schidor agreed to help him filch the ticket. He thought it was all in fun, that Fassbinder wanted Chatel to stay longer in New York out of friendship, only recently renewed after a lengthy break. Chatel, however, believed that Fassbinder was trying to prevent him, by getting him to New York in the first place, from putting on his play in Paris. He had undergone similar interference on another occasion, and then, as now, he was right, though only after Fassbinder's death would he and others begin to appreciate how finely woven was the fabric of interdependence. For the present, heading across the Hudson without his glasses, he had to content himself with the knowledge that Fassbinder was unaware that he had not in fact carried the film can—his mission turned out to have been unnecessary—and had used the ticket merely to pay a surprise visit to a friend in New Jersey.

When Schidor finally arrived at Gaumont's offices with Fassbinder, the woman with whom he had had an appointment was out to lunch. Received by her secretary, an affable person who introduced herself as Lola, they decided to wait and enjoy the view of the city from the forty-sixth floor. Lola asked what they would like to drink. Fassbinder was struck by her friendliness; he himself, whenever he met people for the first time, was extremely shy—a boyhood trait he had simply never outgrown. He asked for a Coca-Cola. Schidor wanted coffee. Both were served promptly, and Lola retired to her typewriter in an adjoining room.

Fassbinder looked out at the RCA building. "It's very small," he said. "The other buildings are higher."

"Do you want a joint?" Schidor asked him.

"You can't do that here."

"Coward."

Fassbinder lit up the joint. He was or wanted to be anything but a coward. He went into Lola's office and asked her if she would like one, too. Lola said she didn't smoke on the job but had no objection if they did.

The telephone rang. It was Lola's boss calling to say that she would not return to the office that day. Schidor got on the line to excuse himself for being late, but that did nothing to change her mind.

On the way down in the elevator, Fassbinder reproached Schidor. "You can't do that in New York," he said. "The people here are very punctual. You can't just show up any time you please."

Schidor pretended to be remorseful. This pleased Fassbinder. If Schidor could get him into the right mood, it would be easier to tell him about cutting *Querelle*.

The next stop was 860 Broadway, Andy Warhol's place, "The Factory." A month or so earlier, Warhol had visited the set during the filming of *Querelle* in Berlin, but though he had watched Fass-

7

binder work, the two had never actually met. Fassbinder, because of his inveterate shyness, had purposely avoided him, and now, outside the Broadway building, he suddenly refused to go upstairs.

You don't talk to any of them. You're all so terribly famous there's no point in talking.

Schidor coaxed him. Warhol had agreed to do the poster for *Querelle;* he had seen the long version and Schidor had provided him with some of the costumes to photograph. Schidor hoped now to see some sketches, but it was not this that induced Fassbinder to yield; he was curious about The Factory's elaborate security system, which Schidor described when he got nowhere with anything else.

"Okay," he said, "but you have to do all the talking. You have to promise me that I don't have to speak to Andreas." Part of his timidity in this case was a reluctance to speak English, though his knowledge of the language was more than passable.

The security system failed to hold Fassbinder's interest for very long, and they were shown into an office to await Warhol. The room was filled with huge pictures of color-intensive dollar signs.

"Do you think I should tell Andreas I want the costumes back after he finishes with them? They cost me eighteen hundred marks," Schidor said.

"If you do, Kitty, I'll scream."

Warhol, wearing short shorts, arrived with a tall Yugoslavian woman.

In Warhol's face you see the horrifying price he has to pay. To exist as a shell. Self-sacrifice. Destroyed by one's own work.

"Oh, Mr. Fassbinder," Warhol said, "I saw *Querelle.* It made me hot for the whole day!"

Fassbinder's eyes opened wide. "We have to remember that," he whispered to Schidor in German. "What a slogan!"

Schidor made a mental note. He could see the placards on the New York buses: "*Querelle* made me hot for the whole day"—Andy Warhol.

8

"This is my gymnastics teacher," Warhol said, introducing the woman. "Do you do gymnastics, Mr. Fassbinder?"

The direct question floored him. He looked down at his feet and said nothing. Schidor wasn't quite sure how to come to his rescue and remained mute. So did Warhol, staring straight ahead. The Yugoslav's eyes darted from one of them to another. The silence grew heavier and heavier.

At last Fassbinder looked up and smiled, answering the question. "Not yet," he said.

No one, including himself, knew what he meant.

"Do you want a Schweppes?" Warhol asked, going out of the room for a moment.

The Yugoslav stood motionless, smiling.

"Do you think he'll give us a picture?" Fassbinder asked Schidor in German.

"I doubt it, but I'll give it a try."

"I can't take much more of this. Besides, I'm hungry."

Warhol came back with two Schweppeses. Schidor eyed a painting, small, gift-size. It was filled with crosses.

"That picture looks like a cemetery," Schidor said.

"Yes," said Warhol.

Fassbinder almost laughed.

"I think *Querelle* will make a lot of money," Warhol said. "All the kids will like it."

"I've got to get out of here," Fassbinder said to Schidor in German.

Back on Broadway, they looked for a nearby restaurant recommended by Warhol, but couldn't find it. Fassbinder bought a copy of the *Advocate*. He wanted to go through the hustler ads. Schidor gauged him to be in a relatively good mood and decided that as soon as Fassbinder's stomach filled up he would tackle the matter of shortening *Querelle*.

They finally wandered into a greasy-spoonish restaurant near the Hudson River. Fassbinder liked the name: the Silver Dollar. He ordered eggs sunnyside-up and began to pore over the *Advocate*, quite content with the world, but Schidor found the place incompatible with appetite and ordered nothing. Fassbinder circled an ad placed by a male prostitute who called himself Ramses II. He had no intention of contacting him, or anyone else in the ads, but the name titillated his fantasy. He was actually having fun.

On the street once again, they strolled toward Union Square. Fassbinder waxed garrulous while Schidor, his courage as gathered up as it could be, searched for his opening words. Then it was suddenly made easy. A stranger came up to Fassbinder and said, "I love your films, thank you," and walked away. Fassbinder puffed up with joy.

You are famous. America knows your name.

It was the purest kind of compliment, so timely that when Schidor later told the story, some of Fassbinder's friends were convinced that the stranger was Schidor's plant.

Schidor and Fassbinder sat on a bench in Union Square. The sun was shining brightly. Schidor's heart pounded. *Querelle* was the first film he had ever produced, and he had done so only after a long struggle against enormous odds. Nevertheless, his career as both actor and producer was almost entirely dependent on Fassbinder's name and whim. Forty-two films had preceded *Querelle,* and no one had ever succeeded in compelling Fassbinder to cut a single frame from any of them.

"Rainer," he said, trying to get it out all at once, "the Americans feel it would be better for the film if it were cut. They said that of course nobody is going to force you to cut it, but if you don't, they said, it's going to have a totally different distribution."

Fassbinder made no reply. It was as if he had not heard a word, but Schidor, knowing he had, was of no mind to repeat himself. Fassbinder stared at the ground. Finally, he said, "You've got to get me some money. I lost ten thousand dollars."

"Lost it?"

"It must have fallen out of my pocket."

Schidor remembered counting about eighty thousand marks scattered around on the floor of the bathroom in Fassbinder's temporary Berlin apartment just after the shooting of *Querelle* a couple of weeks back. He found another thirty thousand in the kitchen sink—two hundred thousand in all, the equivalent of about eighty thousand dollars, floating around a flat in which there was a constant flow of visitors night and day. Fassbinder often insisted on being paid in cash, on some films before the start of every shooting day.

"I'll get you some money tomorrow," Schidor said now.

That evening Fassbinder watched *Dallas* in his room at the Pierre. He then took a large, but for him normal, dose of sleeping pills and Valium and sent for Schidor. When the producer arrived, he was still wide awake smoking, as always, one cigarette after another and drinking Jim Beam, his second fifth of the day. He stood looking out at night-lit Central Park.

> *Real success is success in America. But the Americans warn you. No art film. America is large, and mighty are the hands that caress you. You think of Bertolucci's and Fellini's mistakes. You think of success. Success in America. The cover story.*
>
> *It'll only cost you a burn on your fingers. You forget the cigarette you're holding.*

"I'm not going to cut the film," Fassbinder said. "This is the worst kind of blackmail. They don't tell you you *have* to; they tell you you can do whatever you want, but if you do what you want, this and this will happen. I can't live with this blackmail. I can't stand this anymore."

Fassbinder took more sleeping pills. Schidor went out.

> *Wait. Hold out. Like you waited in Cannes, Venice, and Berlin. You want the prize, the bear, the palm, the lion, the hat trick. You want to win. Why else be this monster? But then when things go wrong you praise rage and disappointment. You destroy hotel rooms, then call your friends and ask about the Oscar nomination.*
>
> *You'll get it, they all tell you.*
>
> *Give it to me so I can survive.*
>
> *For nothing is more fascinating than fame; for nothing is equal to the terror of dreams come true.*

II

Fassbinder slept most of the next day. Schidor spent the morning getting him money. In the late afternoon, they met and walked across the park to the Athlete's Foot on Columbus Avenue to shop for sneakers. Fassbinder, in spite of his weight, frequently played soccer. Schidor noticed a man walking alongside them for a while, falling behind, catching up, then dropping back once more. He was going to remark about it, but suddenly Fassbinder said to him, "Oh, by the way, I'm cutting the film, but you have to give me fifty thousand marks extra."

Schidor stopped in his tracks. He was elated. ("I wanted to jump up and down.") The man who had been following them came up to Fassbinder now. "Hey," he said, "you look just like that famous German movie director, Rainer Werner Fassbinder."

Fassbinder pointed his dark glasses at him coldly. "Really?" Then, as if to himself, he added, "He's much too famous. He wouldn't walk down this street."

2

HE was born in Bad Wörishofen on May 31, 1945, an only child. All his life he would lie about his age, making himself, we don't know why, one year younger, and his mother would go along with this bit of fiction, which gave him an extra year of being a boy wonder and perhaps an edge in the struggle for attention.

Bad Wörishofen is a Bavarian spa southwest of Munich where people come to take a cure, and hence it is a good place to practice medicine and rent out rooms. This was what Fassbinder senior was doing when the child came into the world, three weeks after the collapse of the Third Reich—a time vividly and powerfully captured in some of Fassbinder's films, particularly *The Marriage of Maria Braun,* where we see and feel Hanna Schygulla quietly suffering, walking amid fallen bricks and bathtubs and kitchen sinks blown out of windows, dancing with horny GI's, or standing with other women-left-behind waiting for trains and husbands who will never come home.

The newborn baby's parents were Hellmuth and Liselotte, and he would radically alter their individual destinies. They were a literate couple. No comic books would ever enter Rainer's childhood home. Dr. Fassbinder inclined to art and poetry in a dilettantish way, while Liselotte, a working translator, preferred prose. They named the baby after Rainer Maria Rilke, that tormented giant of a poet who was brought up wearing dresses by a mother pretending he was her dead daughter. Hellmuth and Liselotte, under the impact of their special times, would provide their new arrival with an abnormal upbringing all their own.

"He had a very, very heavy childhood," his mother told the sculptress who brought her his death mask before Fassbinder's funeral.

And Rainer himself told an interviewer a year or so before he died, "Ever since I was a baby I have been what is defined as a manic-depressive, with alternating highs and lows that come on for no apparent reason. When I was a child the way this manifested itself was not much different from today. At times, I was full of joy playing with other children; then I would suddenly lose all desire, and go off in a corner to sulk. The other kids didn't always understand. They thought I was crazy."

The earliest infantile experience Rainer claimed to remember was "homosexual" and occurred when he was two or three years old. "Once," he said, "I stayed a few nights with the family next door. I slept with their boys. We were all in the same bed, and we suddenly got interested in the size of our toes, who had the biggest and who had the smallest. I think having the biggest was more important."

Q. Who were the persons in your early life you could count on?
A. Nobody, even though I was always around lots of people. In our house, there was my father's office in one part, where I was never allowed, and the *pension* in another, where there were several long-staying guests, so as a child I had more to do with those people than with my father. I had a hard time figuring out just who among all these people my parents were, with whom to have a deeper relationship. It was a sort of extended family, though without any structure. All I recall is that I wasn't able to distinguish who was who. For example, there was a woman who lived down the hall, called Anita. To me, she was Mrs. Anita, who at least once a day would ask me who do I love more, her or my mother. As far as I was concerned, one was as good as the other. My grandmother's role, however, was very clear to me. She stayed in the kitchen and gave me what I ate.

One day his grandmother took him to Munich and he wandered off the street into a church. Churches had made a deep impression on him. He was three years old. He climbed up on the altar. His grandmother thought she had lost him. She looked up and down the street, in and out of buildings, and finally found him inside the church, perched on the altar. He wouldn't come down. She tried to drag him away, but he cried, "No, no, I'm not coming down from the altar."

"There's a good scene for you," Rainer told his interviewer, laughing. "I wonder what an analyst would make of that?"

Q. A very important moment in childhood is when one becomes conscious of oneself, when one discovers the individual with whom one must live. What comes to mind?

A. Two episodes, both connected with toys. The son of one of my father's patients had a puppet in the shape of a monkey, and I wanted it and I told him. He didn't give it to me, neither the first nor the second time I saw him, and the third time I took it by force and destroyed it. I was punished: I was forbidden to have toys, and I didn't until later on, when my grandmother gave me a cloth doll she had made herself, filling it with pebbles. Once, I was in the kitchen and I got angry and I threw it at her and destroyed that, too. She had worked hard making that doll and I ruined it. I was sorry then, and I'm still sorry now. That's it: a puppet and a doll.

The home in which no toys were allowed was itself destroyed when in 1951 Hellmuth divorced Liselotte and went off to Cologne, rarely to be heard from again. Rainer was six years old at the time. His grandmother subsequently died. Now he and his mother were living in Munich, in Sendlingerstrasse, prostitute row; he would always remember the street people with fondness. "They treated me well," he would say in a 1981 interview. "The women of Sendlingerstrasse liked that little boy. Prostitution was something quite natural to me, and it was only much later that I found out how other people regard it. I have always felt comfortable with pimps. They have been real friends, people with whom I never have problems."

Q. After your father left, who were the male figures in your life?

A. We took an apartment . . . in a rooming house, and there were plenty of men living there. My mother, to my displeasure, had a seventeen-year-old lover; then, I was about eight or nine. This seventeen-year-old tried to behave like a father to me. All I could do was laugh.

Rainer began attending school. He did poorly. Try harder, his mother told him. If you fail now, you will fail later. He didn't wear the "right" clothes. Look at you, you're ugly; no wonder you always fail.

Rainer could not remain in the company of normal children, Rainer's mother was told in school after school; he had to go to a school for the socially maladjusted. Instead he was enrolled in a Rudolf Steiner school.

Rudolf Steiner was the father of anthroposophy, in which there are still some believers. Anthroposophy, its father said, is knowledge "produced by the higher self in man." Once upon a time, Rainer was taught, people had a dreamlike consciousness that allowed them to partake in the spiritual processes of this world. The consciousness of most people today is too "awake," but it can be "enhanced," and when it is, we can partake once more. Rainer often played hooky, enhancing his consciousness on the street.

Q. Has anything of the ideology of this school remained with you?
A. Only a single phrase sticks in my mind: "Children have to grow like flowers," without punishment when they do badly, without reward when they do well. As an idea I think that's beautiful, but things didn't happen that way.

At age nine he wrote a "theater piece" about flowers that fall in love, and thereafter he never stopped writing. Meanwhile his mother was squirreling out their existence with her translations, but she developed a lung disease, whose name was never spoken in house, and she was often in the hospital for long periods of time.

"Once, after some sort of therapy, my mother began having dreams that she married me, and I didn't like it at all when she told me. It upset me to suddenly discover that I was so important to her."

Q. To a strong maternal attachment, did you respond with Oedipal feelings?
A. No. On the contrary, I treated my mother the way in Freud children treat their father; they're supposed to kill him, they have to kill him. Every time my mother came at me too much with those dreams of hers, I reacted in a way that surely had something to do with murder. It wasn't mere rejection; I protected myself with all my strength. I really tried to reduce her to total silence.

16

He wouldn't succeed until much later, on the film set, where he would take endless revenge on her. He would give his mother a new name and make her an actress, the cold, hovering presence of many of his films. He would scream at her on the set, with a hundred people around. "You tried to kill me when I was a kid! You force-fed me unripe apples!" He would weep and she would reply abjectly, "I didn't know you could die from unripe apples."

Now, with her health failing, she met a man, a certain Mr. Eder, whom she married. He was a journalist and writer of short stories. Rainer himself had started writing stories, but he and Eder never got along, and when Mr. Eder came to call, Liselotte would give Rainer money to go to the movies.

POSTWAR devastated Germany was remade in the image of its victors, and the policy of its most powerful victor, the United States, was the one that to a large extent prevailed. "What we have to do now," U.S. secretary of state James Byrnes said when the war was won, "is not to make the world safe for democracy, but to make it safe for the United States," and Germany had first priority.

One of the initial steps the American occupiers undertook in the reconstruction of Germany was the rebuilding of its motion picture theaters. This was done not for the entertainment of the former enemy but rather in accordance with a 1947 directive that sought to provide the Germans with "information which will influence them to understand and accept the U.S. program of occupation." A result of this directive was that the distribution of films in Germany came under American control, and the new movie houses became the place where much of Hollywood's output of the thirties and early forties —all banned under Hitler—was dumped. This, in the pretelevision era, was part of the spoils of war, an immense economic bonanza, lobbied for with vigor by the U.S. Motion Picture Export Association.

The first image Rainer saw on a motion picture screen was a prairie schooner in a western. By the mid-fifties he had seen everything, the whole Hollywood "dump," and he often went to the movies two or three times a day. He had seen Jane Russell in *The Outlaw;* a *White Heat* Cagney crying, "I made it, Ma, now I'm really at the top"; Bogart telling Sam to play it; and Brando's Kowalski and Vivien Leigh's Blanche Dubois moving across the screen with the authority of planets. By now the cheaply rebuilt theaters were falling apart once more, as in the Germany of Rainer's 1981 film *Lola,* where the ruins of war have not been entirely swept from the streets and the overriding concern of most people is to get enough to eat and to stay warm. Among these people, those on the outermost margins, young Rainer found his friends, the hookers and pimps of Sendling-erstrasse, the Italians and Greeks and Yugoslavs of the train station, so-called guest workers, the menials for whom the rail terminals were the places closest to home.

What he saw in them now went into his bones, and he would later yield it distilled in words and images on the screen. These people, he would say, "have a little more space than people in a bourgeois family to unload their anger quickly and directly. I would rather be with a person who lets off steam immediately when something goes wrong than someone who holds it in until it kills him." He was a mixture of both types. Although he later developed an ostentatious taste for luxury—he would wallow in it like a sow—he always felt at ease among the *Lumpenpack,* where his entire erotic life, which began in 1960, unfolded.

He was fifteen years old and he already had a "sensation" that he was a homosexual. He went to spend some time with his father in Cologne. Hellmuth had given up medicine to become a poet. He had bought a run-down tenement, renting hovels to "guest workers," becoming a slumlord to support his literary pretensions. Rainer would later characterize his father as "completely mad," but now he was quite happy because while his father pursued his muse, Rainer had the job of collecting the rents, which gave him the chance to be with the people he liked most.

"Listen," he told his father one day, "I found out something. I'm really happy. I don't want to have anything to do with girls. I want a man."

"Who is this 'man'?" said the poet, apparently without reproach.

"He's a butcher, a butcher's apprentice."

"Well, if you want to go to bed with men," Hellmuth said, "can't it be someone from the university?"

This parental guidance did nothing to dampen his spirits. "I told everybody," he said later. When he told his mother, "she became hysterical. She said that my upbringing had been entrusted to her until I was eighteen years old, and she would not assume this responsibility. Only then did I understand that being gay is a problem for some people. But it wasn't for me. I never felt it as such and I still don't."

Suddenly, at fifteen and quite pimply-faced, he was going to gay bars, though in those days the word "gay" was neutral and hadn't yet crossed the Atlantic, and no bar, at least in Cologne, favored one sex over another. Some were meeting-points where male prostitutes solicited homosexuals, and it was at one of these that Rainer met Dodo. Dodo, with sky-blue eyes and a presence Rainer would later exploit on the screen, was as beautiful as a boy as he was as a girl, which was how he often dressed. Rainer became his pimp. They became an inseparable couple. Dodo stuffed his bra. Rainer stuffed his crotch. Boys will be boys. They adored the lowlife, the foreign-worker trade, for they had a cause: bringing love and affection to people in despair. This, too, would become the poignant stuff of Rainer's films.

In 1960 movie theaters in West Germany were closing at the rate of one a day. The year 1956 had been the peak in the German movie industry, with nine hundred million tickets sold; but this figure had shrunk by eighty million in each of the next four years. Television had come to stay. Yet a new generation, untainted but not unburdened by the grisly sins of its fathers, was coming of age. Memories returned of the Old German Cinema, of Pabst, of Lang, of Sternberg, of a brooding quest for sinister shadows behind reality. The haunted screen of expressionism haunted anew.

Gone now were the American occupiers, leaving behind them a mark that could not be rubbed out. By the beginning of the sixties, the German film industry had experienced a concentration of power in the hands of a few domestic moguls. Their doors were closed to anyone who wouldn't toe the Cold War line of the day. Vapid television easily preempted the audience for vapid cinema, and the only space for creativity was the short *Kultur* movies being made by young filmmakers who were subsidized by a government throwing bones at discontent. These films began to win recognition at home and abroad, but mostly abroad, and in 1962, at the Oberhausen short-film festival, a cultural revolt broke out. Led by the idealogue filmmaker Alexander Kluge, twenty-six young writers and directors who had gained experience in short movies drew up a manifesto in which the culturally bankrupt and tottering film industry was pronounced dead. It was a declaration of independence. The manifesto read:

> The future of the German cinema lies with those who have demonstrated that they speak the new language of cinema. . . .
>
> This new cinema requires new forms of freedom: freedom from the conventions and habits of the established industry; freedom from interference by commercial partners, and finally freedom from the tutelage of other interest groups.
>
> We have concrete plans for the artistic, structured, and economic realization of the new German cinema.
>
> We are collectively prepared to take the economic risks.
>
> The old cinema is dead. We believe in the new.

It would take three years of infighting to wrest a palpable result from this initiative: the formation of a government agency, the Kuratorium Junger Deutscher Film, to implement the proposals of the Oberhausen Manifesto. By then, however, Werner Herzog and Volker Schlöndorff had made their first full-length films, and Rainer Werner Fassbinder, with an infinitude of life's images in his head and a script under his arm, was ready to roll.

Now, 1965, he was one year out of school. He had no diploma for his trouble, and the lack would always gnaw. Mature, he was short, already pudgy, pockmarked for life, and, he earnestly believed, ugly. He had moved in with an unemployed actor named Christoph Roser. Roser had the money in the bank that would finance Rainer's first short movie, but Rainer didn't know about this money yet. He worked at odd jobs, in the morgue of a local newspaper, the *Süddeutsche Zeitung,* and backstage at the Kammerspiele, a Munich theater. He wrote poetry. He wrote plays. He wrote short stories. He enrolled in an acting school. Sometimes, lured by the scent of "glamor," he made timid voyeuristic sorties to the Little Bungalow, a bar in Schwabing, the bohemian quarter, where the reigning princes of short movies gathered to play the pinball machines, drink beer, and talk the language of the new cinema. Then something did happen. He won first prize in a writing contest, he discovered Christoph Roser's bank account, and he met the first women in his life and art.

4

"IT was love at first sight," Irm Hermann said some months after Rainer's death. She smiled wistfully, radiating tenderness, before recounting life at the Tangente, a smoky Munich bar near the university where, as its name implies, young people on the outside gather.

Rainer had somehow taken it over one evening so that Christoph Roser could read from the piece that had won first prize, "A Slice of Bread." He himself couldn't muster the gumption to face his very first audience. Somewhere among his listeners sat Irm, a pussy-willow person, as thin as the branch, as soft as the catkins. She had been invited by her friend Susanne Schimkus, a classmate of Rainer's in the acting school. Irm was twenty-one, a year older than he. She was a secretary for the Automobile Club, as far from the career that awaited her in films, television, and on the stage as was the stern upright family whence she came. At the moment, she was falling in love.

> I had been warned [she recalled]. My girlfriend Susanne told me that Roser was Rainer's fiancée. But that didn't stop me. I'd had no experience at all with homosexuals, so I guess I didn't hear her or want to. I was innocent, I would never believe it, and even now that he's dead, I don't really believe that he was homosexual. I know he *did* it, but not in his heart of hearts.
>
> Anyway, that night when I first met him was one of those times you can never forget. Christoph Roser was standing under a spotlight, reading Rainer's piece from a podium, and Rainer was with his mother, sitting hunched up in front of Christoph like a schoolboy, so bashfully. He seemed shapeless, he was dressed terribly, he was full of pockmarks, he was ghastly, even

23

repulsive, and he smoked one cigarette after another all night long. So many cigarettes, yet to me he was beautiful. He had an aura, and I was fascinated. After the reading, we all went to a pub, and I sat next to him, never leaving my seat. I was so fascinated. Up until then I'd had nothing to do with artists, never in my whole life. And then the evening ended and everyone went his own way.

A whole summer passed. Rainer was writing a script, more than one. There was another woman. Her name was Hanna Schygulla. She was nothing less than beautiful. She had long blond hair, an I-wanna-be-loved-by-you look in her eyes, and a yen to be like Marilyn Monroe. Rainer had met her in acting school; she was a runaway from her parents' aspirations for her to become a teacher. On Wednesday evenings, after class, Rainer and Hanna had frequented a small café, where they passed long silences together and exchanged a few barely articulate thoughts about books and films and their growing disenchantment with the school. "On one of these evenings," Rainer would later claim, "between one second and another, I had a crystal-clear vision that Schygulla would one day be the star of my films, but I was too much of a coward to tell her." What he did tell her—that "Capricorns are the worst," that he wouldn't have anything to do with them—gave her cause to avoid him. Hanna, though Rainer didn't know it, was one of "them." So when the time came, it was Irm who got the call. She had had no news of Rainer since that evening at the Tangente, when one day that autumn, Christoph telephoned her at the office.

"Rainer would like to see you this evening," he said. "He wants to talk to you about a role in his film."

"But I can't act," said she. "I'm not an actress." She was flabbergasted.

"He will meet you at the Café Monopterus at seven o'clock."

It is ancient memory, Irm's, from which this dialogue unreels. Of course she was there on time, ahead of time, and when Rainer entered the café, she fell in love again.

He was so shy, so, so shy. He said he wanted me to play this part, but he couldn't offer me any money. I told him I didn't know anything about acting, and he said it didn't matter; it was only a small part.

So we shot the film, in Susanne Schimkus's house. The camera, the lights, the sound equipment were all going when I got there. There were five or six people around, and I couldn't figure out who was doing what, but Rainer did a little of everything, acting, too. When it was all over, he gave me his bathrobe as a gift. He said he had always worn it when he needed luck and it had always worked. And from that moment I loved him madly. He was, how shall I say it? My dream of dreams. Oh, the way he treated me! So dearly, so kindly, so courteously, so humbly. He was so fascinating! Nothing like the Fassbinder of later times.

So Rainer had made, or at least shot, his first movie, *The City Tramp.* In the can, it would be ten minutes long, the story of a man down and out in the city who finds a gun in an alley and can't get rid of it. It was Rainer's first filmic statement: life is not a bowl of cherries. Happily he didn't dwell on it. Christoph still had a bank balance, so before very long Rainer laid plans to shoot again. This one needed a "real" actress, not Irm. He saw Hanna in the leading role, but she had dropped out of the acting school, bored stiff, returning to the University of Munich to fulfill her parents' wishes. He went to the university to search for her, but in vain, and finally cast another classmate, Marite Greiselis, in the part.

The second movie, two minutes longer than the first, marked the screen debut of a certain Lilo Pempeit, Rainer's mother with a brand-new name. He called the film *A Little Chaos.* The plot: three young people rob a helpless woman and get away with it. Period. The Real World strikes again.

Making movies was fun, but Christoph ran out of money, and neither film was quite finished. Rainer submitted them to the Oberhausen Festival. Both were turned down. Taking the rejection like castor oil, Rainer didn't know that he never had a chance. It was 1966, and the young pioneers of that New German Cinema born four years ago were already becoming old-boyish. The Real World strikes again. And again: he was thrown out of acting school for having no talent. Rainer then decided what he needed was an agent.

"You have to become my agent," he told Irm.

She had already left her job at the Automobile Club to serve not only as a volunteer actress but also as a secretary for the short-lived Christoph Roser production company.

So I became an agent. I represented Rainer as an actor-director. I withdrew all my savings from the bank, which wasn't very much, and with two heavy copies of the films and a portfolio of photographs, I set out by train to visit producers and television stations all over Germany.

I remember that Easter Sunday sitting on my suitcase in the train station in Cologne. I had run out of money. I didn't have one mark to my name. I couldn't even make a phone call. All I could do was cry. Luckily, I ran into a girlfriend of mine. She lent me five marks and took me to her home. Her father gave me fifty. I called Rainer in Munich and asked him what to do. He said, "Try Hamburg." I went to Hamburg, Bremen, Baden-Baden, Stuttgart. One man told me that Rainer was an interesting type as an actor, but his films were not the kind that were being made in Germany. So I went back to Munich. And Rainer was gone.

Rainer and Christoph were on their way to Turkey. They had been hired by an underworld enterprise as drivers to deliver stolen cars, for which they were promised five hundred marks each and the train fare home. While she waited for the men to return, Irm, dauntless agent, made the rounds in Munich. Suddenly all her labors were rewarded.

"This type I can use," a casting director said, going through her portfolio. He wanted Rainer. He offered a juicy ongoing role in a television series, a windfall of a part for an unknown. The deal was struck. Shooting was to start in ten days, time enough for his return. Irm borrowed money to buy Rainer some clothes—a pair of Bavarian knickers, long stockings, the works. He would love them; she knew it. But no word from Rainer. Shooting started without him. He had lost the job and he didn't even know he had one. He and Christoph were cooling off their driver's cramps doing eight days in a Turkish jail.

26

When he came back and found out that he'd missed his chance, he went crazy [says Irm]. It was terrible. But he never really wanted to be an actor; he tried only for the money. His dream was to *make* movies. He wanted to become the greatest director of all time. And I believed in him. I *knew* he would become the greatest, and I was ready to do anything for that, with all the power of my imagination and with all my capabilities, even though there was nobody I knew who could help him and I was nobody too. The only thing I had was my belief in him and I didn't care what people said, because everyone was saying that this ugly pickle-faced man was only taking my money and using me. But they didn't understand. I loved him.

There is a photograph to prove it, taken when things were good between them. His hand is on her breast and happiness looks out of her eyes. Her love is not unrequited.

Out of jail, Rainer was now also out of work, out of money, and out of prospects. To which he had now to add yet another major disappointment before he could go on to become the "greatest." The wise men of the New German Cinema had wrung two film schools out of the purse-string-keepers in the government. One was to be established in Berlin, the other in Munich. They opened their doors in 1966, and the whole new generation, it seemed, gathered to sit for the entrance examinations. Rainer was in Munich, but the place to *be,* so he heard, was Berlin.

He arrived there during a season of *Sozialkitsch;* Berlin was a frontier town, but all the young people there who wanted to shake the earth believed they were living at its center. If you weren't one of them, if you weren't persuaded that the only good film was a film that fomented class struggle, you were a Fascist. History was getting gang-banged and pregnant with the issues of 1968. The flower child's time had yet to come. So Rainer failed to get into film school, if only for defying the odds against someone who had never passed a formal test in his life. Naturally his despair descended to new lows.

5

BACK in Munich Rainer ran into Marite Greiselis, the young woman cast in his short film *A Little Chaos.* Marite had made her way into a leading role in *Antigone,* the Sophocles play. It was being performed with a little Brecht thrown in by a group that called itself the Action Theater, a threepenny operation patterned after Julian Beck and Judith Malina's Living Theater. He accepted her invitation to a performance, given in a used-up movie house converted into a theater by the tinkering husband of the proprietress. It was in an out-of-the-way street called the Müllerstrasse. Off-off, under-underground. Rainer liked that. He also liked what he saw. The living-theater rapport between player and spectator, he would say later, "took my breath away." Without thinking twice, he decided: "Here in this theater, with this group, I will work. I had no doubt that I would be accepted."

Marite agreed to introduce him. Among the group's members was Kurt Raab, in his twenties. Like Marite, like the tinker and his wife, Kurt was one of the many whose destinies would be radically altered by the chance encounter between Rainer and Marite, and he has remarked on what the Action Theater was like before Fassbinder showed up:

> We were hopeful, courageous, and avant-garde when, in 1966, we transformed a dirty suburban theater and set about to bring something new to the Munich theater scene. Full of sacrifice, convinced, inspired, emitting primal screams . . . [we had] many plans for the future, but no one could manage to execute them; we were in a vacuum, unconsciously waiting for someone who would show us the way. Then Rainer Werner Fassbinder arrived.

At the time of his arrival, everybody disliked Fassbinder, especially Raab.

> The door opened and he walked into the theater behind Marite. He had this round, pale, pimply, ugly-kid face that filled me with terror. I thought he was an intruder, somebody who had followed Marite in off the street. I didn't hear a word he said. All I felt was an aversion. Behind him stood this tall, lanky young woman in a broad-brimmed hat, looking at him full of love, and looking at us full of suspicion.

The lady in the hat was Irm, a gray governess.

Another one of the instant dislikers was Peer Raben, called Willi, the director of the play. "I'd say he was a little arrogant," he recalls. "In walks this person claiming to be an actor. 'I want to work with you!' he said. It sounded like an order."

Rainer was not accepted at first. Nevertheless, he kept coming around, taking a place at the group's round table, where they discussed their work and drank cheap wine. No one but Irm, unable to take her eyes off him, paid him any mind. Rainer was undaunted. *He* had decided that the others were characters in search of an author. Then an actor slipped and broke an arm, a foot, or a couple of fingers—no one remembers what; they recall only that Willi, the director, who was beginning to find Rainer "a not uninteresting type," asked him to jump into the void. Rainer jumped, slipping only on the lines he had to learn within hours.

Somebody then proposed the ill-starred idea that the *living* theater part of the play could be improved. *Real* people from the street were what was needed, and tramps were picked up off the benches of the English Gardens on the promise of a hot meal. One of them was a *real* prince, evidently very down on his luck. He took a fancy to his new job, to Marite, too. Some in the group thought that Marite, who had a reputation for being flirtatious, was toying with the prince, who indeed grew jealous. Others thought, or would later say, that Rainer, who never had toys, was toying with them both, searching, as was his nature, for a play within the play.

There was a mean-looking knife in the theater. It happened swiftly, after a performance. The prince was courting Marite's attentions. His voice rose. "Come with me," he said. She said, "No, I won't." She turned her back on him. He grabbed the knife. He stabbed her. She screamed. He stabbed her again, seven times in all, before somebody smashed a chair over his head. Marite fell unconscious in a puddle of her blood. She would never walk again.

After the arrest and the testimony, the show had to go on. To find a replacement for Marite was no easy labor since there was no pay involved except for a share in the proceeds, and more often than not there were no proceeds. Rainer thought once more of Hanna. He went again to the university; this time he learned where she lived. With fair, noble, celestial Hanna, his shy side took over, as it always would. He slipped a note into her letter box: "How would you like a part in *Antigone*? Opening night day after tomorrow. Come to the movie house in Müllerstrasse. Cheers. Rainer."

Onstage, her teeth chattered and she delivered nonsense lines in place of the speeches that wouldn't come to mind, but she drew energy from all the eyes upon her and she gave back more in return. *Antigone* with Hanna Schygulla succeeded as the play never had before, at least in the Müllerstrasse. From the start she was treated like the first rose of spring. A prima donna, if not yet a star, was born.

No one was more satisfied than Rainer, but to hear him tell it, after *Antigone* the group grew complacent. The actors got "lazy." They "drank too much." They "lacked initiative" and worst of all were unproductive. "I had the feeling," says Rainer, "that they were unconsciously hoping that my perhaps morbid drive to do something would make matters change, even though I was trying to hide it. Finally, I couldn't stand it anymore."

But Rainer decided again to direct. He chose *Leonce and Lena*, a play by the nineteenth-century German playwright Georg Büchner —Rainer saw the political present in the past as Büchner had seen the future. To his surprise and dismay, Hanna turned down the role of Lena. She claimed it was not big enough. But the rest of the group, of which she was never really a part, went along.

"My first rehearsal with him turned out miserably," Kurt Raab tells us. "I was to play King Peter in *Leonce and Lena* and I acted the role superficially, like a lame puppet. Fassbinder sat below in the audience, buried in himself, motionless, dissatisfied. Then he said, 'You must not play King Peter as a fool; you must imagine a petty bourgeois who believes he is a king.'

"I was irritated at first, but I thought it over for a day, suddenly saw the sense in his observation, and returned to rehearsal the next evening, feeling a bit penitent. Serious times began. I also got to know a Fassbinder who could be tender, who listened, gave advice, had sympathy, and was affectionate."

A competition developed for those affections. Willi fell in love with him. So did Kurt. So did the tinkering husband's wife, Ursula Straetz, but not the tinkerer, not at all, and Hanna wouldn't stoop to conquer. Rainer moved in with Irm, and Willi and Ursula took turns living with them, a shifting threesome, sometimes a foursome, in Irm's tiny one-room apartment.

"Unbelievable," Rainer would later remark. "Four people living in a hole in the wall."

"Intimate, wasn't it?" Irm remembers, lifting an eyebrow. "He was always switching people. It was very hard for me, very hard and very new. It went against all my middle-class upbringing, the ultimate horror. But I was so bound up with him, dependent on him and at the same time protective of his needs."

Leonce and Lena opened in October 1967. Rainer's choice and timing could hardly have been better. Playing Peter as a "petty bourgeois who believes he is a king" was at that moment like playing Lyndon Johnson back at the ranch. The audience and the critics were in a mood to rave, especially for Rainer in one of the leading roles. ("I worried that they wouldn't like me, so I played it to show that I disliked them ten times more, so that if they really didn't like me, I could take credit for provoking them. This was my way of protecting myself from being hurt.") The Action Theater got on the local map, becoming an "in" place for the radical young and the radically chic. The concept of the group was still collective, but now Rainer rose quickly to become number one, though not without a play for power.

Later he would be qualmless in describing it:

> Kurt Raab, for example, had a knack for exercising power, which he maintained in very strange ways. He was the only one

in the entire group who had worked in television. He was also the only one who had money. Raab, not all the time, but frequently, would go out and buy food and divide it among those in the group he favored. They could eat with him, the others could not. I tried from the very beginning to protect myself from this trap. I demanded that it be stopped, and it was. Maybe this was how I nipped his ambitions in the bud.

Kurt sees it his own way:

After the premier of *Leonce and Lena,* Fassbinder's grand ambition awakened. He became fanatic, wanting to put on one play after another, without number. He became sly. The easygoing character of our group underwent change. For me, now, he became the Director and I was the actor who had but to obey. His was the proposal I had to accept, the part I had to play, the bidding I had to do. For all of us in the Action Theater he became the Leader, the Shepherd, the Source of Ideas, the Maker, the Mentor, the Motor.

According to Rainer, the transition was anything but smooth:

When I showed up, the Action Theater was headed by Peer Raben, whose personality was so gentle you couldn't even tell he was leading the group. The moment I got the job—who knows why, maybe I wanted it or maybe the others wanted me —you knew immediately who was the director. I never liked a leader who is so kind and soft-spoken that you don't even notice him. To me that's dangerous. I prefer a leader who is vulnerable. In the beginning, when I began to direct, they didn't want to work with me.

As to why, Kurt remarks:

We had to rehearse even when we didn't feel like it; we had to perform even when there were more people on stage than in the audience. He worked with the miserable materials of a small theater, but he staged his plays like scenes in a movie. Each step

32

was exactly established, each movement exactly rounded, each look had to be precise to the smallest detail. Soon we had something resembling success and recognition in the media, with the public.

All dissent disappeared, except for the grudge borne by Ursula's tinkering husband against Rainer for having taken his wife under Irm's little roof. The husband, however, was conveniently in traction, hospitalized after an automobile accident. That winter Rainer wrote his first produced play, a satire on contemporary middle-class mores. It was titled *Katzelmacher,* a disparaging slang word that tore the veil off the euphemism "guest worker." He began to direct Hanna in the big-enough leading role. By now he was being pampered and adored by most of the group, even Kurt, but especially by the women, each of whom believed she was tripping lightly toward the unreachable part of his sexuality. For his part, he adored and pampered Hanna, who would always remain unreachable in her own way.

Life in the Müllerstrasse, for Rainer, was the life of the young genius at work, and to work, he said, he needed to eat steak. The trouble was that the group was always short of money. Some had side jobs and contributed their pay to replenish the Source of Ideas. He had learned, and would never stop learning, how to turn the tensions inherent in interdependence to the service of his art, so one of his ideas addressed the issue of eating steak. Knowing the milieu of the "guest workers" from firsthand experience, he suggested to a couple of the more adoring and pampering women in the group that they frequent a certain bar near the train station as a way to earn some extra money. Prostitution? He wouldn't put it that way. *Ars longa, vita brevis* would seem more to the point. So from time to time, the women brought home foreign workers and Rainer went out to a café across the street to write. He wrote at a table by a window that allowed him to watch the "guests" come and go and told him when to come home for his steak.

Among the expanding audience for whom he was writing was a young man named Andreas Baader, who, together with the incipient clan that was soon to become the Baader-Meinhof terrorist gang, attended almost every night's performance, not at all in tribute to the

33

author-director, but to expound their political views whenever they felt the play dragged, which was often. It was mid-April 1968 now. Half the youth of Western Europe was in revolt. Red Rudi Dutschke had been shot down in Berlin, and from the Wall to Berkeley, California, students were on the march. In a back room of the Action Theater Ursula's tinkering husband, fresh out of the hospital, was making incendiary bombs for the Baader bunch. His name was Horst Söhnlein; a notorious career awaited him.

We never took the Baader people seriously [Willi recalls]. They had a slogan: "Burn down the department stores"—to give comfortable Germany a taste of Vietnam—but *everybody* had a slogan, and only Horst knew about the bombs. It was just around that time, though, toward the end of April, that the Baader group, including Horst, went on a rampage and totally destroyed the theater. Horst, who had built the stage with his own hands, who had built everything we had, did most of the destroying. The idea, so they said, was to put an end to an action *theater;* they wanted just plain action, and the very next day, Baader and Horst and the others collected their bombs, got into their VW minibus, and drove to Frankfurt to set fire to Schneider's department store.

The fire at Schneider's is to the founding of German terrorism something on the order of what the Reichstag fire was to the Nazis, and it consolidated Meinhof with Baader, but the destruction of the Action Theater was a lot more personal. They didn't give a damn about what we were doing; it was Horst who wanted revenge because Ursula had left him to live with Irm and Rainer.

So much for the Action Theater.

RAINER was now twenty-two, with celluloid fever in his veins, and it would be only a year before he would get "to do movies." For he left Ursula behind to pick up the splinters of the Action Theater, and now as undisputed leader, he, with eight or nine other members of the old group (including Kurt, Willi, Irm, and Hanna), staked a claim on a voguish prefix and formed an "Antitheater." They no longer had any real estate, but by the summer they were performing a Peter Weiss play at the Munich Art Academy, and Rainer's adaptation of *The Beggar's Opera* established them firmly at a place called the Witwe Bolte. The Witwe Bolte was only a saloon in Munich's Schwabing quarter, and all the Antitheater got was the big back room, behind the kitchen, but this was upward movement. Playing in Schwabing was as far from playing in the Müllerstrasse as playing, say, in Greenwich Village is from playing under the wrong side of the Williamsburg Bridge. With Rainer as Mack the Knife and Hanna as Polly Peachum; with Irm and Ursula (back in the fold) as hookers singing Rainer's original song "Two Dozen Cocks Every Day (That's the Only Way)," the Antitheater had an enormous "mainstream underground" hit.

It was now February 1969, cold on the streets but hot and uncensored at the Witwe Bolte. The uncensored part was important, because at the Oberhausen festival some months back a filmmaker named Hellmuth Costard had taken a giant step beyond the prancing nudity of *Hair* and the shenanigans of the Living Theater when he projected a staggering closeup of an old-fashioned hard-on on a public screen and, more important, survived the mighty scandal.

By the time of the opening of *The Beggar's Opera,* Rainer had already been making sparks by rewriting, staging, and audaciously "decensoring" (some say sacrilegiously) works of Goethe and Sophocles. He had also written an original play, adapted another, had staged those, too, and so on, while masterminding (and scriptwriting) the passage of the group into films.

In on the scheme—most of the group were unaware—were Irm and Willi, the keystone twosome with whom Rainer shared his bed. (The bed of course was Irm's, and it was Willi and Rainer who actually shared it, with Irm sleeping on the concrete floor.) Irm was given the job, besides being all other things to Rainer, of finding the money—about a hundred thousand marks—to finance their first full-length feature film. Willi, kicked upstairs as a kind of director emeritus, got the task of imposing and collecting a 50 percent tax on the earnings of each member of the group, earmarking it for the filmmaking fund.

The announcement of the project arrived at a propitious psychological moment. Under Rainer's direction, the group had seen its per-performance income rise tenfold, but the price being paid was a loss of solidarity. The poster for *The Beggar's Opera* read, "Rainer Werner Fassbinder and his Antitheater present . . . ," a first. Willi thought it fair enough, but Kurt detected long-range calculation and was resentful.

> I was very disappointed suddenly to find myself a mere sheep in the Fassbinder flock. I became conscious of this by the press coverage. The more he emerged, the more we were shunted to the rear. Yes, he was taking Hanna with him, but we were waving them goodbye. This was during *The Beggar's Opera* and we were happy enough getting thirty or forty marks for a night's work, but we wouldn't have been happy for very long. Then [Willi] came and said, "It has been decided; half of our earnings will be put aside for a film that we will all make together." We'd had no say in the matter, but no one said, "No, I'd rather have my whole night's pay." We thought it was a great idea. At last we would make a film.

It didn't happen quite that way. During this same period—the first half year or so of the Antitheater—Rainer got five acting roles in movies being made by other young directors. In one of these, Schlöndorff's *Baal,* he became friendly with a young leading man on the

36

rise named Ulli Lommel. Ulli's fame was close to being what in the film business is called bankable, that is, capable of attracting production money, and he was even closer, by way of his bride-to-be, to the world of wealth. He had never heard of Rainer Werner Fassbinder, but making discreet inquiries among his friends ("Have you seen any of those plays?"), he faked it well; it was a case of a comer having a good eye for a comer. For his part, Rainer for the first time in his life was exposed to tablecloths and silver, to wine that came in bottles not already opened, and to leather upholstery (he was already a leatherphile) in a car. Luxury, pushed to the absurd—chartered jets flying nothing but cocaine, to take a near-the-end example—would become one of his primary vices, but here he was enjoying it when it tasted sweetest, and he offered Ulli the starring role in his movie. It worked. Now all he needed was a movie.

In the meantime, Irm, gathering proof that love conquers all, had found an angel living in Munich, one Hanna Axmann von Rezzori, heiress to the Bosch fortune. Frau von Rezzori, Irm reported, gleaning from local rumor, was a patron of the film arts who never said no to the worthy. Irm succeeded in arranging an appointment for Rainer and Willi. They made the pilgrimage, as Rainer called it. Soft-spoken, properly reared, minimal Willi did the talking, Rainer hiding his two left feet wherever he could. The first thing they discovered was that Frau von Rezzori had never given away a pfennig to a struggling artist. On the theory that where there's rumor there's fire, however, they tried to persuade her she ought to. They had the famous Ulli Lommel for the lead; they had the up-and-coming Hanna Schygulla (her picture had recently been in the press). They had this and they had that. "Ja, gut, okay," said the Bosch heiress. She would make only a donation, she said, not pay for the whole thing, but she would pay for the film itself—the raw stock, that is—and the rental of the camera, the lights, and the rest of the hardware. Bosch, of course, is in hardware. Ja, gut, okay. Rainer's gratitude was real. Before a year went by, he would be shooting not his first but his *fifth* full-length film, in which von Rezzori herself plays a patroness who finances two young ne'er-do-wells' pipe dream of discovering a lost treasure in Peru.

Now, however, Fassbinder had to shoot the first.

RAINER wrote the script. He called it *Love Is Colder Than Death*. Only later, would life—his and the lives of others—imitate his art. For now art would have to imitate life. Here is how Rainer recounted the story of the film:

> At the start a crime syndicate wants Franz (acted by me) to work for it. But he only wants to work for himself and keep all of what he earns. Bruno (acted by [Ulli] Lommel) works for the syndicate and is sent after Franz. Franz grows to like Bruno. He invites him to his place and wants him to sleep with his girl, just because he likes him and doesn't question his liking. But then he can't question anything, just like Bruno, who does what he's told. Joanne, the girl, does the same. She (acted by Hanna Schygulla) is actually the main figure. Her character reveals that she is stuck in middle-classness, despite her profession [a prostitute], even worse than the others; she wants to save her bourgeois relationship with Franz by being his whore and even by betraying Bruno and a bank robbery to the police. She would rather be alone than share Franz with Bruno. She just can't stand that.

The gangster milieu, which would become a familiar setting in his early films, was dragged right out of the colder-than-death movie houses he had been frequenting since he was big enough to see over the seat in front of him. It had been filtered through postwar Hollywood films and ten years of the French cinema's New Wave, and had been personalized by his boyhood on the streets. The way he saw it, "the gangster environment is a bourgeois setting turned on its head, so to speak. My gangsters do the same things that capitalists do except they do them as criminals. The gangster's goals are just as bourgeois as the capitalist's." The character of Franz is a gangster who doesn't want to play ball. Franz ("acted by me") is Rainer as he saw himself.*

The Hanna Schygulla character, Joanne, is Irm, "stuck in middle-classness," ready to do anything to save her relationship with Franz-Rainer, and unable to share him with Bruno—the prototype of the variable third person throughout Rainer's life. Here, in his first complete screenplay, written from the clash of experience around him, we have the beginning of a pattern he would never abandon: filling his life with followers in order to make movies, then making movies to fill his life with followers; finally, the distinction would disappear.

Love Is Colder Than Death was shot in twenty-four gray days in April 1969, mostly on the streets of Munich and environs. Nineteen actors took part. They all had contracts with the newly formed production company Antitheater-X Film, of which Willi had been made the chief financial officer. He would never keep books (creating future tax problems), and no one would ever be paid. He also wore the hats of producer, composer of the film's music, and bit player. Rainer was director-writer-editor-star. Much to their dismay, the other members of the Antitheater group, with the exception of Hanna, were given the tiniest parts. Kurt played "a lookout," Ursula a "fat prostitute," Irm a "sunglasses seller."

"We all had two seconds on the screen," Kurt has griped, "and naturally I was thinking that I had a right to a big role, as I had had in the theater. But suddenly we were all extras, and it occurred to me that perhaps we were nothing but the extras in his career. Only Hanna had a starring role, and of course he himself. And Ulli Lommel. All of a sudden, Ulli Lommel was playing what should have been my part. I hated him from the beginning."

*From here on any "Franz" in a Fassbinder film (there are nine of them) would always be a self-portrait, whether acted by him or not. The full name is usually Franz Walsch, who would also get nine screen credits as film editor. It derives from Franz Biberkopf, the protagonist in Alfred Döblin's novel *Berlin Alexanderplatz* (a book that Rainer had carried around for years), and one of his favorite Hollywood directors, Raoul Walsh.

Coming years after Kurt had played the title roles in some of Rainer's most successful films, this is pure ax-grinding, but he has his facts straight. Rainer's answer to all the bitching done and yet to come was fair enough: "At a certain point I said to myself that what happens onstage has to be right; everything else doesn't matter." Besides, he would always take pleasure in having at least one malcontent around him.

A N audience composed of nearly everyone who counted for something in the German film world hooted and stamped its feet at the first public showing of *Love Is Colder Than Death* at the Berlin Film Festival, where so many of Rainer's future works would premiere and where in the last year of his life he would finally, for his penultimate film, win the top prize, the Golden Bear. But now, in June 1969, when he came onstage after the screening, the jeers were louder than ever, yet he clasped his hands over his head and paraded this way and that way with the swagger of a fighter who has just kayoed his opponent in the first round.

Rainer's interpretation of the event, as an unbridled triumph, proved over time to be closer to the truth than that of his detractors, and there were those among them who would very soon be scrambling for the nails to hang the star upon his door.

In the meantime, while the critics did their best to forget him, he planned his "comeback" with a film shot that August on an even slimmer budget than the last and in a third of the time. It was his film version of *Katzelmacher,* the play he'd written and staged a year before to much local acclaim. Putting Hanna and himself once again in the leading roles, he continued to make sparse use of the Antitheater group. He completed the cast with several of the players in *Love Is Colder Than Death* and some newcomers, too. In one of the latter he discovered first his alter ego and later a man who would be as close to and as loyal to him as his shadow.

His name at the time was Harry Zottl, but Rainer would rename him Harry Baer and lend him his precious pseudonym, Franz, on the screen.

Harry, plodding, pretty-faced Harry, was still in high school ("during the revolution," says he) when in 1968 he first heard of

Rainer Werner Fassbinder. Four years Rainer's junior, he was appearing in a school play when one of his classmates told him about a "revolutionary theater" that needed a drummer. Harry played the drums, got the job: drummer-actor in the Fassbinder Antitheater.

"It was fun at the beginning," he says. "Some nights, if there was a good-size crowd, you could make fifty marks; others, you came out losing." But he drifted away as easily as he'd gotten in, never even really meeting Rainer and indifferent to any notion of becoming a professional actor. He took his diploma that year, his only ambition being to make a trip around the world. Maybe then he'd go back to school, become a teacher, raise a family. A family—one in which you know who's who—was something he had never experienced. Harry Zottl, the future Harry Baer, had been Harry Koch until he was eight years old—Koch was the family name of his foster parents. When his natural mother married the man she was only fairly sure was Harry's natural father, the boy became a Zottl, though he would never know if indeed he was one.

He became Harry Baer and a homosexual after Rainer, preparing *Katzelmacher,* looked him up and found him in a coal mine, shoveling to pay his way for his round-the-world trip. Evidently Rainer had had his eye on him during Harry's brief drumming stint in the Antitheater.

> He just showed up [says Harry]. I'd hardly spoken a word to him before that. He said he had a part for me in his new film. I said I had other things to do. He began throwing hunks of coal at me. I threw them back. It was suddenly like a pillow fight. We started laughing and didn't stop until he was as black as I was. Then he said, "C'mon. Do the part." So I said okay, and then he said, "You can't be a movie star with a name like Zottl. From now on you're Harry Baer."

Baer is the German word for bear, but Harry was more a cub at the time and perhaps a little cuddly, too. He was cast in the part of Franz, one of the neighborhood jocks who feel intimidated by the imagined sexual attributes of a Greek "guest worker" named Jorgos and played by Rainer, the *Katzelmacher* of the title, which is a Bavarian slang word for a foreigner, especially someone from one of

42

the Mediterranean countries, who is supposed to be good for nothing other than turning out litters of children. The word, or at least the title, has been translated as "cock-artist," and in any case, the girls in the film, especially Marie, played by Hanna, take a fancy to Jorgos. The boys get depressed, until they beat up the Greek to reassert their racial supremacy. Hitler isn't quite dead.

Katzelmacher came out in October 1969, three months after *Love Is Colder Than Death.* Like the play, it was an instant critical success, but now nationwide. The film had cost eighty thousand marks, and though it went relatively unrewarded at the box office, it earned Rainer nearly a million marks in prizes and state subsidies. He was now very much in business.

9

OVER the twelve months between November 1969 and November 1970, Rainer proceeded to produce, astonishingly, nine full-length motion pictures written and directed by himself.

Few interviewers, when given the chance, would later fail to ask him to reveal the secret of his characteristic phenomenal speed. His answers would vary little over the years. "I am extremely sure of myself," he would say, and anyone who worked with him would either grow equally confident or be out of a job. To illustrate his efficiency, he would point out that his first feature-length movie, *Love Is Colder Than Death,* had 129 scenes and was shot in twenty-four days, while his twelfth, *The Merchant of Four Seasons*—made in 1971, the first after the phenomenal year that preceded it—had 470 scenes and was shot in eleven days.

Neither arithmetic nor any other cold analysis can ever explain Fassbinder's *annus mirabilis* of 1970, however. Harry Baer has said of the achievement: "The material that he produces at top speed doesn't come at him; it comes *out* of him with a compulsion— childhood and adolescent dreams, lacking attention, loneliness . . . 'I can sleep when I'm dead,' Rainer philosophizes over his Cuba libre." In that year, says Kurt Raab, "he was afflicted by a true intoxication of film ideas and their realization. He had hardly shot one film when he began to prepare the next; hardly had it arrived in the cinema when yet another was finished. His obsession infected us. We couldn't work enough. . . . Any day when nothing was produced was boring, every break filled us with emptiness. It's no wonder we hated days off and simply abolished Sundays."

The tale of that wildly productive year was spun from a love story. In the fall of 1969, Rainer had met Günther Kaufmann, one of the rarest birds on the planet, a black Bavarian, on the set of a 1969

Schlöndorff film in which they both had roles. Kaufmann was what the Germans call a *Besatzungskind,* that endangered species propagated only between 1945 and 1949 by the crossing of a German female with a male soldier of the postwar occupation forces, in Günther's case a black American GI. The GI in question had returned to the United States, and little Günther, never learning a word of English, black or white, grew up very Bavarian. "Günther," Rainer would often say in his presence, "thinks Bavarian, feels Bavarian, and speaks Bavarian. And that's why he gets a shock every morning when he looks in the mirror."

Throughout 1970 Rainer suffered deeply from being unable to conquer and tame the man he called "my Bavarian Negro." Günther was married and had two children. According to Kurt, Günther "probably liked Rainer a lot, gave himself in regular doses, but never spoke of eternal love, as Fassbinder would have liked."

Nobody knew of Rainer's new love when Günther was cast in the first picture of the 1969–1970 cycle, *Gods of the Plague.* Kurt recalls the impact of Günther:

> We were all attracted to his beautiful body, his radiant sensuality and his mild manner, which could suddenly turn brutal if he felt offended. Everyone fancied this guy and openly showed it. He was to do a scene with a deep bullet wound and lots of blood, and I was asked to make him up. I willingly accepted the job because I finally would have an opportunity to touch this body and I painted it lovingly in every detail. Fassbinder observed me suspiciously and finally shouted at me with irritation: "Leave off fiddling around with Günther's body!" . . . [Then] Ursula Straetz began to seduce the sensuous colossus in moments when Fassbinder was busy editing. As I had a close relationship with Straetz, I sensed what was going on, and when she invited him to her apartment, I managed to go along with them on the pretext that I had to work on some important props, which is how I became a participant and voyeur in a short game of love.

Günther had replaced Harry, who had replaced Kurt, who had replaced Willi, and so on, but Harry never was and never would be one to hold a grudge. "Rainer's real passion was for Günther,"

45

Harry says, and in the moment of transition he dreamed up *Gods of the Plague,* with Harry and Günther playing inseparable friends. As Harry recalls: "In the last scene, we rob a supermarket. I get killed with a pile of cans on my head, while Günther, wounded and half-naked, gets to show off his body, staggering off to die beautifully, delivering Rainer's favorite line for his exit, "Life is so precious, even right now!"

For Rainer, Günther was suddenly everything—but grateful. The black man seems to have been the first and only man in the Fassbinder constellation to have perceived that love unrequited, or requited strategically, could be turned for a profit. As Kurt remarks:

> Suddenly, prosperity stepped into Kaufmann's life. Wife and children were fitted out. Every wish, pronounced or merely read in his eyes, was granted. We, apart from our film work, were sent continually shopping to satisfy Kaufmann's demands. The purchasing of Lamborghinis was an art in itself. There were four in one year, because hardly had Kaufmann wrecked one of these precious vehicles when the next had to be found, and if the color did not meet Kaufmann's approval, he sold it, certain that a new one would soon be on the way.

The golden eggs kept dropping, and the hen was kept brooding by methods for the most part best left undescribed. One of these, however, was a variation on the time-tested "headache," by which Günther would often cite alleged demands made upon him by his wife as an excuse for not being as available to Rainer as Rainer might have liked. Thus, when Rainer was made an offer to shoot in Spain, he saw it as a chance to have Günther all to himself, and he dashed off a script for a western with Weltschmerz called *Whity,* casting Günther in the misspelled title role.

The story of the *making* of *Whity* in Spain, which itself became a Fassbinder film later in the year—*Beware of a Holy Whore*—is far more interesting than the movie, as Rainer agreed: "The thing that counted was that for the first time the group could look at itself outside its customary milieu. . . . Many relationships thought to be solid turned out to be either nonexistent or not at all what they seemed." The remote location where the film was shot became a crucible in which the group was irrevocably altered, and it was the beginning of the end of the Antitheater experience.

The annals of the New German Cinema are replete with this or that version of the filming of *Whity,* and the facts, as opposed to the interpretations, are not contradictory. Peter Berling, who was the line producer of the film and the man to whom it is dedicated on the screen, has written a hitherto unpublished memoir of how he managed to live through it.* It was in Spain, he says, that he discovered the Fassbinder "group dynamic."

About halfway through the filming [says Berling], my eyes were pried open when one day I came on the set—it was in a stable—and Harry ran at me brandishing a pitchfork. "I'll kill you!" he was shouting. "I'll slit your big fat stomach!" Since Harry was about the only one in the group I could talk to man-to-man, I asked him what the trouble was, feeling there had been some dreadful misunderstanding.

While Rainer and some of the others held him back, he cried, "You know perfectly well what's wrong. You did it on purpose."

"Admit it," said Rainer, laughing as never before. "You did it on purpose. You sent him away."

"Me? Who?"

"Juan Carlos," Rainer said. "Harry's friend, the electrician with the nice ass."

I couldn't remember his face, let alone his ass, but I did recall dismissing a supernumerary Spanish technician to save money. "Now what?" I asked.

"Bring him back," said Rainer, offering to pay the expenses out of his own pocket.

It suddenly dawned on me that I was surrounded by homosexuals, something I truly didn't know until this moment. I made arrangements for Juan Carlos to be flown in on the very next incoming flight from Madrid, and now that I'd been initiated, I began to perceive more of the origins of the sharp fluctuations in mood.

*See Appendix I, "The Making of *Whity,*" by Peter Berling.

Everything seemed to depend on where Günther had slept the night before, whether in his own room or Rainer's. When Günther rejected him, everyone grew depressed, knowing how irascible Rainer would shortly become, and Kurti, for one, would drink himself into a stupor. If, on the other hand, Günther was willing, everyone was happy, even euphoric, but if he didn't keep his promise, Rainer threatened suicide. On one occasion he went as far as borrowing a razor, but in the end he simply shaved, and on another, with Kurti alongside him in his speeding Mercedes, he ran a highway intersection blindly. "If a car had come now, I would have died like James Dean," he announced to Kurti after the attempted "suicide" had failed. "Not exactly," said Kurti, still trembling.

No one, not even Rainer, would deny Kurt his own jaundiced assessment:

We experienced a perpetually drunken, insufferable, berserk, foaming-at-the-mouth Fassbinder, who made life miserable for all of us. If he had a fight with Günther, he would then pick a fight with us. His moods were as good or as bad as the relationship between the two was at any given moment, and thus he was soon hated by the whole cast and crew.

"The feeling was mutual," said Rainer. "They said that I exploited them and I said that they exploited me. . . . They had the sensation that I was the only one to profit from all the work and gather all the success. I reproached them for having made me do so much, simply because I was the only one ready to do it. With us it was like this: you watched them hang around, so the only thing to do was to do something and be busy. They practically forced me to make ten films a year. They drove me to the point of collapse, of psychic and physical exhaustion, so that I could say that they sucked the blood out of me." Which he did in *Beware of a Holy Whore,* in a scene where the director, lying on the floor and shaking his fists, cries, "You're all sucking my blood!"

10

THE love story continued. *Whity* was April. May, back in Munich, was *The Niklashausen Journey,* a film about a sixteenth-century religious "revolutionary" who wanders over the countryside accompanied by a twentieth-century American Black Panther, played not by Günther but by a white man. Günther had a small part as a peasant. Rainer was apparently saving him to star in what was to be a Cinemascope spectacular (by German standards at the time) called *The American Soldier,* to be shot during the summer in Berlin. The shooting of the May film went smoothly. Even Kurt didn't complain.

> I played a transvestite bishop [he remembers], and Fassbinder gave me the job of casting a dozen choirboys. Not only did I choose them with loving care, I also chose their costumes. I had them come every day to try on tight, short skirts, and Breuer's Costume House became the place of my naked lust.

Rainer's passion for Günther, however, was not finding a similar sort of outlet. On their return from Spain, the group rented a staggeringly expensive (five thousand 1970 dollars a month) villa in Feldkirchen, a suburban township near Munich. Rainer already sensed that the Antitheater communal concept was a dismal failure, but for now it kept going on its own momentum. The living arrangements at Feldkirchen reflected how the group had become hierarchically structured. Rainer and Günther got the master bedroom and its king-size mattress, though Günther was spending more time than ever with his wife and children in Munich. Rainer had become a business partner with Michael Fengler, who had founded a film production company, Filmverlag der Autoren, so Fengler and his girlfriend, Molly, were given an airy room with a balcony almost as big as Rainer's. Kurt laid claim to a small room next to the master's, having been allowed to oust Ursula, who had got there first, much to Rainer's displeasure. She was dispatched to an even smaller room, while tiny Ingrid Caven, who had lately come under Rainer's aegis, was billeted in the privacy of an attic where she could continue her studies. Willi, falling out of favor in proportion to his attraction to Günther, was stuck into what had once been a broom closet, and Irm was consigned to some long-forgotten corner. Harry shuttled back and forth from a commune in Munich, and Hanna, as always, kept and safeguarded her distance, she, too, staying in Munich.

Nominally, the entire group remained a collective, but Rainer's supremacy at Feldkirchen was as certain as the divine right of kings at Versailles, and he held court every day to display it.

"It was fun," Fengler remembers. "Every day there were dozens of people there. It was interesting. It wasn't really a commune, but it looked like one."

According to Kurt, "the doors were never locked. Some people came to get a free meal, others to enjoy the swimming pool, and still others to watch color TV. Fassbinder behaved like Louis XIV. His court was the large kitchen. His throne was at the head of a big oak table, from which he got up only to go to the fridge or the bathroom. Here he ate, drank, napped, and brooded. Actors, directors, film editors, and others presented their credentials here. Projects were discussed, films were cast, favors were granted, and falls from grace were announced. I survived this period by steering clear of the kitchen."

Irm describes Rainer's state of mind at the time:

He grew paranoid. He was so afraid of not being loved that he began to think everybody was against him. When two people were standing and speaking together, he would strain his ears to listen in. When someone was sitting in a corner talking to someone else, he would immediately rush over to one or the other and say, "What did you tell him about me?" He was always checking. He read every letter that came in the mail, no matter to whom it was addressed. He created situations where people conspired, saying, "Now, we've got to tell Rainer that we

50

can't take this anymore!" He provoked this, and when it actually happened, it gave him some sort of pleasure, and somebody would inevitably fall into disgrace. It happened to Harry, it happened to Kurt, it happened to Fengler, and of course to me. One member of the group always had to be in disgrace to show the others how terrible it was. What he was saying was "Look, this is Irm. She is in disgrace. But you are my friends." He switched from one person to another, but there was always a black sheep in the flock. . . .

The tenderness between us and the belief we shared in love was in the past now. He put me through so many trials that I truly believed I was all weakness and evil. I tried suicide. Again and again I tried to leave him, but he would always come and fetch me and I would always return. I was bound to him spiritually and physically, and it was impossible to lead any other life, even part of the time. I was with him day and night. A marathon. It was crazy. If you wanted to go to bed before he did, even at five o'clock in the morning, he called you "traitor."

My only hope was that things would get better. I knew he dreamed of having a child, a small and proper family, though an instinct told me not to have children with Rainer, and I used the pill. That year, nineteen-seventy, we wanted to get married, and we almost did. We came so close. He sent me to Bad Wörishofen, the town he was born in, to get his birth certificate. I have it still today.

What Irm didn't know at the time was that he had already sent someone else on the very same errand. It was true; he did want to marry, and on August 26, during the lunch break in the shooting of *The American Soldier,* the wedding took place in Feldkirchen. The lucky bride was the woman in the attic, the fiery, diminutive redhead Ingrid Caven. Until now she had played only minor parts in Rainer's films and seemingly even lesser ones in his life; nobody had taken her as a serious candidate for his affections, not even when the two of them had gone off to Italy and Greece on what was announced as an "engagement trip." The wedding-day gossip was that Rainer was using Ingrid to spite Günther, to show him that he, too, could have a wife, and perhaps even children. He had already fired him from the starring role in *The American Soldier,* relegating him to a bit part, though he made him the best man at the wedding. The "real" women in Rainer's life, Irm and Hanna, accused Ingrid of slick calculation; whether or not that was true, Ingrid would shortly discover that being Mrs. Fassbinder was more a liability than an asset, at least during their marriage. Anyway, Ingrid denies it, saying, "I was a petit bourgeois with kitsch dreams of submission and a quiet family."

As usual, however, Rainer's apologia would prove to be nearest to the truth, as is shown in this case by the closeness of the relationship he would have with Ingrid for the rest of his life, even though they would be divorced within two years.

"We got married," Rainer would say long after the event, "because we understood one another very well. It was a relationship that had deepened because of what had happened at Almería [during the filming of *Whity*], in spite of Ingrid's not being there. Both of us— she in Munich, me in Almería—suddenly understood the importance of our relationship."

Was this marriage an attempt to become heterosexual? No, that he had never tried to do, "because I know very well it's senseless," he would later say. "I know how to treat women, but the possibilities are limited." Ingrid concurred: "My relationship with Rainer was always very friendly and very intellectual."

On the wedding day, however, this was something the bride was yet to learn. "She went along eagerly," Kurt remembers, "because on the one hand the crazy game excited her and on the other because she could get back at her rivals."

Irm, the most jilted of the jilted, laughs when she thinks now about that day, but she felt quite different then:

> I met him in the bank that morning, and he said, "I'm getting married today." I couldn't believe it. He had just withdrawn a lot of money, about forty thousand marks, and he peeled off five hundred and handed it to me because he somehow always owed me money. He left me in a state of shock, expecting me on the set the next day.
>
> I was insanely jealous. I felt I'd destroyed everything with my jealousies. If I hadn't been so jealous, he'd have had a different image of women. I ran into Hanna outside the bank. She was

jealous, too. She was also in love with Rainer. There was a lot of love between them, and it was a good love, while Ingrid was only conscious of her career.

Hanna and I went to a bar called the Kulisse. By two in the afternoon we were so drunk we'd spent the whole five hundred marks.

At the same hour, Rainer and Ingrid were already married, back on the set, and Ingrid was drunk, too. By all accounts, she showed up at the civil ceremony in that same condition.

The mayor of Feldkirchen, already taken aback when Rainer in a white suit (you can see him in it in *The American Soldier*) and black Günther presented themselves, alone, at the registry office at the hour announced for the wedding, was only slightly relieved when Ingrid finally appeared. She made a staggering entrance, singing a street song from World War II in her Edith Piaf voice:

> Everything passes
> Everything ends
> Comes next December
> Comes another egg*

Peter Berling's recollection of the wedding party is graphic:

"Tout-Munich" came out to the Feldkirchen villa that evening. I had flown in from Rome for the festivities. I guess I was late, because by the time I arrived that splendid August night, people were already fucking in the garden or by the pool. It looked like a gym class, with the coupling under the instruction of a pair of monkeys (a souvenir from Rainer's and Ingrid's pre-honeymoon in Greece), who were going at it with exemplary spontaneity.

I had known Ingrid longer than Rainer had, and when I had congratulated both bride and groom, she called me aside for some "girl talk." In view of what I had learned in Almería about the sexual predilections of Rainer and his male friends, I took

---

*"Another egg" because that was the wartime December ration: one egg per Christmas.

it upon me out of friendship to dampen her exaggerated expectations. Ingrid was convinced that she could turn Rainer straight, so I said, "Ingrid, you're crazy, those are things women can't do." And she said, "But you don't understand how fantastically we make love together!" I said, "You're talking like a kid, Ingrid; that doesn't mean anything, believe me."

Naturally, she didn't believe me, and considering that my own sophistication in such matters was of so recent a vintage, I was being little more than pretentious, but I was as drunk as she was. But when, long after midnight, it came time for the great nuptial moment, Ingrid found the door to the wedding-night bedroom locked. I'll never forget those bloodless little fists drumming on the door, drawing all of us around her. Rainer was inside, fucking the best man.

Since not even Ingrid put an eye to the keyhole, what Rainer was doing on the inside is only an educated guess, but whatever it was, he was doing it for old time's sake. Günther, Kurt's "sensuous colossus," had already been deemed undomesticable by Rainer and he was cast aside in the morning, taken up by Willi of the broom closet. A few days later *The American Soldier* was finished, and the newlyweds, accompanied by one of Rainer's old lovers, Daniel Schmid, went off to Rome as a threesome for the honeymoon.

They checked into the luxurious Parco dei Principi, which adjoins the Borghese Gardens. Rainer sat under the palms by the pool, putting the finishing touches on the script of his next film, while Daniel and Ingrid, lovers of a sort themselves, had no trouble finding amusement.

THE idea going through Rainer's mind for months now was to make a film about the shooting of *Whity*—"a film," to use Rainer's words, "about why living and working together as a group doesn't function, even with people who want it to and for whom the group is life itself." In July, on the so-called engagement trip, he had stopped off in Rome with a six-and-a-half-page treatment for the movie, asking Peter Berling to produce it. A film treatment is normally ten times that length, about half as long as a finished script, but as Rainer told Berling, pressing the treatment into his hands, "Each page corresponds to ten pages of *my* finished script. Multiply that by two and you've got the length you're used to. You can count on it!" Berling, charged with making up a shooting schedule on this slim basis, was skeptical, but the completed screenplay would be as precise as Rainer predicted. He would call it *Beware of a Holy Whore*.

In mid-September, the group began to assemble in Sorrento, south of Naples, where Berling—nicknamed Mutti by Rainer*—had found a hotel setting reminiscent of Almería, a place where the *Whity* shooting had rendered them all personae non gratae.

The newlyweds arrived last, driving from Rome in Rainer's new Chevrolet Stingray. If Ingrid had ever hoped to draw immediate advantage out of being Mrs. Fassbinder, her calculations were thwarted on the way down there. She later described this in a letter to Mutti:

"My wife is no actress!" This is what I heard when we were barely onto the highway, and I was driving Rainer in the Sting-

*See Appendix I.

ray to Sorrento. What amused him was to have "such a little chatterbox behind the wheel of this gigantic bug." The only thing louder than our screaming was the stereo music (Modugno's *Amara Terra Mia*), but both were welcome distractions from the absurd speed racing us south to the showdown with the group, who were already there waiting. I was set on working, at least to assist him somehow. But not so: "My wife puts on a hat, takes a book and goes out to lie in the sun."

Ingrid, though she was to get a good tan, resisted valiantly. She landed a small part, and Rainer would grow to appreciate her uninhibited criticisms during the shooting. On their arrival in Sorrento, the familiar tension among the players was already apparent. Since *Holy Whore* was to be Rainer's critique of the group itself, Mutti worried less about a repetition of the high jinks and tantrums that had characterized the filming of *Whity* than about the danger of outright rebellion. But in the end, Berling says, "we would all jump through the hoop whenever the master summoned." There were in fact high jinks and tantrums galore, but they were only variations déjà vu.

The "plot" of *Holy Whore* was simple: A film troupe with nothing to do but gripe and get drunk waits in a Spanish hotel for the arrival of Jeff, the director. When he finally shows up, he finds only utter chaos and struggles for order. The film they are supposed to shoot is about state-sanctioned violence, but the troupe itself cannot rise above the petty everyday violence that welds or shatters human relationships. Finally, but only after Jeff imposes dictatorial rule, the shooting starts.

"It's strange to see this film today," an interviewer said to Rainer years later. "It's clear that it marked the end of the first period of your work and represents very real self-criticism. Were you aware when you made it that this was the end and a new beginning?"

"I wasn't sure that it was a new start," he replied, "but I knew it had to be the end. With that film we buried the Antitheater, which was our first dream. I didn't know what would happen from then on, but I knew it had to change."

Harry Baer mocks this *a posteriori* talk.

Rainer was always one to amuse himself by leading film critics up the garden path. That the oh-so-clever critics who saw the film fell for his subsequent interpretation doesn't say much for their profession. "One of his most desperate films . . ." "Mercilessly coming to terms with his own persona . . ." It makes my sides split. A whole truckload of color had to be added to turn us ill-mannered slobs into birds of paradise with a Fellini-like tinge of madness. And that the film within the film was supposed to be against state violence was just another slick piece of mischief to inject meaning where Rainer's only concern was to fabricate myths out of trivial inside stories and to crown our lord Fassbinder with a halo around his head.

Mutti calls the film Rainer's "day of reckoning with the 'bloodsuckers,' " and Kurt claims it was an outright vendetta:

He avenged himself on us bitterly and in a very self-righteous fashion with the film *Beware of a Holy Whore,* which recounted, in a way, the Spanish filming. He represented us all as egotistical, whining, selfish rabble who heartlessly walked by and overlooked the existential wanderings of the director. . . . When I read the script I recognized myself despite the name change, and I was outraged at how one-sided Fassbinder had portrayed me. I could have refused the part, of course, but my dependence on him was far too strong. What was I to do alone in Munich while the others were shooting in Sorrento? The thought of it made me so miserable that I preferred to bear the humiliation.

In the many roles we played for him, you could always find a piece of your own personality, but mostly one side—the uglier one, of course.

All of this is partly true, the uglier part, let's say. The film itself, however, contains many layers of truths, and what impressed the critics was its startling frankness. It is not coincidental that this film, like the others of the 1970 series, deals with washouts of radical attempts to live free. We are now in "that strange postrevolutionary period," as Fassbinder himself once called it. The "revolution" of 1968 by now was being seen as a failure. It had begun to consume its own force, turning inward, eating its heart out, so to speak, only to soon reemerge as heartless political terrorism. Fassbinder was not alone in having reached that dead end, and he would never be far from violence, identifying with, say, the Baader-Meinhof group. "They are very clever people," he would say later. "They have great intellectual potential, but also an oversensitive despair which I don't know how one would use constructively. Because they themselves don't know how either, they've flipped." He was, he said, eager to find out "how one can use the great strength those people have." Making *Holy Whore* was a key moment in the search.

For anyone who was present at the filming of *Whity,* or has since heard any reasonable version of the "war stories," there is no doubt about who's who in *Holy Whore,* though only two roles—Hanna's and Kurt's—are played by the persons they are meant to represent. The character of "Jeff," the director, is of course Rainer; "Ricky," his lover, represents Günther; "Sascha," the producer, is Mutti; and so on. It was not who was who, however, that carried the most clout among the group; rather, who *played* whom was considered a better measure of Rainer's judgment of this or that member of the group. Thus only by knowing that Irm, for example, was given no part at all other than dubbing the voice of the actress who plays her on the screen can we understand just how low she had fallen. In the same vein, Ulli and his wife, Katrin, were cast in degrading roles. His part in the making of *Whity,* as producer-financier, is preserved in *Holy Whore* as the character "Manfred," but he himself is made to play an errand boy, while Katrin, real-life scion of an haut bourgeois family in Hamburg, is transformed into a scriptgirl, always seen naked. Harry is reduced to the unctuous husband of a mere extra (played by Ingrid), and Günther is as gone from the cast as he was from Rainer's life.

On the other hand, Rainer is etched in three dimensions: "Jeff," the director in the flesh, is played by a blond Swedish actor named Lou Castel, who dons Fassbinder's beat-up leather jacket but never fails to look if not behave like Prince Charming; "Ricky" is Günther semi-idealized, who shows comprehension of Jeff's creative and sexual needs, though he is really only "in it for the money," and the part of "Sascha," i.e., Mutti, is acted by Rainer himself, providing him the opportunity to show his den-mother, human side.

58

Holy Whore ends with a quotation from Thomas Mann's novella *Tonio Kröger:* "I tell you that I am often weary to death of portraying humanity without participating in what is human." Considering the source—Tonio, who is convinced that artists cannot be normal, decent human beings—it sounds a little like pompous self-pity and is in any case a post-production afterthought. More down-to-earth is Jeff's curtain line, spoken to himself in a sort of epilogue; the film within the film has been made and has turned out, as Hanna predicted, "incredibly beautiful," whereupon the camera zooms on Jeff, who murmurs, "Almería n'existe pas."

It was all over but the packing. There was one last film to be made in 1970, *Recruits in Ingolstadt.* It was shot in November, in and out of Munich. Nobody had his heart in it, above all Rainer, and it shows. He had been hoping that Günther would come crawling back to him and had cast him in *Recruits* as the first and only black soldier in the Nazi army, but Günther had gone home for good to his wife and children.

In the meantime, the rented villa in Feldkirchen had been turned into a high-priced hovel. The antique furnishings had thinned out in the comings and goings of the film crowd, purloined or in pieces rarely swept away. One day that apocalyptic autumn, Rainer and the hangers-on woke up and found the entire contents of the kitchen missing, only to discover them, smashed and splintered, in the empty swimming pool. The chief suspect was Harry, who was thought to be "flipping out," but nobody cared. With the first frost, the garden, already ravaged, took on the appearance of a battlefield, and the love-happy monkeys, who lived in the gazebo, nearly froze. When the Munich zoo refused them shelter, they were left anyway on the doorstep with an Alice in Wonderland–like note: "Take care of us."

Suddenly, to the delight of the landlord, Rainer wanted to leave Feldkirchen. "It happened at the right moment," says Kurt. "Not only had a crazy year come to an end but also a depraved period in Fassbinder's and our lives. Everyone was sick of him. We'd had our fill of Fassbinder for a while."

"Rainer," Harry says, "was disgusted with everybody, including himself. He wanted a pause for reflection. And I'd had enough, too!"

Harry took the first offer that came his way from another director. Kurt tried his acting luck in Bremen. Rainer and his bride rented an apartment in Munich, taking in Willi to complete the ménage, whereupon Irm ran away in desperation, seeking Buddhahood on a macrobiotic diet.

To start the new year, Rainer "dissolved" the Antitheater, which the authorities discovered had never been legally constituted in the first place. Willi, who had been given the job of group business manager when nobody else would accept it, now had to do the dissolving. He had "kept the books" in his broom-closet room at Feldkirchen, in an in-basket that looked more like a wastebasket. The only thing in it that impressed the authorities was his signature on this or that piece of paper, and by virtue of his title, he was saddled with a four-hundred-thousand-mark debt for back taxes on the group's unreported income. Rainer, as director, was ordered to pay half, but there the matter ended, and when Rainer got the bill, he threw Willi out of the household. The reason given was punishment for Willi's having paired off in a way with Günther, but Willi knew better. Thus, he left the fold, too, to write his music for other directors.

NOW Rainer was alone with Ingrid, a bickering husband and wife ensconced in a flat near the English Gardens. An ordinary Münchener couple, so to speak. It didn't last but a moment.

On January 21, 1971, the *Süddeutsche Zeitung*, Munich's leading daily, ran its review of one of Rainer's 1970 films, *The Coffee House*, based loosely on the Goldoni play. The critic wrote: "[Fassbinder's] 'new' style is nothing more than an often boring device: theatricality. The sugar coating with which Fassbinder glazes everything tastes insipid because he does not make it clear that he is interested in the people with whom he is dealing. Prodigies and child prodigies come and go quickly. Antitheater, who believes in you now?"

Five of the nine films shot since the electrifying success of *Katzelmacher* had come out by now, and the reception was nothing like what it had been for *Katzelmacher*. The money had dried up, and the *Süddeutsche Zeitung* review rang like a death knell.

"Everybody was under the impression," says Fengler, who, after Feldkirchen, departed even more precipitously than the others, "that the Fassbinder phenomenon was just a flash in the pan. Nine films in one year, and now it's all over."

Kurt says: "It looked as if everything else had been dissolved along with the Antitheater. The visits from friends were less and less frequent. It was thought that Fassbinder had already scraped the bottom of the barrel and that he was finished. The critics who had said he'd been burning the candle at both ends seemed to have been borne out. I was trying my luck in Bremen, but I felt uprooted and lonely. I yearned for the 'old days,' wanting only to work for Fassbinder again."

The "pause for reflection" was real but only on the speeded-up

Fassbinderian scale. In the early part of the year he wrote three plays, which were staged; two opened in the spring and one in the late autumn of 1971. The themes of all three show what Rainer was reflecting about: a search for a new beginning.

The first one he called *Blood on the Cat's Collar* and subtitled "Isn't It a Shame About People." In it a naïve extraterrestrial named Phoebe makes a study of earthlings. Thinking she has finally understood them, she tries to make contact but succeeds only in alienating them, demonstrating complete miscomprehension.

The Bitter Tears of Petra von Kant, subtitled "Real Feeling," is the story, transexualized into a lesbian love affair, of Rainer's relationship with Günther. Petra von Kant, a highly successful fashion designer, falls in love with Karin, a would-be model who has drifted into Petra's life from the margins of the lower middle class. Petra is continually wounded by Karin, who refuses to give up her male lovers, including her husband, and Petra can never be sure of Karin's affections. Rainer never challenged the view held by those closest to him that every word in the play was spoken either to or by him. But it goes much further than mere revelation or even soul-baring. A year later he would turn it into one of his most powerful films, both versions making a deep descent into the nature of love.

The third play of that year, which would also become a film, is *Bremen Freedom.* It is based on a historical incident, a series of murders by poison committed by a mid-nineteenth-century woman known as "pretty Gesina." Its starting point is another play, *Maria Magdalene,* written at about the time of the case by the great German dramatist Friedrich Hebbel. In both plays bourgeois society is seen as a system of oppression, especially of women, but whereas Hebbel's work ends by questioning the old order, Rainer's questions the "new," that is, the liberated order contemporary radicals still dreamed of in 1971. Rainer's Gesina, renamed Geesche, decides to do something about her plight; everyone responsible for it must die. Her domineering husband, her demanding children, her husband's carbon-copy replacement, her haughty brother, her dunning creditors, and so on, are eliminated one by one by arsenic, but the relief is never more than ephemeral since the oppression always returns, embodied in someone else. Finally, she's caught and she herself must die. Freedom is not what Geesche achieves, nor could her perversion of the quest ever attain it. Later, Rainer would come under severe attack from the extreme left as well as from the women's movement, but with *Bremen Freedom* he had already begun criticizing them, although they hadn't yet caught on.

With these three dramas Fassbinder was playing to an audience larger than he had been accustomed to, by addressing popular sentiments and issues. During the same "pause"—which may be reckoned as the eight-month gap between the making of the last of the 1970 films and the start of the next film in the summer of 1971— Rainer, the movie buff, went into the packed archives of his mind in search of a way to reach, with artistic integrity, as many people as possible.

"The only cinema I can take really seriously," he would conclude not very long afterward, "is American cinema, because it's the only one that has really reached an audience." There were exceptions, he said, but that only proved the rule. He, like most European directors, did not have the courage of the Hollywood masters to tell a story simply, without the complications of the art film. "That takes guts," he said, and maybe one day he'd succeed in telling "naïve stories." "I am constantly trying to do that, although it's very hard. American directors can work from the idea that the U.S.A. is the land of freedom and justice. . . . I find that very beautiful."

His search led him to an intense study of the films of the Danish-born American director Douglas Sirk, and he quickly grew to idolize him. Sirk was forty-five years his senior and was then in virtual retirement, living in Switzerland. He was known in the United States for his schmaltzy melodramas—such as *Magnificent Obsession, Written on the Wind,* and *The Tarnished Angels*—many of them box-office hits of the 1950s, though American critics never placed him in the front rank. Rainer, however, screening film after film in the first months of that year ("The most beautiful films in the world were among them"), experienced in Sirk's large body of work a sensation of discovery that he would later regard as decisive. Here was a man, Rainer saw, who had long ago solved the very dilemma he was now confronting: how to make films that deal honestly with human feelings in a way that has impact on a mass audience.

63

"My encounter with Sirk," he would say later, "removed the fear I had of 'selling out.' . . . Sirk gave me the courage to make films for the public. Before that I believed that serious work meant shunning the Hollywood model. Hollywood movies, which do in fact emulate precise models, seemed quite stupid to me. Until then, my semicultured European scruples held me back, but Sirk, no matter how one regards his films, made me understand that it was possible to pursue this path."

On a wintry day early in that year, Rainer, after writing to the director, made a pilgrimage to Sirk's retirement home in Lugano. Rainer was twenty-five, Sirk past seventy. Years later, at the age of eighty-three, Sirk would recall that meeting:

> Lugano, usually flooded with sunshine, was covered with snow when a group of young Germans, bundled up in overcoats and fighting an icy wind, trudged up the difficult road to my front door. "It's us," he said, "Rainer Werner Fassbinder and a couple of my friends." My wife and I have unforgettable memories of the hours that lay ahead.
>
> We discussed art and literature, theater and cinema, until the wee hours of the morning. For some reason I no longer recall, I began to speak of classical Spanish theater, mentioning the extraordinary productivity of Calderón and of Lope de Vega, to whom his contemporaries attributed a thousand plays; Calderón had, I think, gotten to about half that number. And all of this work, I told my guests, had been created with strictest adherence to formal language and style. To make a long story short, Rainer, who had listened to me attentively, suddenly said, "I would like to be as prolific as they were." As we know now, those words were not merely the expression of a desire.

Rainer traveled a lot in those months. One stop was his favorite watering hole in Paris, the Arab sauna in the Rue Wagram. Along with Ingrid and Daniel Schmid, he had fallen in love with Paris, and the affair would last his lifetime. It was only an hour's flight from Munich. He would keep an apartment there on and off for years, and even at that time he had already learned enough French to impress his friends.

The so-called Arab sauna, frequented by North Africans, was a meeting point of the Parisian gay world. A year earlier, Rainer had taken uninitiated Harry there on a weekend. Harry, before meeting Rainer, had dreamed of traveling, becoming a teacher, marrying and raising a family. The weekend in Paris was his first trip abroad. After being overwhelmed by Rainer's ability to order a meal from a French menu, Harry, his jaw still hanging, went with Rainer to the sauna in Rue Wagram.

> Rainer didn't like the fact that I was still a virgin [Harry remembers], and he had already presented me with a wide range of choices, all boys, of course, but I'd held out. In Paris, though he could charm waiters and bellhops, his enterprise seemed to have come to an end when we went to bed. He just turned over and fell asleep. The trap was sprung the next day in the Arab sauna, where I suddenly found myself stumbling through a labyrinth of dark passages. Grabbing hands came at me from all sides. Behind me I could hear Rainer's now legendary Mephistophelian laughter. He was staging this play, too. Either I was pushed or I lost my balance, but careening to the bottom of the flight of stairs, I fell into the arms of an older man. A father figure. I had my first sexual experience. Short and painless.

Now, in the same sudorific corridors, Rainer met the second of the three great loves of his life. El Hedi Ben Salem was a dark-skinned Berber from Morocco with placid eyes and a volcanic soul. Like Günther, he had a wife and children, five of them, but they lived over the Atlas Mountains on the edges of the Sahara. Salem, a self-made literate, had also taught himself French, and Rainer considered him a "cultural phenomenon," to speak only of his mind. Rainer brought him home to Munich, to install him alongside Ingrid and to put him in movies.

Rainer set himself at once to the task of creating a part for Salem. In those same early months, he was writing the screenplay of what would be his next film. It was spring now and *Petra von Kant,* the play, was due to be staged for a Frankfurt opening in June. Rainer suddenly couldn't be bothered. He gave the job to Willi, making a beginning in drawing some of the group back to his side.

Shortly after *Petra* opened to so-so reviews, one of the 1970 films, *Whity,* suffered an even worse fate, premiering at the Berlin Film Festival in early July. Not only was it poorly received, but it was an instant box-office flop. The pause for reflection was over.

"His call made me leave everything and rush off to Munich," Kurt remembers. "Finally Fassbinder wanted to make another film." He didn't care about what role he'd be given. "The most important thing was that I could work with him again."

Harry ("I can't stand it anymore") responded with Pavlovian glee when Rainer rang the bell of his single-occupancy-only apartment and announced, "I'm making a new film in Munich." Taking one look around Harry's new quarters, he added, "Great, this can be our production office!" Hanna and Irm jumped, too, Irm getting the leading role, if not as a reward for her inextinguishable love, then at least for her troubles. Rainer, budgeting the film on scant financing, founded a production company called Tango Film, though it wasn't any more legal than Antitheater-X. Ingrid, for the first time permitted to call herself Mrs. Fassbinder, was named the producer, and Rainer's mother, Lilo, was given Tango's purse strings. Her husband, Rainer's hated stepfather, Mr. Eder, had just died, and a new beginning between mother and son was in the making here too. For years, ever since Rainer had come to call on Eder and Lilo arm in arm with a transvestite as blatant as a vibrator, he had been allowed to visit his mother only on Sunday afternoons, when Eder would go out for a walk. Now Rainer could look forward once again to Senfbraten roasts and Königsberger meatballs as only Lilo knew how to concoct them, and Eder, by leaving the scene, was spared the merciless portrayal of his persona that Rainer was writing into the new script.

After the mourning, Rainer took his mother for a summer holiday in Rome in the company of Ingrid, Daniel, and the new light in Rainer's life, El Hedi Ben Salem. In Rome he renewed his acquaintance with Peter Chatel, who was to become one of the most enduring members of the group. Their first meeting had taken place well before Rainer began making feature-length films, and Chatel was one of the few people who knew and admired his early theater work, but Rainer had taken an immediate dislike to him. "He called me a 'fashion queen,' " says Chatel. Chatel had gone on to a successful acting career in Italy, and now, in Rome, Rainer would see him in another light.

> I remember one tea party in my apartment that summer [says Chatel]. Ingrid and Rainer were there, and Daniel was there, and Lilo and Salem. And Rainer simply would not talk at all to me. Then, something strange happened. By pure chance, a lot of famous people called me. Visconti called and Zeffirelli called and I don't remember who else called. After the calls, though, there was this sudden interest on Rainer's part, though he still didn't say a word. Later in the day, it was evening, we all went to the beach at Fregene, where I had the keys to [actor] Walter Chiari's house. Rainer went off to a corner to write and we all went swimming. It was not until the end of the evening that he finally spoke to me, saying, "Well, if you ever want to work in Germany, just let me know." I was pleased, of course, but sure it had to do with all those phone calls.

The offer in any case was genuine. A few days later Chatel received word that Rainer wanted him for a small part in the new film. "I signed for an enormous salary," he says, "three thousand marks for one day's work, but of course I never saw a pfennig. I suppose it looked good on their books."

The new film was *The Merchant of Four Seasons,* the first since his recent discovery of Douglas Sirk and the first with a wide-audience orientation. It was shot in Munich in eleven days of August at the incredibly low cost of 178,000 marks. These facts alone ought to make *Merchant* the first lesson for every aspiring filmmaker, since it is almost always ranked among Rainer's best, having been an outstanding critical and commercial success.

The actual almost around-the-clock shooting could make a lesson, too, though little of it recommendable. The tension on the set was particularly excruciating. Ingrid, sporting a queen-size cigarette holder as Mrs. Fassbinder, the producer, rubbed Hanna, Irm, Harry, and probably everyone else the wrong way—except Rainer, who always enjoyed volcanic eruptions. Rainer's new friend Salem seemed likable enough to the others, but it was quickly noted that when he had a few drinks he could become truly fearsome. Harry, without a drop, managed to get angry enough to throw Ingrid out of a ground-floor window and go after Irm with a knife. "I was treated like filth," says Irm—particularly by Rainer, who continually reduced her to tears in the filming. Later, recalling the intensity of her performance on the screen, others would see Rainer's cruelty to Irm as a triumph of directorial technique; her undeniable acting achievement would in fact bring her the prestigious National Film Award for the role she created in *Merchant.*

All of the roles had once again been drawn out of Rainer's autobiographical hat, but this time that was merely the starting point for a great departure from the previous films. Set in the West Germany of the economically booming fifties, *Merchant* is the story of an ordinary rotten family, Rainer's own. He was only a kindergartener when the events he recounts actually occurred, and his mother was astonished by the accuracy of his recollections, mainly about his favorite uncle, who was the victim of the family's middle-class pretensions.

In the film, Hans Epp, the fictionalized uncle, is a former foreign legionnaire, an ex-policeman, and a would-be engineer. Unable to live up to his mother's expectations, rejected as an underachiever by his "one great love," and cuckolded by his wife, he earns his daily fare by peddling fruit in the alleys and courtyards of Munich. After he has a heart attack, his wife tries to leave him, and he grows increasingly despondent. A fight with his treacherous family sends him off to a bar, where he drinks himself to death.

"It is a story," Rainer would later comment, "familiar to almost everyone I know. A man wishes that he had made something other of his life than he did. His education, his surroundings, and circumstances frustrate the fulfillment of his dream."

No other Fassbinder film would gain such unanimous approval as *Merchant* did when it opened the following year. More than one critic would call it the best film made in postwar Germany. What amazed them was how Rainer had succeeded in breathing life into so many of the timeworn stereotypes—complete with a domineering mother and a shrewish, unfaithful wife—that could be found any day of the week jerking tears on TV or at the neighborhood movie theater. The leap forward was Rainer's realistic, unsentimental treatment of characters who are merely playing the roles bequeathed them by the existing social structure. What he created in *Merchant,* wrote Thomas Elsaesser, one of his most perspicacious critics, was "the uneasy awareness of watching a documentary about people playing out a fiction." The wholly positive feedback from his public, coming so soon after his appreciation and conscious emulation of Sirk, led to an outpouring of successful films over the next few years, in which Elsaesser, writing in 1976, detected the Sirkian-inspired pattern:

> The typical situation in a Fassbinder film, where a mother/father, wife/husband or friend/colleague makes demands on the hero/heroine that are sadistic, or betray, deceive or abandon him/her, is dramatized in such a way that these dominating figures, from whom there is objectively or subjectively no escape, also have their reasons, are sometimes well-meaning or possess complex motives over not all of which they have control. ... The hero, by contrast, is given a moral/emotional innocence that almost makes him the holy fool in a Dostoevskian world of universal prostitution. His simple-mindedness, his obstinacy in hanging on to simple truths and direct feelings, become a form of higher wisdom, the gesture that unmasks the stupidity of self-interest, prejudice and oppression. Evil then appears depersonalized, as somehow inherent in the social system as a whole. What the films ultimately appeal to is solidarity between victims.

"When I show people, on the screen, the ways that things can go wrong," Rainer would tell an interviewer, "my aim is to warn them that that's the way things *will* go if they don't change their lives."

O UT of the utter discord of his life he had found a way to create what others saw as harmony and beauty in his work. It could hardly have been intentional, but the process of refining his art was accompanied by further departures from normal human behavior. Thomas Mann has written: "The artist must be inhuman, extra-human; he must stand in a strange, aloof relationship to our humanity"; only "the frigid ecstasies of the artist's corrupted nervous system" could generate art. Rainer, of course, had read this, but literary authority was not at the root of his amoral comportment. He had issued himself an unrenewable license to traipse around heaven and hell, and it went unchallenged until it expired.

Like most of the years of the mere decade that lay ahead, 1972 was very little heaven and a lot of hell. Hell is what Rainer would make of his relationship with Salem.

Charged to the full by the impact of his latest work, Rainer whipped himself into a frenzy of stage and filmmaking activity that would last until a relative slowdown five years later. In terms of titles, 1972 would add "only" four to his filmography, but that is deceptive. The great central workpiece of the year was a five-part television miniseries, each segment of which was as long and as complex as a feature film. The series, called *Eight Hours Are Not a Day,* was a dramatization of the everyday lives of a community of factory workers and their families. Telecast at prime time on the nation's number-one channel, it gave Rainer the widest audience he'd had so far and at the same time multiplied his political enemies on both the right and the left. The former saw to it that the series, which had been conceived in eight, not five parts, was canceled when it became clear, at least to them, that Rainer was carrying out an enunciated threat "to make things dangerous to the so-called ruling class," while the left saw the danger in Rainer's failure to raise a Marxist fist.

In January he had shot the film version of *The Bitter Tears of Petra von Kant,* and before starting *Eight Hours,* he made a film based on a work by a contemporary German playwright, Franz Xaver Kroetz. Called *Wildwechsel,* it has no established English title, though *Jail Bait,* which is what *New York Times* film critic Vincent Canby would call it in his 1977 review, is quite apt.* *Wildwechsel,* a poignant story of a pregnant teenager, would become a cause célèbre on its release at the end of the year, and when even the playwright denounced it as obscene, Rainer would trade off a penis in close-up for access to the general market. But that was all unforeseen during the shooting, when Rainer often repeated a defense of his artistic immunity that went something like this: "If you're always trying to avoid being misunderstood, you're finished."

Uppermost in his mind in the early part of the year was a half-baked notion of becoming the third parent of Salem's children. Nobody remembers exactly when, but around this time, Rainer and Salem made what must have been a quick trip to the oasis in the Algerian hinterland where Salem's wife and five children wrung out an existence. Presumably to lighten the burden on the Mrs., Rainer and Salem returned to Germany with two of the boys, Abdelkader, eleven, and Hamdan, nine. Back in Munich, Rainer instructed Kurt to find suitable living quarters in Cologne, where *Eight Hours Are Not a Day* was due to start in April and roll over a four-month period. In the meantime the boys, cutely outfitted as twins, were handed over to Rainer's mother for Senfbraten and sympathy. By the time they all got to Cologne, where Kurt had rented a huge penthouse that looked out on one of Europe's most awesome cathedrals, Rainer had decided that one son was enough to start with. He farmed out the younger boy, Hamdan, to the actor Hans Hirschmüller, who had played Rainer's uncle in *The Merchant of Four Seasons* and now had a juicy part in *Eight Hours,* and who couldn't say no. Hirschmüller, however, had three children of his own, and they treated the younger "twin" cruelly, provoking extremes in unsavory conduct on the part of the

---

*Variety, reviewing it in 1976, translated the original title—which refers to the movement of wild animals from one part of their habitat to another—as "Game Pass."

newcomer. Soon, but probably not soon enough to prevent lasting trauma, Hamdan would be shunted off to Salem's sister in Tunis, getting off nevertheless luckier than his brother. Rainer, like most prospective mothers or fathers, had no idea what he was in for, but unlike his more orthodox counterparts, he was unendowed with parental scruples. Within a few weeks, his "son" was declared an intolerable nuisance and treated like Cinderella, virtually imprisoned in a back room; and when the flat got crowded, which was often, he was left out on the terrace. Salem, unable to deal with such a fundamental and heart-wrenching conflict of interest, let out his frustration on the boy, maltreating him to the point of violence.

This situation was relieved when Kurt volunteered to take in Abdel, but since Kurt already had a confessed weakness for young boys in the style of the ancients, surrendering Abdel to Kurt's hospitality was yet another act of irreparable thoughtlessness. On the other hand, by now it was becoming clear that Abdel's natural father was a homicidal maniac.

Salem, Kurt says, "was an affable, affectionate man, ready to be of help, but could, after enjoying whisky, become a furious, demolishing devil. We all liked him, but sometimes also had to fear for our lives when he had his drunken attacks."

Rainer, reflecting later on his relationship with Salem and additional empirical experience with other Arabs gained in the sauna in Rue Wagram, would formulate the undoubtedly erroneous opinion that "many Arabs, who are not supposed to drink alcohol, never get completely drunk if they stick to beer or wine or stuff like that. But when they drink whisky, even if the amount of alcohol is the same, they go wild. I don't know how to explain it, unless they feel the word 'alcohol' is synonymous with 'whisky.'" In any case, he went on, "whenever Salem drank whisky, being with him became really dangerous."

In the early part of their relationship, Rainer made light of Salem's dementia, even employing it as his latest "secret weapon" to create the kind of tension that fascinated him. Peter Chatel, who was in Cologne during the filming of *Eight Hours,* remembers one such incident. Chatel was to have one of the leading roles in the series, but he had been in an automobile accident and his face was too freshly scarred ("Don't worry," Rainer had wired him, "I'll write you a

Frankenstein movie"). Well enough for a minor part, however, he had come to Cologne for one day's shooting, and Rainer had invited him to stay a few days longer as his guest.

We were having a drink in his penthouse just across from the cathedral [Chatel recalls], when all of a sudden Salem came at us with a knife. He was very, very jealous because he thought I'd had an affair with Rainer. But when he was approaching us with this knife, I didn't take the situation seriously, and I said to Rainer, kind of like a character in a Noël Coward play, "For whom is this knife?" And Rainer said, "Why, for you, I suppose."

I realized then it was quite serious and I started not running but walking away, and Salem followed, threatening me. Then Rainer took off the chain he was wearing around his neck and threw it over the balcony, so Salem rushed down and retrieved it on the square I don't know how many stories below, because it was a voodoo or something. But when he got back he started chasing me through the apartment. He wanted to throw *me* over the balcony!

I hid in the bedroom, pushing the wardrobe against the door, and all of a sudden, I heard Rainer's voice saying, "Well, anyway, I have to go out to get cigarettes." And I said, "You must be out of your mind to leave me alone here," and eventually Rainer calmed him down. But I really believe he provoked such situations because it somehow made you dependent on him.

The incidents began to pile up, and Chatel, now more and more a regular in the group, became the butt of Salem's jealousy. Rainer had accepted an offer to stage a number of plays in the industrial city of Bochum, and toward the end of the year, the group moved into a house on the edge of town. The house was promptly laid waste by Salem in one of his alcoholic seizures.

I was to live there, too [says Chatel], but when I arrived, two weeks later than everyone else, Ingrid met me at the station and said I'd be wiser taking an apartment elsewhere. Which is what I did. Then the others followed, moving out of the wrecked house and renting in my building. Salem had a part in the first play and I didn't, so one night he came home and walked in on Rainer and me in my apartment. We were sitting in the dark, drinking champagne after a meal of caviar and lobster. We happened to be simply watching television, and the caviar, lobster, and champagne happened to be the only food the restaurant would send over, but I guess it looked to Salem like a producer romancing his starlet, and he went crazy once again. But the worst came the next day.

I was sitting in the lobby of the theater when Salem approached me and leaned over. I thought he wanted to whisper something in my ear so I sort of met him halfway. Then he bit me. He bit me on my cheek drawing blood. Everybody had his back to us and when I started screaming they all turned around and Rainer asked me what was wrong. "What's wrong?" I said, showing him the gaping wound on my cheek, "Salem just bit me!" "Oh, bullshit," said Rainer, "you did it yourself!"

The unconcern stopped when Rainer himself felt in jeopardy. Three films after *Eight Hours Are Not a Day*—we are now in 1973 —Rainer made a movie he called *Fear Eats the Soul,* from an original screenplay he had written with Salem in mind for the starring role. Until now Salem had acted only in minuscule parts in some of the films and plays since *Merchant,* and casting him as Ali, the Moroccan immigrant protagonist of *Fear Eats the Soul,* gave rise to the suspicion among the group that Salem was being handed a farewell gift. Salem was unaware of the gossip, and considering the performance he turned in and the success of the film, he certainly gave more than he received. In any case, Rainer had in fact concluded that Salem was dangerous to his health, and immediately after the shooting in Munich, he dispatched Salem on a false mission to get him out of the house.

Rainer was scheduled to stage Ibsen's *Hedda Gabler* in Berlin, and Salem was sent ahead to rent and furnish an apartment they would share. Doggishly obedient when sober, Salem went to great lengths to prepare for Rainer's home comforts, but the master, when he finally arrived, never moved in.

"I was so busy [working]," Rainer said later, "I didn't have much

74

time to devote to him, so I guess he felt very alone in Berlin. For the first time in the three and a half years that we were together he turned against me."

Rainer, unbeknownst to Salem, went to stay with the owner of a Berlin gay bar. The man was reputed to be a sexual Titan, though Rainer seems to have been more attracted by his rags-to-riches-to-rags personal story, which would in fact form the basis of his next film, *Fox and His Friends.* This professional interest was not on the grapevine at the time, however, and when the rumors that were eventually reached Salem, the manhunt was on.

Informed and alarmed, Rainer closed the *Hedda Gabler* rehearsals to "outsiders," meaning Salem, slipped in and out of the theater with stealth, and shifted his sleeping quarters from one hotel to another. Salem continued to lurk around the theater, sulking in the company of the group, and when Rainer skipped town on opening night, Salem became bent on revenge.

"I'm going to kill somebody," he told Kurt and some of the others. "It's going to get in the newspapers and that'll be the end of Rainer."

Nobody doubted his capacity to do so, particularly when he flashed a long knife to illustrate his intentions, but neither did anyone worry. The threat was actualized in his next drunken fury, in which he stabbed and seriously wounded three strangers. He was spirited out of the country by friends before the press could put it all together, though a warrant for his arrest was issued in Germany. Kurt says that Rainer took the news coldly and refused to answer Salem's desperate calls for help from abroad. The couple, however, were reunited briefly once more, in Marrakesh, where Rainer, filming *Fox and His Friends* some months later, gave Salem a small part.

Salem, according to Rainer, had by then rid himself of his compulsion to violence, somehow articulating his belief that his aggressiveness was related to his submission to Rainer. "Most people have no understanding of this phenomenon," said Rainer, "but he just looked at me and came out coldly with, 'You don't have to be afraid anymore.' That was really one of the most captivating moments of my life. It's subtle things like these that restore one's faith in Freud." It was a restoration destined to be shattered, though they would never see one another again. Over the next few years, Kurt says, rumors reached the group "that Salem was running around Western Europe like a maniac." In 1977 Salem hanged himself in a prison cell in France. Not until the final year of his own life would Rainer receive the news, which "he took silently," says Kurt. "He only gave instructions to preface the film he was then making, his last, with the dedication 'To my friendship with El Hedi Ben Salem.'"

14

NOT without some irony, it was the "farewell gift" film in which Salem had played the leading role, *Fear Eats the Soul,* that catapulted Rainer to the threshold of world fame. His twenty-first film, it was released in the spring of 1974 at the time of their definitive parting. Some months back, a leading German newspaper, unimpressed with Rainer's recent work, had revived an earlier refrain, writing his artistic obituary. He was a "tired boy wonder," it said, "a genius ruined by too much success too soon." But *Fear Eats the Soul,* followed closely by *Effi Briest,* which had a dazzling premiere at the Berlin Film Festival in June of the same year, laid to rest once and for all any further talk about burnout.

By now, at twenty-nine, he had established his name in West Germany, was a closely watched favorite on the European film festival circuit, and was being noticed among the cognoscenti in New York and London. Film critic Andrew Sarris of the *Village Voice,* who, along with Vincent Canby of the *New York Times* and Penelope Gilliatt of the *New Yorker,* was among the first American observers to recognize and even champion Rainer's talent, has recorded his initial filmic encounter:

> He first began attracting attention at the New York Film Festival in the early '70s with *Recruits in Ingolstadt* and *The Merchant of Four Seasons.* I recall David Newman's raving to me about the erotic attraction of a new German actress named Hanna Schygulla in *Recruits.* It was something, Newman insisted, in the way she wore her lipstick. When I caught up with Fassbinder and Schygulla in *The Merchant of Four Seasons,* I was entranced by an extraordinary mixture of stylization, sensuality, passion, and disgust. At first glance, his mise-en-scène

77

seemed sluggish and undeveloped. Nothing in my aesthetic had prepared me for his shallow field, obtrusively static blocking, and ritualized line readings. There had been many campy filmmakers on the fringes of the festival scene around the time of this unlabeled period of film history. But from his earliest work, Fassbinder displayed an unusual degree of rigor and control for a filmmaker with such a playfully perverse sensibility. He never wallowed in self-mockery or self-hatred, and he could cut away from his most painful traumas. I became aware of his razor-sharp artistry. . . .

In England critic Tony Rayns was preparing a book for the British Film Institute, bringing together a collection of analytical comments on Rainer's work by some of his earliest discoverers. Rayns's purpose, according to his introduction to *Fassbinder,* was "to confront the discrepancy between Fassbinder's status at home in West Germany and his status abroad." In Germany, there was a "relentless bombardment" of Fassbinder productions on the screen, stage, television, and radio, frequently generating scandal and controversy in the mass media, while elsewhere there was only a sprinkling of art-house movies, inspiring either acclaim from or dismissal by a small circle of insiders.

Among the writers published by Rayns in *Fassbinder* was a Danish journalist named Christian Braad Thomsen, who had been following Rainer's career and interviewing him at intervals since 1971. It was Thomsen, in fact, who had conducted the first in-depth interview with Rainer by any writer, at the Berlin Film Festival the year *Whity* had been thumbed down by the German critics. Thomsen, who tagged after Rainer for the rest of his life, was not the first in print, but the Rayns book brought out all of his interviews thus far, making them the first to appear in English. The most exhaustive bibliography on Rainer—the posthumous edition of *Reihe Film 2*—lists more than one hundred major interviews, so Rainer's answer to Thomsen's first question is notable because it shows Rainer ready from the start to be candid.

Q. Before you began making films, you wrote and produced plays in the theater—or rather the "anti-theater," as you called it. Why did you gradually turn to cinema?

A. ... I wanted to make films from the start, but it was much easier to begin in the theater. And it has paid off: when I *did* start making films, my previous work in the theater made it much easier to get credit. The success of my early films, the very fact that they were invited to festivals and that sort of thing, had something to do with theater enjoying more respect than film in Germany. You'd hear, "Well, yes, he makes films, but he's done plays, too, so the guy must have something."

Among the discoverers, the true Christopher Columbus of all the critics was the West German writer Wolfgang Limmer, who in 1973 brought out the first Fassbinder book anywhere. In 1969, after seeing Rainer's first feature-length film, *Love Is Colder Than Death,* unanimously panned by his colleagues, Limmer decided on the spot that they were wrong.

I didn't write about this film [Limmer later recalled], but I felt something peculiar, that there was someone very talented behind it. It took a year or two, then the whole German cinema world began to realize that there was a big genius coming up, mainly because the Fassbinder films were so different from the rest of the German films. There was something about the quantity as well as the quality. If you didn't like one film, you knew that within a few weeks there would be another, so it was hard to be completely disappointed.

The quality aspect was harder to explain. It had to do with energy, with honesty, with the way he handled feelings. At that time, the rest of the German directors were eager to make political and social statements about how bad life was in Germany, and a few of them were quite good at it, but they couldn't deal with human feelings, especially their own. Fassbinder could, and he did it with immediacy, which was almost unique on the German scene.

I remember when I finally met him. It was when he was screening those Douglas Sirk films. I heard about it and called him, asking if I could come. He said it was all right with him, but when I showed up he was very aloof. Later, I understood that he had a problem with people he considered as "intellectuals," and because I wrote about film, I was one of them. The

79

tension that that created between us lasted for years. My impression of *him* was that I had never met a guy like this before, a person of such force and determination, who knew exactly what he was going after and how he was going to get it. I saw him as a planet drawing more and more satellites around him.

We never really became friends, but little by little the distance between us narrowed. Still, not once did he say a word about my reviews of his films, and they weren't always favorable. That was class, because all the others would read your criticism and call you up and say, "You're just bullshit, man," and that sort of stuff. He understood how criticism worked in his favor. He knew that if one person writes that's a bad film and another says it's great, people go to the theaters to see what it's all about and decide for themselves who's right. He didn't lobby, like the others. You had to go to him.

The year that Limmer's ground-breaking Fassbinder book appeared, 1973, also saw the publication of the first book on the New German Cinema, which contains the first published interview with Rainer. The book, titled *Die Filmmacher (The Filmmakers),* was compiled by two German cineasts, Barbara Bronnen and Corinna Brocher, and Brocher had interviewed Rainer just prior to the filming of *Effi Briest.* The encounter took place at the Venice Film festival, with Rainer buoyant if not flamboyant after back-to-back successes at the Cannes and Berlin festivals, with *Merchant* at the former and *Petra von Kant* at the latter. He had affirmed his Sirkian influence and now he spoke easily if not flippantly about his own style.

Q. How did you learn to make films?
A. By making them. I did the sound in one film, assistant direction in another, and I acted in a few. I was assistant director on a film about polio-crippled children and how they do sports. I did the sound for a documentary on unmarried mothers in northern Italy, and I acted in army films that were made to show the poor soldiers that when you work as a mechanic in the motor pool, if you put oil on the brake shoes you're likely to cause a fatal accident. That's how I learned to make films. And then I often

went to the movies, three or four times a day. I didn't care what was playing. I just did what I could in a day. . . .

Q. How were you able to make so many films in so short a time?

A. Because I worked so fast. The less shooting days you have, the cheaper everything is, and the more films you can make.

Q. Isn't it also because you had a team that worked so well together?

A. Almost any team could, because I am extremely sure of myself. With Ballhaus, when he became my new cameraman, it took him a week or two until he got it. At the beginning, he was incredibly slow and it nearly drove me crazy. He had to learn to set up his lights in one hour instead of four. . . . The same with the actors. Hanna Schygulla, Irm Hermann, and others became a lot more confident along with me as the years went by, which makes everything go faster. When I was less confident, I had less discipline and I was a lot more hysterical during shooting than today. . . .

Q. Many of your films were made without paying salaries. Don't you think this altruistic system goes a little too far? You can't always depend on the idealism of others.

A. That's not my system. If I make a feature film and nobody gets paid a salary, the people who work for me know with one hundred percent certainty that a month later I'll film another one of my stories and that this time they'll be paid. Maybe another reason is that I make my films so fast that they say to themselves, "I'm better off playing a part that'll be seen by a lot of people who may make me offers than hanging around Munich, so why not stand in front of his camera for a couple of days." If I were making a film once every three years and still counting on people's idealism, then of course I'd be exploiting them.

The nonsalaried people in question did not always agree with that assessment, even when they *were* getting paid. During the filming of *Effi Briest,* which coincided with the publication the *Filmmakers* interview, Hanna led a revolt of the group, protesting low wages. The wages remained unchanged, but Hanna's insubordination, which Rainer usually tolerated in silence, brought their relationship to a breakup that would last almost five years. To her demands for a collective hike in salary, Rainer responded by shouting at her, "I can't stand the sight of your face anymore! You bust my balls! You bore me so, I can't imagine ever having an idea that would make me want to work with you again. You're used up!"

Peter Berling remembers:

> We were coming out of the Zoopalast theater in Berlin, where *Effi Briest* had just overwhelmed the festival crowd. The cries of "bravo" from the standing ovation could still be heard. I was walking alongside Rainer, who looked a little sheepish in his joy. "The way I see it," I said, "I just saw your goodbye film to Hanna." Rainer shushed me, murmuring under his breath, "Stop talking so loud; she's right behind us!" Then he added, "How did you know?" I knew because I knew Rainer in his own way had fallen in love with his new leading lady, Margit Carstensen, who had eclipsed Hanna by then. And besides, I knew what a goodbye film looked like since I'd seen the one he made for Salem.

That was on June 28, 1974. Many of the people who had been closest to Rainer either in duration or intensity of feeling were gone or fading. Berling in fact had been right about Hanna's swan-song appearance. Günther and Salem and sons were of course gone too, and by now Rainer had divorced Ingrid. Although that was a mere bookkeeping adjustment, she too would soon be off on her own. Even abiding Irm was going out slowly. She had come under the spell of a guru, and had added abstinence from coffee and cigarettes to her vegetarian ways. So it was probably her new religion and good living that had given her the wherewithal to turn down two consecutive roles in which Rainer had cast her. She had reached the peak of her career with her award-winning performance in *The Merchant of Four Seasons,* and when Rainer "rewarded" her with a nonspeaking bit part in a play in which she had to climb a ladder to exhibit herself without panties, for the first time in her life she said no. Her pride still shows when she recalls that moment:

> I knew it was a test, but I said, "No, I won't do that," and I persisted. He couldn't conceive of my refusing him, and he

tried everything. He almost beat me to death on the streets of Bochum, but I screamed and I yelled, knowing in my heart that I was finding the strength to leave him. Then, in the very next film, he wanted me to play a whore in a garter belt, and when I said no, he came around early the next morning holding a bottle of milk, and he hit me on the head with it. But I didn't do the part. He tried again and again to dissuade me; then he stopped. I had defeated him with my inner strength.

Irm's "inner strength," considering its initial underdeveloped state, still needed nurturing on an all-grain diet before she would take the final step, but after Hanna departed, Irm did disappear for a while. The void that was "colder than death" inside him was filled for a time—the last time—a month later when his third and ultimate love entered Rainer's life.

15

GOING on thirty, Rainer had slimmed down to play the title role of the working-class homosexual in *Fox and His Friends,* and when Harry remarked that he hadn't seen him so fit since the Antitheater days, Rainer beamed.

"With my looks," he said, "I could still make a couple of fast marks on the street."

It was not Rainer's looks but those of his new lover that had kindled the final passion. Kurt was there when the lightning struck. They were eating in the Deutsche Eiche, a saloon and rooming house with a lively gay scene in Munich's Reichenbachstrasse. Rainer was in the process of adopting the Eiche and would soon make it famous as *his* place. Kurt remembers:

> We were having the Eiche's usual "dish of the day,"
> Schweinebraten mit Knöll [roast pork with dumplings], when
> Rainer suddenly stopped eating and nudged me. "Look at him,"
> he said; "he looks like James Dean."
>
> I glanced up. He was pointing to the fellow washing the beer
> mugs. He was a typical Bavarian country boy who was no
> longer a boy but around thirty. He was okay but I couldn't see
> any resemblance to the mythical dream man and said so. But
> Rainer insisted and he sent me to find out who the pretty-boy
> was. He told me he was a butcher and that his name was Armin
> Meier. He worked in the neighborhood and had a room in the
> Eiche, where he sometimes helped out in the evenings, which
> was when the place filled up with leather freaks and male danc-
> ers from the nearby Gärtnerplatz Theater. I reported back to
> Rainer, who didn't have the nerve to approach him. He made
> me come back with him the next night and then night after night

84

just to keep him company while he stared at Armin. Finally, we invited him for a drink after hours, but Rainer was still too shy to go any further.

On my birthday, Rainer rented the whole Eiche and made me a party. First he had to get totally drunk, but near the end of the evening he disappeared with Armin, and when I saw him the next morning he said, "Last night was our wedding night." His happiness was literally glowing.

Armin, like Günther, was another biological offshoot of the war in Germany. He was a product of the *Lebensborn,* a sinister sexual fantasy hatched and put into practice by Hitler's SS chief, Heinrich Himmler. Himmler, a onetime breeder of rabbits, had had a notion about improving the stock of the Master Race by crossing the best with the best. Armin could remember only one encounter with his mother and none at all with his father. The Master Race was redefined when conquered, and Armin was brought up by nuns with conventional pretensions. He was still illiterate when at the age of fourteen he fell into the clutches of a country doctor, who took him in as a domestic, went out of his way to arrest his mental development, and abused him sexually for the next twelve years. Shown the door when the doctor finally lost interest, Armin drifted into Munich and got a job in a slaughterhouse, the likes of which would become the setting of a memorable scene of a 1978 Fassbinder film, though Armin would not live to see it.

"For me," Rainer said later, explaining what he had seen in Armin, "he represented the only possibility of putting some order into my life." This statement was ridiculed, behind his back, to be sure, by people who had witnessed one or another aspect of their inchoate and tragic relationship, but in the context of Rainer's ineluctable search for a family we can believe this is what he felt at the time. He may also have been attracted to Armin the butcher. Rainer had a faculty for anticipating his own future, both in life and film. His very first discovery of the joys of sex, he has already told us, was with a butcher's apprentice. In his 1969 play *Pre-Paradise Sorry Now,* he speaks of a murderer who once worked for a butcher, and in *Blood on the Cat's Collar,* staged four years before he met Armin, one of the characters is a butcher who had been repeatedly molested by his first employer. The male lead in the 1972 film *Wildwechsel* works in a factory where chickens are butchered, frozen, and packaged, and he bears Rainer's self-representational film name, Franz. Butchers, butchery, and butcher shops continually filed past his camera, and, he told some of his friends, they were also a theme of his dreams.

Several other instances of Rainer's "clairvoyance" can be cited— usually having to do with the destiny of characters he created and identified with himself—but in the case of Armin it borders on the uncanny. Rainer dedicated *Fox and His Friends* "to Armin and all the others," and this has fostered the belief that the character of Fox, played by Rainer, is modeled after Armin.

Ronald Hayman observes:

> Fassbinder chose to play the working-class part he identified with Armin, Fox. . . . Fox, when we meet him, seems almost a latter-day equivalent of Rousseau's noble savage, unspoiled, with, apparently, a great potential for happiness. But he will be dead at the end of the film . . . he is unable to understand his lover's perfidy. Finally he kills himself with an overdose: Fassbinder was accurately anticipating the suicide Armin had not yet committed.

Hayman is correct except on one score. Not only had Rainer "foreseen" in 1974 Armin's 1978 suicide because of his failure to comprehend what he would perceive as betrayal, he had done so before ever laying eyes on Armin. He had written the script for *Fox and His Friends* and the filming was all but finished before that evening when he first noticed the "James Dean" washing beer mugs in the Eiche. What makes it somewhat more spooky is that Fox's real name in the movie is Franz (again, Rainer's filmic name for himself). Fox-Franz-Rainer played by Rainer, done in by drugs on the screen, would of course end up that way in real life, and the character often sounds more like the Fassbinder persona than that of anyone else he knew.

The release of *Fox and His Friends* provided Rainer with further acclaim and another tier of enemies to go with it. He had hardly shoveled his way out from the scorn heaped on him by the right and left for *Eight Hours Are Not a Day* when feminists showered abuse on him because of the way he portrayed the quietly suffering heroine

86

of *Effi Briest,* and now, with *Fox,* he was provoking sharp divisions among gays.

Whoever else the character of Fox may have been patterned on, the gay-bar owner with whom Rainer had stayed in Berlin when hiding out from Salem is in there somewhere. Rainer had collected all the threads of his story and had rewoven them. The man had been penniless when he hit a lottery jackpot, whereupon his lover contrived to make him put more and more of the winnings into a foundering paper mill, until all the money was gone.

More or less the same thing happens in the film, though Rainer adds elements of his own life, culled from his past on the streets: Fox is picked up in a public toilet by an antiques dealer, who introduces him to Eugen. Fox and Eugen become lovers, and when Fox wins a lottery, he puts the money into Eugen's family business, a printing plant. The money runs out, Eugen leaves him, returning to a former lover, and Fox, his heart broken, dies of an overdose of drugs.

Rainer claimed that his use of the gay milieu was incidental. "Precisely because of its setting," he said, "I think people look at it more carefully, because if it had been a 'normal' love affair, the melodramatic aspect would have loomed much larger." But film critic Andrew Britton, writing in the British publication *Gay Left,* saw *Fox* as a "version of homosexuality that degrades us all, and should be roundly denounced."

Not all homosexuals agreed with him, but the interest generated by *Fox* caused female gays to take another, or a first, look at *Petra von Kant,* and one critic, Caroline Sheldon, compared it with *Fox* and concluded that "it appears that male gay filmmakers are no more sympathetic to lesbians than straight ones." While *Fox* was apparently sensitive to the problems of male homosexuals, *Petra,* she said, was in the "freak show genre," stressing the inherent "unwholesomeness" of women in a lesbian relationship.

Repeatedly accused by women of being a misogynist, Rainer told his habitual interviewer Christian Braad Thomsen, "All in all, I find that women behave just as despicably as men do." As for the male gays whom he had "degraded," he said, "Homosexuals have always been very self-pitying and also most of them are dominated by a sense of shame." The criticism continued, but Rainer, taking an apartment with Armin and Kurt in Frankfurt, went on to the Next Big Thing.

16

THE man who for years had run the pioneering
Oberhausen Short-Film Festival, Hilmar Hoff-
mann, was in a certain sense the father of the New German Cinema,
and he had gone on to become culture czar of Frankfurt. Unlike most
czars, he had the vision of democratizing one of his country's great
institutions, the Theater am Turm (TAT), Frankfurt's center for the
performing arts. All decisions about the arts performed, so went the
idea, would henceforth, as in any good democracy, be taken with the
participation of everyone concerned. Playwrights, directors, actors,
and technicians down to the gaffer's assistant would all have a voice.

Paradoxically, the person invited by Hoffmann to fill the office of
artistic director of TAT and bring off his good intentions was the
same person whose spirit he had deeply wounded by turning down
his short films at Oberhausen: the Great Democrat himself, Rainer
Werner Fassbinder.

"Let's go up there and have some fun," Rainer told Peter Chatel
when he accepted the three-year appointment, to begin in the fall of
1974.

There is nothing to suggest that Rainer still bore a grudge over the
turndown at Oberhausen eight years earlier. By now he had worked
his "shortcomings"—his failure to get into film school, for example
—into his interview spiel, playing them for their "absurdity," so it
is unlikely, in the honeymoon days of his love affair with Armin, that
he was in a sadistic frame of mind when he went to Frankfurt. On
the other hand, Hoffmann was certainly asking for punishment when
he picked, of all people, Rainer at this stage of his life to lead an
experiment in group self-determination.

Having already purged himself of the Antitheater illusion, Rainer
gave only lip service to Hoffmann's scheme, not having the slightest
intention of being anything less than absolute monarch of all he

surveyed, in Frankfurt or anywhere else in his purview. In the beginning, however, he went through some of the "democratic" motions. He put together a broadly based ensemble of talent, though he packed it with the most trusted members of his own clan—including Irm, lured back from her self-imposed exile. Kurt, his very own John Alden, was "elected" to represent the interests of the actors. The assemblies, called by Rainer to make decisions affecting the entire company, looked good on paper, but in practice they resembled some of the early party congresses of the Soviet Union, at which Lenin would sleep through the democratic debate and rise at the end to declare, "Comrades, this is what we will do . . ." Rainer didn't sleep; he read a newspaper.

Peter Chatel, whose memories of the experience are especially vivid, describes one such assembly:

> We were all waiting interminably for Rainer to show up, and to pass the time, I did a reading of a short story about life at Berchtesgaden, where Hitler had his mountaintop retreat. The story was about how the atmosphere changed there according to whether the Führer was absent or present. But what I did in the reading was to leave out all the names, Hitler, Albert Speer, Göring, etc. At a certain moment, Irm leaped up from her seat and shouted back at me. "This is outrageous," she cried. "How can *Der Spiegel* print such an article about Rainer?"

Chatel, who was a member of the "politburo" carrying out Rainer's desires, admits to being part of the conspiracy.

> It was an out-and-out manipulation of the idea of self-determination [he recalls]. I remember when the proposal came up. It was going to be our own deal, Rainer, Kurt, and me, the purpose being to go up there and have some fun. Everyone else fell for it. Rainer had a way of creating an atmosphere of family in which everybody thought he or she was participating, feeling completely certain of being a handpicked member of a brain trust. Everybody, above all Rainer, used the word "we"; but Rainer's "we" was the "we" Adorno meant when he said, "Some people say 'we' for 'me.'"

89

It didn't take long, however, for Chatel himself to fall under the same spell. Fresh from his starring role in *Fox and His Friends,* he had been dubbed by Rainer as "my second-best girlfriend." The Frankfurt offer had looked to him like a big chance to direct in the theater, and he made that a condition in exchange for his complicity in the Fassbinder takeover of TAT. Rainer put him in "an enormous villa" in Frankfurt and accepted the challenge. This is how Chatel tells it:

I had always wanted to direct the Georg Büchner play *Leonce and Lena.* It was the first play that Rainer himself directed, and I knew he had a sentimental attachment to it, but it simply didn't fit into our program. So I asked him to figure out something, because whenever he had to sell an idea that was hard to accept, he came up with his best arguments. That was one of his enormous powers. When he didn't believe something, he could seduce anybody. So he got the assembly to accept me to direct the play, but when we were ready to open, something strange happened, and that was when I first understood the way his mind worked.

After the final dress rehearsal, he invited me for dinner, and he said, "Well, you could postpone the opening night for a couple of weeks; it'll be very expensive, but I'll do it for you as my second-best girlfriend." I found this rather odd, but he drank another cognac and said that the play still needed work. "What is it you want me to change, Rainer?" I asked him, because he was hedging on specifics, and he finally pointed out a few moments he didn't like. Those were the moments I cared most for, and I felt very strange, not knowing just what to say. After a few cognacs more he suddenly blurted out, "You have to change what I tell you, because your production is as thinly elegant as a Chabrol film and as useless as a Peter Stein play!" I knew, all of us knew, that Chabrol and Stein were the very directors he was most jealous of at the time and I thought, "Well, that's all right for me."

The next day, I went to him, and speaking kind of how you'd speak to the high authority, I refused to accept the responsibility of postponing. He didn't fight me, so we went ahead as announced. Opening night came, and it was clear that the play was a hit. I had a TV interview scheduled for after the show, but I was a bit late because the applause was so long, and when I got there, I found Rainer sitting in front of the camera. I was just in time to hear the tail end of what he was saying, which was "Yes, I'm proud of my films, but besides that, I'm very, very proud that I have discovered Peter Chatel as a director."

So there it was. His first impulse was to destroy this thing of mine, and when instead it succeeded, he absorbed it into himself, which is destruction by other means, isn't it?

An atmosphere of intrigue began to develop at the Frankfurt court. The Fassbinder people formed one camp and the long-term TAT actors another. The hostility between them heightened, and as either a cause or an effect, the quality of the performances fell off, as did the ticket sales. Onstage drunkenness and brawling in the aisles became features of the Fassbinder "reign of terror," as some were to call his tenure, and TAT's reputation began to plummet. By Christmas of that first season, Rainer had directed Zola's *Germinal,* Strindberg's *Miss Julie,* and Chekhov's *Uncle Vanya,* all to faint praise. Rainer's three-year contract began to look like a monkey on Hilmar Hoffmann's back. He'd have done better to have given weight to a warning launched by one of Rainer's most careful theater critics, Peter Iden. Commenting favorably on Rainer's appointment to TAT, Iden had nevertheless observed that while Rainer invariably returned to the theater because of the possibility of controlling one's creative work more than in filmmaking, he was "invariably repelled by the prevailing limitations." As for Rainer himself, he felt far from having reached those confines, but with the Christmas season upon him, he went off on a holiday with Armin, his—and Armin's—very first trip to America.

They had barely come back from a preholiday jaunt to the Bahamas, where they had gone with Kurt as a threesome. Armin liked the setup, describing it this way: "Rainer is the father, I'm the mother, and Kurti is the child." The free-spending "father" picked up all the tabs, and they enjoyed themselves immensely, basking in the winter sun and shooting off picture postcards to Frankfurt written to green the stay-behinds with envy. Kurt did all the writing; Rainer couldn't be bothered and Armin simply couldn't write. The trip must have been fun indeed, for Kurt remarked years later that "in the relationship between Fassbinder and Armin there were some of the only happy moments of love that Rainer had ever experienced. . . . I witnessed a quiet, even unproductive Fassbinder. He willingly obeyed Armin's often crude orders and did things that had nothing to do with his passion for work, even if it was just visiting a 'dirty bookshop.' "

It had been Armin's idea to go to the States, to visit all his "leather friends," he said. The America they saw was brand-new to all three. Kurt tells the story of their trip:

> In San Francisco we were met at the airport by a dozen leather freaks in fabulous polished-steel-studded getups. They took us everywhere. On one sightseeing tour, they showed us an entire neighborhood for homosexuals only, and we went to all the bars and saunas. By the time we got to Los Angeles, though, I was bored with the whole scene. Going around with all those people just didn't suit my personal tastes. I didn't want to offend our hosts, but finally Fassbinder explained my long face. I saw one of them smile and say, "Oh, he's a chicken hawk," and we then proceeded to make the rounds of bars that featured the underage set.
>
> The whole New York Motorcycle Club, its leather-clad president out front, received us splendidly in their city. They said they were honored to be the first to take us on a tour of the bars on Manhattan's waterfront. It was there that we were introduced to the ill-reputed Anvil, which was to become Rainer's favorite club in New York. It had enormous rooms and the de rigueur fucking room was a dark chamber packed with people watching the ongoing spectacles.
>
> Exhibitionists occupied various platforms, striking self-satisfied poses. Some of them had their penises pierced with gold needles or wound in barbed wire. Suddenly somebody with a suitcase and looking like some sort of traveling salesman who'd lost his clothes got up on one of the platforms. He opened his

bag and began to unpack rubber cocks of all imaginable sizes and he lined them up in a neat little row, each one bigger than the one beside it. He then went on to quietly shove them up his ass, working in ascending order. It took a handful of Vaseline, but he even managed to take on an enormous object which he ended up sitting on like a bar stool. This drew a round of applause and he went off looking quite pleased with himself. His place was taken by three other men wearing nothing but chains. One of them was strung up by the others, hoisted by his arms with his legs spread wide. The second man greased the hanging man's asshole, and the third with his hand clenched in a fist penetrated him slowly but relentlessly until his whole arm nearly disappeared. The "victim" simply hung there limply, his eyes closed and a dreamy smile on his face. This of course was the famous fistfuck we'd heard about but had never seen before, and we were quite taken with it. Fassbinder, in fact, was absolutely fascinated. We came back night after night to watch it, and when Armin and I finally lost interest, he stayed on long after we'd gone back to our hotel. One night, when Rainer was fast asleep, Armin and I sneaked out of the hotel and went to a big sauna filled with Puerto Rican and Jamaican prostitutes. The hours flew by and when we got back we found Fassbinder very much awake. He went into a rage about having been left alone, insulting us in the vulgarest language he knew.

These eruptions became frequent as the trip wore on; one of them was ominous. They had picked up two hitchhikers in their rented car and the strangers ended up going off with Rainer's toiletry bag. When they stopped for the night, he discovered the theft, and he went out of his mind. He put the blame on Kurt and ran around in circles, raving and stamping his feet. Both Kurt and Armin were left dumbfounded until he explained why he was so disturbed. The bag contained his Valiums, and without them, he admitted, he couldn't fall asleep. It was too late to attempt to buy some. His fear that he wouldn't sleep until he could obtain a replacement was devastating. "Luckily," says Kurt, "Armin found a bottle kept as a spare, and Fassbinder calmed himself with two pills."

Only two.

. . .

Rainer had written a play in New York. It was based on a novel by Gerhard Zwerenz, *The Earth Is As Uninhabitable As the Moon*, and back in Frankfurt, the city where it is set, he began to rehearse it as the next TAT production.

He titled it *The Garbage, the City, and Death.* It is about big-city squalor and real-estate speculation, of which Rainer had some firsthand knowledge from his father's slumlording days in Cologne. One such character in the play is a successful developer who specializes in razing dilapidated neighborhoods, putting the poor on the streets, to make way for the construction of high-rise office buildings. This unsavory figure falls in love with a prostitute who began life as the daughter of a Nazi drag artist and didn't get much further. Now she wants to die. He obliges by strangling her, and the corrupt social system sanctions the act by allowing him to get away with murder.

The play is archetypically Fassbinderian, suiting to a tee Thomas Elsaesser's definition: the holy fool—in this case the prostitute—in a Dostoevskian world of universal prostitution. Rainer, however, made the unpardonable error of giving the real-estate character in the play the same sobriquet he had in the novel. The difference was that in the book the distasteful appellation is justified by circumstances, whereas in Rainer's work it is an unqualified mere transfer. The villain of the piece is called The Rich Jew.

The most offensive line in the piece reads, "The Jew is to blame for everything because he has put the blame on us. If he had remained where he came from or if they had gassed him, I would be able to sleep better today." It was invariably quoted, and continues to be to this day, as the proof of the basest kind of anti-Semitism. But whenever it was, at least toward that end, the quoters failed every time to say that these words are spoken by an unrehabilitated Nazi. Rainer would later defend himself by saying that the play "points the finger at anti-Semitism," and undoubtedly he believed it. But it was one of the most costly acts of frivolousness he ever committed. It precipitated events that truncated his career in the theater and seriously harmed others as well. The play was never performed. Rehearsals were canceled when word leaked out that Rainer's work was "anti-Semitic" and governmental authority intervened. No one was more surprised than Rainer, who was about as far from being anti-Semitic as he was from joining the priesthood. Indeed, it was his inexplicable naïveté about Jewish and West German sensibilities that led him into an even graver error. He had planned to turn the play into a film, but when it ran into trouble and no one would even consider financing it as a film, he produced it himself, hiring his friend Daniel Schmid to direct. The idea was that Schmid, the scion of a wealthy Swiss-Jewish family of hoteliers, was unassailable. He was, but Rainer, who had avoided a public controversy in Frankfurt by quietly canceling the play, would take the brunt of the international scandal that erupted a year later on the release of the film, retitled *Shadow of Angels*. He would be branded an anti-Semite worldwide, and though the charges would be eclipsed by his future work, they are still dying hard.*

Before making *Shadow of Angels*, Rainer, fulfilling critic Peter Iden's prophecy, had reached the point of repulsion by the limitations of the theater. He was ready to quit. But he had one more score to settle with culture czar Hoffmann and the various cabals eager to be rid of him and his dictatorial ways. Peter Chatel recounts the denouement:

> When Rainer had that trouble staging his play *The Garbage, the City, and Death* he grew fed up with the theater. We all began to sense that he wanted to leave, and Hilmar Hoffmann asked me, along with Peer Raben and Gottfried John, if we would care to take over as a kind of triumvirate if Rainer were to go. We agreed, but as soon as Rainer got wind of it, that there was a possibility that we would go on without him, he called a

*In 1983, when the film was shown for the first time in New York, the Yiddish-language daily *Forward* ran an article as blistering as it was jaundiced under the headline "A film imported to America outdoes Hitler-Göebbels-Streicher outpourings of poisonous hatred against Jews." Rainer, dead more than a year, was accused of copying the pages of *Mein Kampf*. In the fall of 1985, Rainer's stage version, still never performed in public, was scheduled to open in Frankfurt, generating new charges of anti-Semitism. On the night of the first performance, with about one thousand boisterous protestors outside the theater, a group stormed the stage when the curtain went up and refused to leave. The actors pleaded with them to be allowed to go on, voicing their conviction that the play was not anti-Semitic. After two and a half hours of confrontation, the performance was canceled and stricken from the program.

big meeting in his house. He served us coffee and cake and asked us all to walk out on our contracts along with him.

He gave us a long list of what he called "good reasons" why we shouldn't go on. We'll form a new theater company in Munich, he said. We'll put on plays and we'll tour. We'll rent a big house and we'll all live there, etc., etc. It was the old family dream again. And then he said suddenly, "Who's giving back his contract tomorrow?" and he asked for a show of hands. Everyone went along except me.

"Peter," he said, with utter surprise, "why isn't your hand up?"

"How can I give up a three-year contract just on a word from you?" is what I said.

He said, "Don't you trust me?"

"No, of course I don't trust you. Why should I trust you?" I said, knowing well how he gambled with what could pass for truth.

"Well, then," he said, "you have to leave." And I got kicked out of the house while the meeting went on.

That evening, the two actors staying with me in my villa, Y Sa Lo and Peter Bullock, came home from the meeting and they couldn't bear to look me in the eyes, trying their best to avoid me. Suddenly the telephone rang and Peter Bullock answered. It was for me and he held out the telephone like the Holy Grail, dropping his voice, saying, "Rainer wants to talk to you." Y Sa Lo and Peter Bullock—and me, too, I guess—were sure the death sentence was about to be handed down. I took the call and Rainer said very calmly, "Shall we have dinner tonight alone?" I said, "Sure," and he said, "Didn't you like how I handled this whole thing today?" I said, "Yes, very clever of you. I think it's terrible, but as an act of manipulation it worked wonderfully." He thanked me for the "compliment" and we made an appointment to meet later.

At dinner, he tried his best to win me over. He said it was a question of principle. They had censored him, preventing him from putting on *The Garbage, the City, and Death,* and that was scandalous, so now he would do so anyway by founding a new company in Munich. I suppose he wanted me to think that

96

would be a triumph for freedom of the arts, but I didn't believe a word of it. "If you really want to make a scandal," I said, "why don't you force the issue, going ahead with the play as a TAT production here in Frankfurt, where all of us have a place to live and where we're all paid by the theater? You try to open the play, they stop you, we all say our contracts were broken, we quit, and take the play on tour." I felt that was sound thinking, economically as well as politically, but he just stared at me without expression and said I didn't understand and didn't "trust" him.

After a long silence, he looked at me and played his trump card. "Anyway," he said, "everyone else has quit, so what can you do here now?"

"Nothing," I said, "but I have a three-year contract and at least I'll be paid."

"Well, I love you very much," he said, "but you're asking too much expecting me to stay with this theater for years so that you can direct. If you want to direct, come to Munich, and I promise you one of the new company's productions."

"There aren't going to be any productions," I blurted out, certain by now that all he wanted was the big scandal of everyone quitting along with him so it would look like the whole world stops when he does.

He didn't deny it. Instead, he called me a traitor. What happened in the end was that he got his headlines and came out the hero of his pocket revolution. When it was all over, though, the company in Munich, far from being formed, was simply forgotten, and everybody was out of a job. As for me, the traitor, I got paid for three years doing nothing, and Rainer gave me a part in his very next film. Maybe I'd won his respect. Much later, a few weeks before he died, in fact, he said to me, "You know, you're the only one who never freaked out."

17

Q. Do you plan to go on with this staggering rate of production, or are you considering taking things a little easier?

A. Sometimes I think of taking it easier, but at the same time I've discovered that work is necessary for me. I get very depressed when I'm not working. For the time being, my plan is to make my thirtieth film when I turn thirty.

WHEN Rainer told this to interviewer Christian Braad Thomsen at Cannes in May 1975 he was a week or so shy of his thirtieth birthday. He had just shot his twenty-sixth and twenty-seventh films back-to-back over the past four months. Not even he, however, could have hoped to make the necessary three additional films in the paper-thin slice of time remaining to reach the vaunted goal. The reason the statement went unchallenged was that the curious fib subtracting one year from his age had already rooted, and here we find him cultivating it unabashedly.

Since any director, given the nature of the art, would be considered precocious having made his *first* feature film at thirty, what Rainer said immediately after catering to his vanity with this little anachronism is more to the point. He really, if secretly, was turning thirty and this is how he said he felt at the moment:

> I've achieved a lot of things that directors aspire to. I've had more success than most and I earn more than most. But none of that has made me any happier. I can't see any reason to be happy when I see how people live. When I come in contact with people in the streets and in railway stations, see their faces and their lives, it fills me with despair. I often want to scream out loud.

Not even his fiercest enemy would question Rainer's assessment of the intensity of his feelings. He defined himself in Freudian terms, claiming to be both manic-depressive and sadomasochistic. He was certainly all of those to extremes, though a combination of sado- and depressive may have been up front most often. According to Rainer's analysis, "Relationships between people are always sadomasochistic as a direct result of their upbringing. . . . The parent becomes the figure which in one respect the child accepts as dominant, meaning that all through his life he will accept dominant figures while at the same time trying to destroy this dominance in order to exist. Actually, a child develops a dual need for dominance and destruction, which is to say that one becomes sadistic and masochistic at the same time." This sounds as if he made it all up as he went along, but it's black-and-white tone seems applicable at least to himself at thirty.

Daniel Schmid, another "Freudian," has put it this way: "Rainer felt that all people, including himself, were pigs, that the relationship between him and others was pig to pig. I am a pig and you are a pig; therefore we can do anything we want to one another."

Daniel said this in what he called "the Year One p[ost] RWF" (it was February 1983), but even in 1975 their friendship was being recast.

They had been lovers once upon a time; they had met in Berlin in 1966 taking the film-school entrance examination. "I walked in," Daniel remembers. "The room was full, and I don't know why, but I sat down next to him." They had gone their own ways for a while and then, when Daniel showed up in Munich in 1969, they became close companions, with Ingrid forming a third pole of the friendship. Three years later Daniel directed his first feature film (at thirty), and in 1974, in his second, he launched Ingrid as his own star (à la Hanna), as well as on a career as a chanteuse that would grow to international proportions.

By now, the structure of the three-way relationship had changed. Daniel and Ingrid, after her divorce from Rainer, had become inseparable friends, and Rainer, committed to producing his "anti-Semitic" play as a movie, *Shadow of Angels,* with Daniel as director, had become his boss. Daniel had cast Ingrid in the principal female role, asking Rainer to play the male lead. When he accepted, it looked as though it had been a wise maneuver, since the financing had not yet been completed. But when it was—probably because of Rainer's name—he used his position as producer-star-coscreenwriter (with Daniel) to consolidate his control of the project. Daniel was thrust into the unhappy situation of personifying Rainer's "child," forced to accept dominance while fighting back for his own survival. But he was not as submissive as some of the others—all of which made for a very unpleasant summer when a whole group of them went off to Greece and Turkey on a disastrous vacation.

The trip began pleasantly enough just after the Berlin Film Festival in July. The first of the two films Rainer had made earlier in the year, *Mother Küsters's Trip to Heaven,* had premiered at the festival, drawing fire and bile from the left, who are shown in the film to be as capable of opportunism as anyone else. On the very next day, however, the made-for-television second movie, *Fear of Fear,* was telecast to a much larger audience than would ever see *Mother Küsters's Trip,* and it was warmly received. So Rainer was at least in a neutral mood when he set off, with a kilo of pure hashish, for sun and fun on the Greek island of Skópelos, accompanied by Armin, Kurt, Ingrid, and Daniel and his lover, Raul Jiminez.

The hashish was stashed behind the radio of Rainer's pale blue BMW, unbeknownst to the occupants of the car, who had to clear multiple customs inspections that grew less friendly as they proceeded south. Rainer flew. Customs proved to be outwittable, but the contraband, even when smoked, did little to soothe the petty quarrels that continually erupted among the smokers.

Daniel recollects a ploy invented by him and Ingrid to deflect the tension:

> Rainer would always stay home and write, and it bothered him that we went off to have a good time. So when we came back from a glorious day at the beach, we would separate before we got close to the house, and I would go inside first, pretending that I was very angry. I would huff and puff and throw things around. Before very long Rainer would look up from his writing and ask me what was wrong, taking a genuine interest in my being so obviously bugged. Then I would let out my "anger,"

blaming it all on Ingrid, which would please Rainer no end, and when she finally came in she would play her part, too, to the hilt. It was all a game to keep him off our back.

Rainer played a holiday game, too, an "adult" game he called Chinese Roulette. Eminently suitable for sadomasochists, it was his favorite and would become the basis of a film he would make the following year, giving it the same name. Normally called Truth, the game involved guessing the identity of one or another of the participants by the answers given to questions about his or her character. Provoking such questions as "What job would this person have held under Hitler?" or "If this person were an animal, what kind would he be?" or "If a ship were sinking, who would this person leave behind?" and so on, the game, as played by Rainer, invariably turned vicious and ended in tears. In the film, which he was then writing when he wasn't playing, it leads to murder and suicide, and Peter Berling remembers one session elsewhere that brought on an immediate divorce, but on the beach in Greece it was only more sunburn under the skin. Which was as good a reason as any to go on to the next leg of the tour.

Joined by Rainer's mother, Lilo, they flew to Turkey, rented two tiny Fiats, and drove off to examine the ruins of ancient Ephesus. It was on the way back, after they had admired the Hellenistic theaters and the Church of the Seven Slippers, that what came to be known as *the* accident happened.

Rainer loved to take the wheel of any car, but true to form, he'd failed his driving test numerous times. The only license he had was a clumsy forgery that couldn't have fooled anyone, and he evidently knew it, because when he drove he would always change places with whoever was beside him if he thought he might have to show it.

That afternoon, at dusk, he was driving the lead car, his head close to the windshield because he'd forgotten his glasses. Armin was beside him and Kurt was in the back. Suddenly, as Kurt remembers it, "there was a fence in front of us, Rainer jammed on the brakes, we went into a skid and slammed a trailer truck loaded with empty bottles."

The bottles went crashing as Armin was jettisoned through the windshield, landing on the road. He was followed by Kurt, who sailed over the front seat, went through the shattered windshield, and ended up sprawled on the hood. Rainer was stuck behind the wheel, looking lifeless. Kurt was the only one conscious. He saw Armin lying in a puddle of blood and began to shake Rainer, who came to his senses, shouting, "You saw it, Kurt, it wasn't my fault!" A truck driver rushed them all to a hospital, and the moment they were gone, the other half of the traveling party arrived on the scene. Daniel was in the front seat of this car alongside Raul, and Ingrid and Rainer's mother were in the rear. Daniel says:

> We hadn't yet stopped when we saw the wreck in front of us. It looked as though there couldn't possibly have been any survivors. There was blood and glass everywhere, and I saw one of Rainer's shoes on the road. I happened to glance in the rearview mirror and what I saw there was almost as horrifying. Rainer's mother was fixing her hair, certain, I suppose, that the press would soon be there to cover the latest news of her famous son.

Daniel had never been very generous when speaking of Lilo, and now that he had become Rainer's underpaid employee the old thrill was gone forever, but something that happened later that evening deepened his disdain for Rainer's mother:

> Rainer called from the hospital and spoke to his mother. He told her that everything was going to be all right and that he wanted to see Ingrid and me, but not her. But we didn't know this until we got to the hospital, since his mother, after she'd hung up, feeling terribly slighted, I'm sure, put it this way: "Rainer wants to see you—for the last time." We rushed over in a panic, but when we arrived, he was waiting for us on the street outside.

His leg was in a cast, the knee broken. Kurt was patched up and released, but Armin, his face badly cut, was flown to Geneva for plastic surgery. Rainer, of course, paid all the bills, but everyone had to swear that Armin had been at the wheel, not he.

. . .

Sadomasochism, the real stuff, would remain close to the surface now, and later it would be manifest in the practice of sex. Rainer, whose streak of cruelty had grown in before his beard, seems to have been turned on by what he called "the beauty of pain," or at least he said so before he is known to have actually sought it in the bedroom. "It isn't easy to accept that suffering can also be beautiful," he told Thomsen. "It's something you can only understand if you dig deeply into yourself." Of this, boring a shaft into his inner self, he was certainly capable, and into the next three films, which brought him to the magic number thirty, he put much of what he mined regarding submission and aggression on and off the screen.

Two of these three films, *I Only Want You to Love Me* and *Chinese Roulette,* consider the consequences of a lack of parental love, the former being one of Rainer's most poignant works, and both showing the consequences to be violence. The other film is *Satan's Brew,* made in between the above; it deals directly with the sadomasochistic condition in comedic form, and a lot of the same condition obtained in real life on the set.

Along with *Beware of a Holy Whore, Satan's Brew* gives us a self-portrait, warts in the foreground. "I tried to make a comedy about me," he said later, "looking at my negative side from a distance; it's a comedy about maybe the way I am, though I don't think so." The maybes and the don't-think-sos can be termed Fassbinderarch.

Here is Rainer's negative-side self-portrait in the words of one of the few West German critics who enjoyed looking at it, Peter Buchka of the *Süddeutsche Zeitung.* Reviewing *Satan's Brew,* he wrote:

> The main character of this spectacle of savagery is Walter Kranz ([played by] Kurt Raab), a disgusting fellow indeed. He is a total egocentric, once celebrated as a "poet of the revolution." Since we all know what happened to the revolution, the bard now keeps his mouth shut. All that remains of his days of glory is a mountain of debts, a complaining wife, a retarded brother, and his never-ending flight from the middle-class conformism he loathes so deeply. After he murders his rich lover, he recovers his inspiration, but a burst of creativity produces nothing but a plagiarism of poet Stefan George's *Albatross.*

What makes matters worse is that it is Kranz's own family who accuses him of being a plagiarist. Swept by a madness, he begins to believe he is Stefan George reincarnated, and by a stroke of luck, one of his few remaining admirers, Andrée, turns up. She gives him her life savings, which allows him to establish a following of "disciples"—hired young male prostitutes, who drop him as soon as the money runs out.

Kranz in the meantime surrenders all to his megalomania. He steals from his parents as well as from a prostitute, with whom he is supposed to be writing a book, which he intends to claim as a work of his own. His wife grows more and more hysterical. The prostitute's protectors beat him up, and after he admits to having enjoyed the pain, he loses Andrée's admiration. When the original murder is on the point of being blamed on his idiot brother, whom Kranz has accused, the brother shoots this demonic incarnation of the noblest art. Is that it? Wait! The bullets draw only stage blood . . . so we're back where we started from. Is this what life is all about?

The first thing that ought to be said is that Rainer, when he wrote *Satan's Brew,* was under an accusation of plagiarism for having stolen the idea for *I Only Want You to Love Me* from a television play of a few years earlier. This was rather insignificant in itself, but it weighed heavily on his mood because of a more serious incident. Creating something of a scandal, it occurred in 1974, after the release of *Martha,* which bears a remarkable resemblance to American author Cornell Woolrich's short story "For the Rest of Her Life." Confronted with the similarity, Rainer expressed amazement but insisted that he was the sole source of his script. The Woolrich estate, however, belatedly succeeded in convincing the producers, Westdeutscher Rundfunk, to buy the rights to the short story, which added salt to the wound.

Secondly, Rainer at the time of *Satan's Brew* was also laboring under the impact of his failure at Frankfurt; massive rejection by left, gay, feminist, and other "revolutionaries"; being labeled an anti-Semite; and the slow but steady diminishment of critical acclaim that had begun after *Effi Briest,* six pictures back. Moreover, his latest effort did nothing to win friends, and one Fassbinder-watcher, Wilfried Wiegand, of the *Frankfurter Allgemeine Zeitung,* called *Satan's*

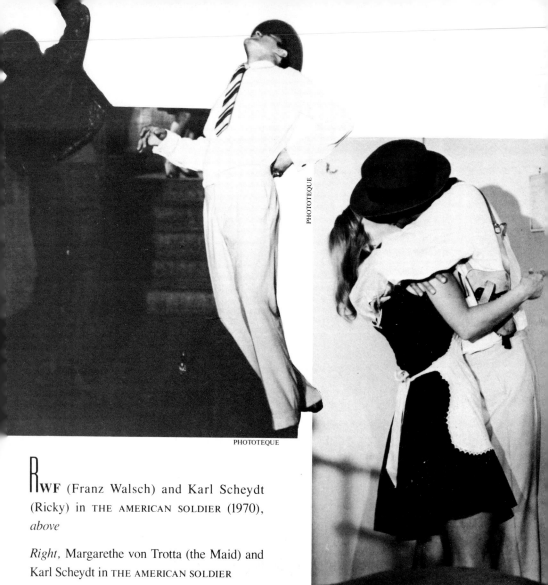

RWF (Franz Walsch) and Karl Scheydt (Ricky) in THE AMERICAN SOLDIER (1970), *above*

Right, Margarethe von Trotta (the Maid) and Karl Scheydt in THE AMERICAN SOLDIER

Below, Hans Hirschmüller (Hans Epp) and In-grid Caven (Hans's Ideal Woman) in THE MER-CHANT OF FOUR SEASONS (1971)

Hanna Schygulla (Karin) and Margit Carstensen (Petra) in THE BITTER TEARS OF PETRA VON KANT (1972), *above*

Left, Eva Mattes (Hanni) and Harry Baer (Franz) in JAIL BAIT (1972)

Ulli Lommel (Major Crampas) and Hanna Schygulla (Effi) in EFFI BRIEST (1974)

VOLKER Spengler (Ernst) and Y Sa Lo (Lana von Mayerbeer) in SATAN'S BREW (1976), *left*

Below, Ingrid Caven (Lilly), Kurt Raab (Walter), Armin Meier (Stricher), and Volker Spengler in SATAN'S BREW

ELISABETH Trissenaar (Hanni) and Kurt Raab (Bolwieser) in THE STATIONMASTER'S WIFE (1977)

DIRK Bogarde (Hermann Hermann) in
DESPAIR (1977), *above*

Right, Hanna Schygulla (Maria) in THE MAR-
RIAGE OF MARIA BRAUN (1978)

RWF and Dieter Schidor on the set of
THE WIZARD OF BABYLON, Schidor's
documentary on the making of
QUERELLE (1982)

VOLKER Spengler (Elvira) and Karl Scheydt (Hacker) in IN A YEAR WITH THIRTEEN MOONS (1978), *above*

Below right, Günther Lamprecht (Franz) and Barbara Sukowa (Mieze) in BERLIN ALEXANDERPLATZ (1980)

Left, another view of Günther Lamprecht in BERLIN ALEXANDER-PLATZ

GÜNTHER Kaufmann (Anton) and RWF (Lieutenant Jansen) in Wolf Gremm's KAMIKAZE '89 (1983), *above*

HANNA Schygulla (Willie) in LILI MARLEEN (1980), *above*

Right, Annemarie Düringer (Dr. Katz) and Rosel Zech (Veronika) in VERONIKA VOSS (1981)

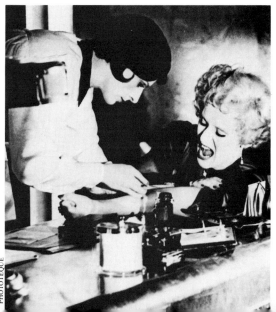

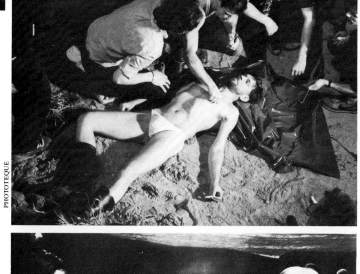

THE set of QUERELLE (1982), *above*

Left, Dieter Schidor (Vic) on the set of QUERELLE

Below, Franco Nero, Dieter Schidor, RWF, Brad Davis, and Andy Warhol in THE WIZARD OF BABY-LON (1982)

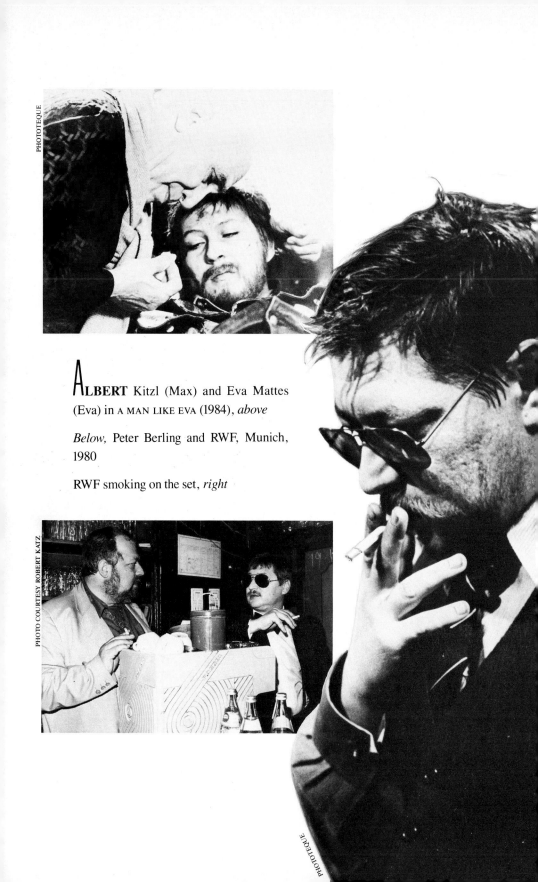

ALBERT Kitzl (Max) and Eva Mattes (Eva) in A MAN LIKE EVA (1984), *above*

Below, Peter Berling and RWF, Munich, 1980

RWF smoking on the set, *right*

Brew "an act of hatred of the human race" and accused its director of using the mass media to heap his private suffering on the public.

Be that as it may, the brew we are left with is one of introspection about as pure as it comes. Daniel Schmid says that Rainer "believed himself to be a monster and so he behaved like a monster." He rode his actors particularly roughshod while making *Satan's Brew.* "Rainer's aggressiveness was implacable," says Harry. "He projected himself into the character of the slimy and sordid poet, which Kurti played marvelously, by the way. He wanted him to appear as hateful as possible."

Kurt claims he was virtually tortured and driven deeper into habitual drinking. Rainer overworked him, sober or not, humiliating him in front of others when they screened the rushes by demeaning his performance as the work of a drunk. Margit Carstensen, creating the role of Andrée, one of the chief victims of the poet's foulest behavior, was forced to wear surrealistically thick glasses that caused severe pain to her eyes. When she complained, Rainer accused her of not having her heart in the role. The script called upon actors to spit on and slap one another and to strike undignified poses; in one scene the retarded brother destroys his pet flies by burning them with sunlight focused through a magnifying glass. The heterosexual sex scenes, performed by Kurt, were a little too demanding for his liking. Feigning naked intercourse with Y Sa Lo, who played the female prostitute, "filled me with horror and made my skin crawl with goose bumps," he says. He was also required to fellate one of the young homosexuals of the story, played by Armin (a performance that ended up on the cutting room floor), and to flagellate the retarded brother with a leather belt, though he claims to have done the latter "with bliss."

"Everything has to go faster!" was Rainer's shouted refrain on the set, and anybody who couldn't keep apace, which included one of the main players, was fired under a barrage of verbal abuse. Attempts to ascribe Rainer's behavior to a known directorial technique, by which actors are spurred on to give more of themselves than they would otherwise, do not succeed. He was just as capable of disarming kindness as he was of ruthlessness, but not, it seems, in the making of *Satan's Brew.* Rainer in this case was simply being what Michael Fengler, who had known him since he was a stray pup, said he was: "a bad, bad guy."

18

THIS was a season of malice, but the three people who would love and worship him with Irmlike devotion now came into his life. They would also receive, Irmlike, back-of-the-hand treatment from time to time, but their adoration would survive him.

Irm herself had not yet packed her bags for the last time, but she had met a man during the Frankfurt debacle, and although that union had yet to blossom, it did have sap. By now Rainer was addressing her in the formal second person only, and she was very much on the sidelines, not having appeared in a Fassbinder film since *Mother Küsters's Trip*. Her swan-song performance was already germinating in his mind, and the ax was being honed for Margit Carstensen and a most unsuspecting Kurt. Lining up for the vacancies were two much younger women and a man who had already been secretly adoring Rainer for years.

The man was Dieter Schidor, a bespectacled young actor, four years Rainer's junior and a doctor—in the German sense of his having completed his university studies. It was Dieter's doctorship that made Rainer feel a little uneasy (another "intellectual"), but Schidor would certainly do everything he could to help him get over it. Schidor wears his zeal on the outside when he remembers how he first got a foot in the door:

I'd wanted to meet him since I first got to Munich in sixty-nine. He was already a known figure, and even though we were moving in the same circles, it was a very difficult thing to get to know him. The people around him, even if they were your friends, were totally reluctant to introduce you, and anyway it didn't work that way. Then Armin arrived on the scene, and Armin and Rainer became lovers, and I knew Armin. I knew many of his friends, Peter Chatel, Ingrid, Daniel Schmid, and I was even at one or two Christmas parties in his apartment. But he never said a word to me, good or bad. I couldn't stand it. His were the films I wanted to act in more than anything else.

Finally, the whole thing started. I was staying with Daniel Schmid in Paris. The phone rang, I answered it, and there he was at the other end of the line—it was one of those strange moments in a lifetime—Rainer Werner Fassbinder calling from Munich. Daniel wasn't in and he asked who I was. I stuttered it out and he grunted. Then, as he was about to get off the phone, he mumbled, "Oh, by the way, do you know you're playing in *Satan's Brew?*" I had heard a rumor about that from Peter Chatel, but I answered as coolly as I could, saying, "No, I don't know that." "Well," he snapped, "now you know." And he hung up. I was *very* happy; I was elated!

The foot in the door proved to be the wrong foot, however, when during a two-month break in the shooting of *Satan's Brew* Schidor went off to the Ivory Coast for a small part in a French film being made there. Peter Berling had a leading role in the movie, *Black and White in Color,* which would win the Oscar in 1977 for best foreign film. He was also a player in Schidor's premature fall from grace. Mutti recounts:

> Dieter had been joined by a friend from New Zealand, Michael McLernon, and in Africa they fell in love. They disappeared on a honeymoon among the rhinos and monkeys in the wildlife reserves, and were still incommunicado when Rainer began to call me every day in a frenzy, demanding Dieter's return to the *Satan's Brew* set. He simply couldn't believe one of his actors capable of such high treason, and he soon suspected a plot. The producer of our film was Arthur Cohn, a German Jew who had recently denounced Rainer publicly as an anti-Semite, and now Rainer thought Cohn and somehow Dieter and I were scheming to sabotage *Satan's Brew.* When I got back to Munich, Dieter still hadn't shown up, and Rainer, faced with serious continuity problems, rewrote the script, and pronounced Dr. Schidor dead.

There he would lie and await resurrection, the miracle occurring only after many lean years had gone by. Meanwhile came the women.

"I was born not far from Frankfurt in 1950. My father was a teacher in our town. I went to a school in Mannheim run by nuns. And the first time I saw a play, in a theater in Mannheim, I decided to become an actress. I was thirteen."

The actress-to-be is Isolde Barth. You can see her in half a dozen Fassbinder films, always in a small, unrewarding part, always in one or another phase of undress, timid, voluptuous, her large dark eyes floating on tears ready to be shed at the sound of an unkind word. Only she's not acting. She's smitten with love in its most bewitching form. She's under the spell of the director. She was from the moment she met him, and only in death would the spell be broken, or rather, slowly wither and die on its own. A bit-player on the screen, she'd have little more than a supporting role in his life, but he'd be the whole volume of hers, and he alone would know it.

Isolde was twenty-four when she pasted enough courage together to introduce herself to Rainer. It may have been her boldest moment. She had become an actress but not the actress of her adolescent dream, and after having played a lot of "stupid stuff" in provincial theaters, two years in Munich had added little to her name. An unknown was what she was, unknown to most but not to Rainer. She remembers it well (how can she forget it?):

I used to see him sitting in restaurants and I always felt he was watching me, following me with his eyes. It happened once in a coffee place in Schwabing, where he had his production office, and another time at the Maske, which is where actors would go because it was practically run by the Fassbinder crowd. It was there that I talked to him. I said, "Hello, my name is Isolde," and before I could get any further, he said, "I know. I just saw you in a film," and he knew the film—it was my only one—and he told me where he'd seen it, so I knew it was all true. A strange coincidence, wasn't it?

She told him she was going to be in a play in a theater in Munich several weeks later. Without further bidding, Rainer and his entourage showed up for her performance. You could hear the heads turn. They left in the intermission, but he apologized to her afterward, saying that she at least had been good. He must have meant it, because he put her in the road company of *Petra von Kant* as the indomitable lesbian lover created by Hanna. By now, the spell had been cast, and when after the tour she was invited to Rainer's famous kitchen in the Reichenbachstrasse to be present beside the throne, her enchantment was complete.

The movie under discussion at the time was the upcoming *Chinese Roulette*. Isolde would have to wait for the next film to get her call —unlike the future second Mrs. Fassbinder (so to speak), Juliane Lorenz.

Juliane was born in Bad Wörishofen, the little spa that was also Rainer's birthplace, but he was eleven years old, gone and becoming a flower, when she first opened her eyes. She would be the last Fassbinder person, the last of a long line of small-towners, born and bred as Catholics by parents or stepparents or surrogates who paled out early. Her lastness is what distinguishes her point of view about the Fassbinder saga. "I always felt like an outsider," Juliane would say after having lived with, for, and by Rainer in the final years. On the master's time scale, Juliane was a second-generation Fassbinder person, the only one.

What did you hear about Fassbinder when I was in my teens? You heard that he's a young guy, very strange, very self-centered, very unlikable [Juliane remembers]. I had a "personal" experience then. My stepfather was a projectionist and he once told me that this guy Fassbinder came to the movie house where he worked to deliver a print of his latest film, and my stepfather frowned and said, "Ugly guy, ugly guy." Then I saw him on television. He was one of the celebrity contestants on a quiz show called *Dolly Dolly*. He made a very good impression, because you always saw him in the newspapers and magazines looking mean and messy, but here he was slimmed down (he'd just played the lead in *Fox and His Friends*), very gentlemanly, and dressed in a suit and tie. He and his partner lost, but maybe that was a plus, too, because the next day I heard people say, "Hey, did you see Fassbinder? How did such an ugly guy get so handsome, and nice, too?"

Having a projectionist for a stepfather was like having a free pass to the movies, and Juliane used it again and again. Her mother worked in the cutting room at Bavaria Studios in Munich, handling film but never reaching the exalted level of cutting. That was a craft that required years of training and experience, or so said those who were doing the snipping. Juliane would snip. "I willed it," she says. "I knew it was impossible, but my heart told me that I was going to be a cutter before I was twenty. I swore I'd leave it for something else if I wasn't." She made herself look older than her age, colored her resumé, and landed job after job, uncurling, numbering, and hanging strips of cut film like clothes on a line, and even doing a little snipping, but nothing worthy of her heartfelt destiny. She was only nineteen, however, when Rainer Werner Fassbinder walked into the cutting room and, as he had done for so many others, made every wish come true.

She was working as an assistant to film editor Ila von Hasperg, whom Rainer had hired to cut *Chinese Roulette*. The film had been shot in a castle far from Munich, and Ila had left Juliane behind to uncurl, number, and hang, so she had never met the big boss. But now the shooting was over, and Ila, back in Munich, turned to Juliane one day and said out of the blue, "Now, Rainer is coming." Juliane recalls:

I got *really* anxious. People had told me how difficult he was. Even Ila, who'd worked with him for pretty long now, was nervous, so I was so nervous I didn't know what to do with myself. And suddenly the door opened and in walked this very silent person looking like a boy. He was wearing jeans and leather boots and a leather jacket, and a beat-up old felt hat. He didn't look this way or that way. He just said hello and sat down to see Ila's cut.

He was very calm and said very few words, but his way of speaking was so smooth and so gentle that it astonished me, considering what I'd heard about him. After ten minutes it was all over. A few days later, the same thing happened again, and when we were finished, Ila asked Rainer if he would give her a lift into town. He said it was okay, but when she asked if it would be all right if I came along too, he looked at me in this funny way, and he didn't answer for what seemed an eternity. I didn't know then how hard it was for him to take somebody he didn't really know in his car, or even to be among strangers, but finally he said, "Why not?" and we all went off in his blue BMW with him at the wheel. Ila and he were joking with one another, and I was totally confused. Somebody had told me he was a homosexual, and I had never met one before. I had expected to see the "difference," but all I saw was somebody very funny, very nice, very sensitive. When we left, Ila gave him a kiss goodbye, and I thought, "Oh, dear, he got a kiss from a woman." That's how naïve I was. From that moment on, though, I knew this man would always be in my heart.

After that I ran to the movie houses to see as many of his films as I could, and I had a sense from the beginning that they all had something to do with his life. Then came the first time he reacted to me. We were in the cutting room with Rainer and Willi, who was working on the music, and I made a joke at Willi's expense, a play on words I don't remember anymore. I don't know how I dared to do such a thing, and when I did, I thought, "Oh, my God, what did I say that for?" But Rainer burst out laughing, saying, "I knew it, she's crazy. I knew it all along." He began to speak to me while we worked, saying would you be so kind as to do this or would you mind doing that, always so terribly polite. And watching him with other people, I never had the feeling he was anything but friendly.

Once, after working late, he took Ila and me to dinner. I remember what he ordered, caviar with potatoes and butter. It was his favorite. The first thing he did was give Ila a taste, putting some caviar in a spoon. I was wondering if it was going to happen to me, when he suddenly went through the same routine and gave me a taste, too. It was the first time I ate caviar. Later, when Ila and I were alone, she said, "He likes you. Yes, he likes you."

When the film was over, Rainer made a party in a French

restaurant in the Rotekreuz Platz and I was invited. I was so scared, I didn't want to go, but of course I did. I was terrified by the thought of being with all those people I'd heard of but didn't know. That was the first time I saw Ingrid and others whom I recognized from photos and films. They were all having such a good time together. The atmosphere was loud and strong, and suddenly this guy wearing dark glasses came running in, totally drunk, I'm sure. He ran across the full length of the room, screaming and shouting; finally he threw himself on the floor. He screamed and screamed, got up, walked over to Ingrid at the bar, and splashed a drink in her face. Then he went out. I was too shy until much later in the evening to ask who the madman was. "Who? That was Emma Potato!" I was told, and so I'd had my first glimpse in person of the famous Kurt Raab, and I'd learned something about life in the bargain. It was a new world coming up for me in my own very small world.

At the party for *Chinese Roulette,* Kurt had been driven to new lows, fired by Rainer for having "run out of ideas." This Juliane would learn only later. Along with spoon-served caviar she would experience countless other novelties, but her naïveté blinded her to the fact that the man of so many kindnesses who had stolen her heart had begun during *Chinese Roulette* to surrender his body and soul to drugs.

19

"**H**ARD drugs? There was nothing, nothing at all, only a little joint now and then—until, I know exactly, we shot *Chinese Roulette,*" says Michael Fengler, adding: "My girlfriend at that time was an ex-junkie. And Rainer would talk with her for hours on end just to know what she had felt, and he was very impressed with everything she said. He had had no direct experience with drugs, and suddenly he started. Heavily. Cocaine, heroin, mixing one with the other, everything. That's when it all began."

Chinese Roulette was shot in an isolated Franconian castle owned by Rainer's cameraman Michael Ballhaus. Many of the people who were in *Satan's Brew* moved over to the new project with hardly a break in between, and neither the onset of spring nor the pastoral setting nor Rainer's experiments with drugs did anything to ease the slave-driving that had characterized the making of the earlier film. Kurt was stripped of all his creative functions and Margit Carstensen, under pressure from Rainer to relinquish her leading role, tolerated worse humiliations than ever before. None of this can be guessed at from viewing the finished product, a tour de force of directorial virtuosity, much less that it was made under the influence of drugs.

The film, another Fassbinder study of the plight of the unloved, revolves around a handicapped child who tricks her parents into going to their house in the country with their respective lovers on the same weekend. The child herself arrives on the scene purposely to create further embarrassments. The truth game "Chinese Roulette" is played, and the exchanges of malice escalate tragically.

When released, the film was received with many reservations but with almost no dissent about what Andrew Sarris, who would later give an entire course on *Chinese Roulette* at Columbia University, describes as its "razor-sharp artistry." Rainer attributed much of this breakthrough, at least in style, to his discovery of the effects of certain drugs, particularly cocaine. "Using drugs," he would say later, "can have a positive influence on art. On the other hand, I don't think this is true for everyone, because all drugs carry with them the risk of addiction. That's true, for example, with cocaine. It is possible to use it creatively, though for some, imagination alone is sufficient. In any case, the danger exists. If you write under the influence of drugs, however, you can work on it afterward, and that can really be useful." He used as examples writers such as Rimbaud and Proust, as well as Freud's experience with cocaine as a way of exploring the unconscious. All this was said in connection with a film he planned for years but never made. It was to be based on the Pitigrilli novel *Cocaine,* and in it he hoped to tell the story of a man who chooses to use drugs in the full awareness that they will shorten his life but at the same time make living more intense. "Everyone must decide for himself," Rainer believed, "whether it is better to have a brief but more intensely felt existence or to live a long and ordinary life."

In 1976, on the remote and secluded set of *Chinese Roulette,* his own decision was in the making. The troupe not only worked but lodged in Ballhaus's castle, yet few were aware of Rainer's being under the influence of drugs. Kurt, himself still in the dark, remembers taking notice of Rainer's "never-ending state of wide-awakeness." Unfortunately, someone who did see Rainer in rather compromising situations was the puberty-aged actress who played the part of the handicapped child. She evidently passed some of the time when she should have been fast asleep peeping through keyholes and writing detailed letters to a girlfriend back home about whose bed was being shared by whom and for what. At least some of these letters fell into the hands of the young actress's grandmother, who, as might be expected, complained. The child had claimed to have seen Rainer running naked at dawn through the garden, whipping Armin, both in a state of some exaltation.

Somewhat less direct testimony about the condition of Rainer's psyche during the filming can be found in a book coauthored by Rainer himself and German critic Hans Günther Pflaum. It is a thoughtful case study of filmmaking, based on the production of *Chinese Roulette* and the two previous films. In it, Ulli Lommel, who had one of the leading roles in *Chinese Roulette,* gives a description of Rainer at work with his actors at the time. He felt that Rainer's direction did not come from his consciousness. "There is," he said, "an incredibly strong connection made between his subconscious and those of others and it takes place with remarkable frequency. It's almost a kind of magic . . . an extraordinary current of enormous power." Macha Meril, another leading player, said, "Working with him is like making love. Often you mustn't say anything. There's an automatic understanding. I don't ask him the why and how. I try to guess or sense it."

So convinced was Rainer of the creative value of cocaine that in his next film—*Bolwieser,* based on Oskar Maria Graf's pre-Hitler novel of provincial middle-class life—he insisted that Kurt, cast in the title role, play the part drugged. The film was made for television in the fall of 1976, in two parts lasting three hours and twenty minutes in all (shortened to two hours for theatrical release years later—in the United States as *The Stationmaster's Wife*). It marks the final appearance of Kurt Raab in a Fassbinder film and the prelude to his exit from Rainer's life. As Bolwieser, the epitome of the small-timer, the universal nobody, Kurt gave Rainer what may be his finest performance—in spite of himself. "It had become clear to me," he said later, "that in both big and small roles I was always playing the petty, petty bourgeois, the grubby, wretched commoner. So I dared, during a charming tête-à-tête, to ask what his motives were in having me play such characters. 'After all, you *are* one,' he responded laconically. I was flabbergasted."

Kurt describes the role of cocaine in his creation of Xaver Ferdinand Maria Bolwieser:

> On the first day of shooting in Munich, [Rainer] took out a pillbox and showed me this famous white powder. There must have been about ten grams. He spoke in a whisper. He said I had to try it, that it would lift me to the heights of the art of acting. It wasn't at all dangerous, he said. All I had to do was sniff it and it would free my spirit. All of my neuroses and complexes would vanish. I would create a Bolwieser far beyond my normal range. I would be greater than I had ever been in my life. I hesitated. I reminded him of my alcohol habit, saying that I was afraid I'd become addicted to this, too. For the next three weeks I held out, in spite of his never letting up.

Then, on one dark November day, I had to do a scene in which I visit a very sick man dying in front of my eyes, and I was very depressed. Fassbinder saw this and shoved me into a nearby room. He opened his ever-ready little box, ground the crystals into a powder, and as I looked on with some interest, I suppose, he formed it into lines and showed me how to sniff it up my nose.

When I went through the same motions he had, I felt a sudden change in my brain. I felt free, a relaxation I'd never known before, a release from all the nastiness around me. My frustrations disappeared, and I did the scene euphorically, believing that I was truly a wonderful actor. I was convinced at once that this was the way of self-liberation, of freeing my inner strengths, my courage, and my self-confidence.

So I took the powder every day, and Fassbinder was always ready to divide this treasure with me. He even let me take charge of the pillbox, and I used its contents as freely as sugar. During the shooting, my concentration was total. I heard nothing and nothing could disturb me. Everything was crystal clear inside me and my thoughts were unimaginably profound, knowing as I did that I was creating a marvelous Bolwieser.

That nothing of these feelings was transferred to the screen, that my acting became stiff and my movements poor was something I would only learn later. Fassbinder just left me in my dreamworld, where I had become great.

What Kurt, undrugged, believed was bad acting was regarded by many critics as an extraordinarily uninhibited performance bearing the unique Fassbinder trademark. Fassbinder-watcher Wilhelm Roth wrote: "Kurt Raab [as Bolwieser] has little in common with the Bolwiser of the novel other than his petit bourgeois mentality. . . . He is a weak man from the very beginning, a born loser, while Graf gives his main character an awareness of being certain that he is a winner. . . . What Graf construes as a 'fall,' Fassbinder sees as being nothing but the slow revelation of a preexisting condition." Rainer may very well have left Kurt in the lurch, but true to his Junkerish obsession with the play *über alles,* he apparently got what he wanted.

20

RAINER'S contract with Fengler's Albatross Productions for *Chinese Roulette* provided for a fee of one hundred thousand marks plus half the profits. This made him the highest-paid German director at the time, and while on a Hollywood scale one hundred thousand marks (about forty thousand dollars then) would have been scoffed at by even a middle-ranking American director, considering Rainer's phenomenal output, and the time and place, his annual income and earning power made him a relatively rich man. In any case, he was well-heeled, and when that same year Armin found a large apartment across the street from the Deutsche Eiche, Kurt was told to sign a ten-year lease and deck it out—money being no object—according to Rainer's precise instructions. The result was a most unusual reflection of his taste.

He may have been inspired by an apartment he had seen in Rome that summer. He had gone there to discuss a film project with an Italian producer who, apart from being successful in business, had made it as a Latin lover, and his apartment was part of his legend. It was a penthouse that looked out on Saint Peter's Basilica (and the pope's apartment, by the way), and it had panache, including a bathroom that had a wall of mirror on the inside but was, at the flick of an external light switch, transparent glass from the outside. Thus, privileged people, and Rainer and Armin were among them, could watch famous movie stars, but more often starlets, powdering their nose, for example, in what the Latin lover called his aquarium.

Rainer's new apartment was to be in a similar style, befitting not a Latin lover, of course, but rather a Teutonic sensibility. Kurt remembers his instructions:

> He wanted everything very dark, nothing lighter than dark
> brown. He told me to make the carpeting dark, to cover the

walls with dark brown velvet, and to put up dark brown drapes, too, so that no outside light would enter any of the rooms. He wanted his bedroom black, except for a long narrow mirror to run along all four walls at the height of a man's cock. In the middle of the room, I was to put a large leather bed. There were to be two bathrooms, one for himself and the other for his guests. Both were to have big, round tubs to accommodate four persons in each tub. Only in the kitchen did I have a free hand, and I used a lot of blond polished wood along with some beige. This turned out to be his and Armin's favorite room.

When it was done, Rainer was immensely pleased. He showed it off proudly, and Peter Berling was among the first to get an invitation. Says Peter:

> I was shocked. It was terrible, in utter bad taste. There wasn't a ray of natural light coming in. You couldn't even see the windows. It looked like a cheap disco, and it felt like a grotto, a very expensive grotto. You felt buried.

Still starry-eyed, Juliane, who thought it was seventh heaven merely to be asked to come ("Rainer said, 'I want you to see how I live' "), found it a "very, very nice apartment":

> They had two bathrooms, with gold trimmings and all. Dark brown rooms, brown carpets, lots of mirrors, which was Rainer's style—glass and darkness. The kitchen was perfect. My God, was it perfect! It was equipped with everything you could think of, because Armin liked to cook.

Berling adds:

> Rainer was always sitting in the kitchen, half-dressed, watching television like your everyday provincial German. Anyone who had an appointment with him had to meet with him in that kitchen and sit at a greasy table with dirty dishes everywhere, and since he was now rich and famous, you could find some of the most important people in the film world looking for a place among the crumbs to put down a briefcase or even an elbow.

That was during "business hours." Alone, Rainer, Armin, and Kurt, who had his own bedroom, were a family of weird sisters. Kurt, as production designer of *Bolwieser*, had gotten into trouble with the producers for having gone seriously over budget, and there were accusations that he had pocketed some of the money. His career as an actor was jeopardized, too, by Rainer's refusal to cast him in any upcoming project, telling him frankly, "I have no more ideas for your face." Rainer promised not to abandon him, however, saying that perhaps they could work together on a script and that he would continue, as his "best girlfriend," to provide him with room and board. He dictated a thirteen-page letter for Kurt's signature in which Kurt confessed to "moral responsibility" regarding the charges of the producers. When it came to typing it up, Kurt demurred, but Rainer—insisting, says Kurt, that "repentance is good for the soul"—prevailed. The confession turned out to be a death warrant to his career, and Kurt was regarded unemployable, reduced now, in the Reichenbachstrasse household, to the role of Emma, the maid.

The family lived by night. Emma would scrub the overworked kitchen ("until it gleamed," says Emma) while Rainer would leave his earth-colored crypt with Armin, sailing out like Dracula in search of not blood but "snow." Releasing time-curdled bile, Kurt would later recount, in details that bear no repetition, how he was repeatedly awakened by the groans of leathermen dragged home by Rainer from places with names like The Black Jail and The Eagle or simply off the street. Suffice it to say that the groans were the result of the pain of his labors to perfect his skill at that fist-oriented practice that had so beguiled him when seen at The Anvil in New York. And practice he did, both in his leather bed and in one or another of his four-man tubs ("I did it like a fish in water," he told Kurt).

Emma would clean up, but that was only one of his jobs. With Rainer dead and buried, Kurt would recollect those days and speak to him "directly" in this voice:

So now I'm your private secretary. And if there's nothing to do, you'll think of something to keep me busy. The telephone rings. You don't answer anymore. That's beneath you. Mostly, you lie in bed, getting up only when it's dark. . . . I'm left to invent the excuses and the lies. I'm also your nurse. Not only do I have to cook, and serve you in bed, I must also look after you like a child, to make sure nothing bad happens to you. All night long you've taken cocaine and now it's four o'clock in the morning and you want to sleep. But you're too stimulated, so you have to take three Mandrax pills to calm you down. Then you remember you have to call Ingrid in Paris, to argue with her, so you take two more lines of coke and you're more awake than ever. More Mandrax. Suddenly the telephone receiver falls out of your hand and you collapse on the floor. My God, I think, now it's over. He's had a heart attack. I bend over you and listen to your chest. You're still breathing. You start to snore, so I drag you to bed and try to go to sleep myself. A little later, I find you in the bathroom sleeping very peacefully beside the toilet. I bring you back to bed again. You keep me going day and night.

Rainer's relationship with Armin was rapidly deteriorating, too, and both Kurt and Armin were finding themselves more and more frequently locked out of the apartment and searching for places to sleep, sometimes for a week at a time.

In March, Rainer shot his version of Clare Boothe's 1937 play *The Women,* which he called *Women in New York.* It was filmed in seven days just as he had staged it in Hamburg some months back, his final work in the theater. There were forty actresses and no men in the piece, and when released it was hailed as brilliant by some of his critics and as antiwomen by others.

During the staging of *Women in New York* in Hamburg, Irm had gotten pregnant. As she's said, she always used contraceptives with Rainer, and whether he knew this or not, whenever her period was late, he would fill up with childlike delight, says Irm, "thinking at last it's happened." Their sexual relationship, however, left much to be desired, at least as far as Irm was concerned, and copulation between them was sometimes unnatural, if Rainer's indiscreet confidences are to be believed: there had been vegetable and mineral phallic substitutes. So it was not surprising that when conception finally took place, Rainer was somewhere else.

The father was the young man she had met during the Frankfurt fiasco, Dietmar Roberg, a writer and a painter. "He was the absolute opposite of Rainer," Irm says, "and we loved each other very much. But right after I became pregnant he went to Munich and I was with Rainer in Hamburg, unsure of that love." Her doubts grew along with the fetus, and by the spring of 1977, when both conditions began to show, Rainer, in a white suit and walking down a street with plump Irm on his arm, made her a serious proposal of marriage, offering to adopt the child. Somehow it became an either/or proposition: either a lifetime of *Sturm und Drang* with the glory-bound Rainer Werner Fassbinder or the straight and narrow path with someone called Dietmar Roberg. Irm was thrown into a fateful dilemma:

> My heart told me one thing, my head said another. I had been weak for so long. Even though I had seen less of Rainer since Frankfurt, I had only to lay eyes on him and I would start to cry out of love. Though Dietmar loved me and I loved him, our situation wasn't that rosy, and my ties to Rainer were so, so strong. It was so difficult for me, but I decided—for what I believed corresponded to the truth—to have the child all alone. I never regretted it, and today I'm still thankful, very thankful.

So it was all over between Rainer and Irm, and she would be thankful. Thankful but tortured to the very end.

> Until his death, the years since that decision were very hard. He went on to have more and more success, and I had always dreamed of sharing it with him. He became so famous, even in America, and whenever I opened a newspaper he was in it—in the headlines, in the photos, in the articles that spoke of him. It was so hard for me because my heart would beat fast, and I would dream about him. Surely I dreamed about him almost every night. No, I did not get him. I wanted him, always, but I did not get him.

Irm, her decision made, would be joined by the father before the baby came, and they would go off to live on the Chiemsee, a lake near the German-Austrian border. Rainer would now be out of her life, but when she went into the hospital to have the child, he somehow got the news and he called her repeatedly. She had a boy, and Rainer sent her a telegram suggesting his favorite name. The couple liked it. The boy was christened Franz.

Throughout Irm's pregnancy, Rainer never looked over his shoulder, and consuming as much as three grams of cocaine a day now, according to Kurt, he went on to plan his most ambitious project up to then: a big-budget international film based on Nabokov's novel *Despair,* adapted for the screen by Tom Stoppard, the first screenplay of a Fassbinder film not written by himself, and starring—another first—world-famous actors Dirk Bogarde and Andrea Ferréol. During a pre-Easter break, he flew to Berlin with Armin to a convention of leatherphiles. Just like Shriners. Kurt, left behind to brood in the kitchen, went off to visit with Ulli on the French Riviera, but when he got back, Rainer was in a fury over his unscheduled absence, and Kurt, finding a new lock on the door, was given entry only to pack one suitcase with his personal belongings. It was all over, except for the pretexts.

Kurt later claimed that he left of his own volition, and that because he had wounded Rainer's vanity, "I was from then on considered an outcast, one who would never again be given the honor of being allowed to work in his films." Work he would not, but the reason Rainer gave was that Kurt had tried to have him murdered.

Both stories are pure invention, but Kurt admits that in a drunken stupor and bristling with a lust for vengeance he hired a musclebound young man, found in the Munich gay bar Bel Ami, to teach Rainer a lesson, bruises included. The contract backfired when the youth took the money and ran, blabbing to his friends. Rainer, hearing the tale, invited the unscrupulous hit man to his apartment, paid him twice as much as he'd gotten from Kurt, and taped his "confession." Thus was his best girlfriend's plot to murder Rainer Werner Fassbinder exposed. Kurt, found guilty by Rainer, was sentenced to be redubbed "my greatest enemy."

A ROUND nine o'clock in the morning, on October 18, 1977, Peter Berling, a late sleeper, was awakened in his apartment in Rome by a phone call. On the other end of the line, in Munich, was Rainer, often an even later sleeper but now very wide awake. "Mutti," he said, with a note of despondence riding the wire, "they've murdered our friends."

Peter, late sleeper but quick riser, made a fast count of the friends they had in common and asked Rainer who the hell he was talking about. The news had just come over the radio, he replied, that Andreas Baader and other members of his terrorist gang had that night "committed suicide" in their fortresslike prison at Stammheim.

Baader, of course, was the strident political heckler from Rainer's Action Theater days who had gone on to bigger things, leaving their "friendship" behind him, and he was certainly no friend of Peter's.

"Rainer, you're talking on the telephone," Peter reminded him, implying that the same "they" who did in Baader and the others might be listening to the postmortem discussions of their "friends."

Rainer rattled on, as undaunted as he was enraged. The suicide story, at least at the time, carried almost no weight at all, even among Baader's enemies, let alone his friends. It had come as the cataclysmic ending to a long season of shootings, police repression, and one of the most sensational acts of terrorism ever mounted.

Six weeks earlier, the so-called Red Army Faction had kidnapped a leading German industrialist, Hanns-Martin Schleyer, after slaying his bodyguards, and had demanded the release of Baader and almost every other terrorist then in prison. When Bonn said no once too often, four Palestinian terrorists, led by an insane twenty-three-year-old killer who called himself Captain Mahmoud, hijacked a Lufthansa jet with eighty-six persons and a Yorkshire puppy on board.

By the time the pirated plane ended up in Mogadishu, Somalia, Mahmoud had murdered the pilot, so when radioed that his demands had been met, he may have believed his crime had paid off; but it was all a play to gain time, and with the terrorists' guard down, the plane was stormed by a German antiterrorist squad. Captain Mahmoud was killed, along with two of his henchmen, while the passengers, including the puppy, were freed. Back in Germany, the news of the raid brought on the murder of the kidnapped industrialist and the collective suicide, if that's what it was, of Baader and the rest of Rainer's "friends."

The German government later presented a body of evidence to substantiate the suicide contention, and many more-or-less impartial observers have declared themselves convinced. But in 1977 it was difficult to find even one believer, and out of the telephone conversation between Rainer and Berling, and many like it, the idea was born to make a movie about the "truth" of these events.

The assumption that Baader and his comrades had been executed by the state was so widespread that when Berling made the proposal of reconstructing the prison setting and asking each of seven or eight of Germany's top directors to shoot his version of how the terrorists met their end, Rainer queried him wryly, "And who do you think you will get to shoot the suicide version?" The project, however, was not abandoned. It reemerged almost instantly, and under the Filmverlag production banner, Rainer, along with Heinrich Böll, Alexander Kluge, Volker Schlöndorff, and other important West German filmmakers and writers, was asked to produce an episode of his own creation that might show what postwar Germany had become. The film, among the most memorable achievements of the New German Cinema, is called *Germany in Autumn*.

For a long time now, Rainer had been troubled by his social conscience. He had been among the first of his generation to point out the fallacies in the dreams of the revolutionary students of the sixties. This had earned him their scorn, and along with the charges of being a left-wing fascist, antifeminist, and so forth, he was accused not only of abandoning the ideals of the New German Cinema but of impeding the way for new talent. After a second experience of being branded an anti-Semite, which occurred in the spring of that year,* he made a public declaration that he would emigrate from Germany and settle in America. In this, he joined several other leading directors, including Herzog and Wenders, who believed that the police-state atmosphere at home, brought on by the unbridled violence of the Red Army Faction, stifled creativity and freedom of expression. Indeed, a form of censorship—not to speak of loyalty oaths—had been installed, and Rainer, interviewed by *Newsweek* about his decision to relocate in the United States, stated that the only kind of movie that could be made in West Germany was one that bore no resemblance to reality.

What seems to have bothered him most, however, was his inability to come to terms not with his critics but with himself. "He was often faced with the question," says Harry, "why, after sixty-eight, he had not chosen the path of Baader and Meinhof, and he always avoided coming up with an answer, telling himself that making films would be more important for the 'cause' than going out on the street."

Two years earlier, he had received a message from the underground. Ulrike Meinhof, by far the most brilliant activist of the "revolution," wanted to speak with him. Rainer was cast into turmoil and in the end remained deaf to her invitation. After her arrest, he was sorry he had not responded, and he was sorrier still when in 1976 she died in prison, the first of the zero-credibility-rated suicides.

Now, after Stammheim, Rainer renounced his plans to emigrate. He was in a mood to go out on the street, and in a sense he did in *Germany in Autumn.*

All of the eight directors of the film sought to rattle the nation's complacency. The dean of the New German Cinema, Alexander Kluge, for example, created startling effects juxtaposing the state funeral for Hanns-Martin Schleyer with the funeral for Baader and his comrades, the latter encircled by mounted police with the mourners observed and photographed with telescopic lenses. But none of the others had the impact of Rainer's contribution, which is one of the most intense short films ever projected on a screen. It is another

---

*His projected ten-part miniseries based on a book that had been popular during the Nazi period (Gustav Freitag's *Soll und Haben*) was rejected in 1977 on grounds of the novel's indisputable anti-Semitism. Rainer, however, had purposely chosen the book because he felt he could show that Nazism wasn't an accident but was an extension of pre-Hitler Germany and that national attitudes "haven't altered to this day." Obviously, he said, such a project was bound to run into trouble.

self-portrait, but this time there is absolutely no boundary between the artist and his creation: The British critic Tony Rayns describes it thus:

> RWF's contribution cross-cuts between two domestic situations: (1) RWF returns to his apartment in Munich from a trip to Paris, to work on his script for the projected film adaptation of *Berlin Alexanderplatz*. He is greeted and ministered to by his lover Armin Meier . . . but RWF repeatedly picks quarrels with Meier over the political crises caused by the Mogadishu hijacking and the deaths in Stammheim. At one point RWF orders some cocaine to boost his spirits, but flushes it down the toilet when he fears a police raid on the apartment. (2) RWF has a kitchen-table discussion with his mother, Liselotte Eder, about the political situation. Ms. Eder evinces orthodox bourgeois outrage at the tactics of the terrorists; RWF agitatedly points out the flaws and holes in her reasoning. . . . [RWF] is at pains to dramatize (-externalize) his personal anxieties: he presents himself both as a "concerned" individual and as a domestic tyrant, taking out his own insecurities on his long-suffering lover.

Many of the reviews that followed the film's release at the Berlin Film Festival in March 1978 echoed a phrase in *Die Presse* of Vienna: "an honesty close to the edge of bearability." The moviegoing German-speaking world was shocked by the dramatic irony of the figure of this brutish homosexual, drug addict, great despiser of all things bourgeois weeping on hands and knees in a plea for the continuation of democracy.

The picture we are shown of Rainer acting the part of Fassbinder, sitting naked in his velvet-walled apartment, with his hairless chest, his droopy mustache, the telephone and a cigarette in one hand, his sex organs in the other, starving for love, glutted with drugs, and aching to make sense of his times is about as true as a picture can be. The horror of it all was that when the lights were turned off and everyone went home, the actor carried on the play to his death.

22

THE script Rainer comes home to work on in *Germany in Autumn* is, as already noted by Rayns, for *Berlin Alexanderplatz,* the monumental (fifteen-and-a-half-hour) film he would not shoot until four movies later. Fengler, who knew Rainer when he was still walking the streets in pancake makeup, attests to the actual existence of the legendary dog-eared copy of the novel that was supposedly always sticking out of his pocket as a boy. *Berlin Alexanderplatz* was to be the Big Film, the story of Franz Biberkopf, with whom he so identified, and now as the German autumn passed into winter he was getting ready to make it. He had already made four films in which the leading character, played either by himself or by Harry, is named Franz; the Rainer-like character created by Kurt in *Satan's Brew* is Walter Kranz; and Franz, as we've seen, ended up tagged on to his pseudonymous film-editing credits as well as Irm's real-life baby.

Rainer had been about fourteen years old when he acquired his first copy of Alfred Döblin's epic of lowlife in Berlin of the twenties, and by his own testimony it bored him, at least at the beginning. The novel, strongly influenced by Joyce's *Ulysses,* depicts the harshness of the economic crisis in 1928 as it bears on life among the lumpen proletariat. What Rainer, when he finally got into it, found fascinating was the relationship between Franz Biberkopf and another man, Reinhold, who, according to Fassbinder, are brought to ruin by the unexpressed and inexpressible love they have for each other. This teenage interpretation was far from mainstream, but by the time young Rainer had turned the last page, he felt "released from the tormenting anxieties that were almost crippling me because of my homosexual cravings; the fear of giving in to my repressed desires was gone." The book had saved him from becoming "completely ill, from breaking down," and if he hadn't practically forced himself to read it, his life, he says, would never have taken the turn it had. The book had so penetrated "my head, my flesh, my whole body and soul," says Rainer, that when he reread it at nineteen "it became clearer and clearer that an enormous part of myself, my behavior and reactions, almost all of what I had thought was *me,* the me-ness of my existence, was nothing more than what Döblin had described in *Berlin Alexanderplatz*. Without realizing it, I had, quite simply, made Döblin's fantasy my life."

This is what Rainer said much later to help sell the film, the book, the book about the film, and so on. It contradicts his freer-wheeling recollections about the ease and naturalness of his "coming out," in which he even admits that the book had little to do with his saying to himself at fourteen or fifteen, "Okay, I'm gay." Nevertheless, says Rainer, "the novel helped me a lot."

One of the things it helped with was the maintenance of what by now had become an enormously expensive drug habit. Rainer had always envisaged *Berlin Alexanderplatz* in the format of a conventional feature film. It ended up ten times the normal length, however, and a major reason was the attraction of a long, uninterrupted stretch of moviemaking and a steady flow of cash, money needed to purchase drugs. The financiers had proposed the project to Rainer and Fengler, whose Albatross Productions had acquired the rights to the novel, as a six-part television series. Rainer, who was to be paid on a per-episode basis, drew it out to fourteen, contracting, apart from his directorial fee, to receive three hundred thousand marks for writing the script. This amount, paid first, was not enough to keep him in drugs, according to Fengler, who, while Rainer wrote, was working with Harry Baer on drawing up a one-year shooting schedule.

> He was now so heavily into drugs [Fengler recalls] that Harry and I came up with a precise plan on how we would manage the whole thing. We estimated that during the filming he would spend forty thousand marks a month to satisfy his need, about half a million for the whole year. We thought it would be idiotic to leave it all to chance, so we decided to buy all the stuff

ourselves in advance and sell it off to him piecemeal, without his knowing that it came from us, of course. The idea was to have some control over his habit by knowing what and how much he was getting.

The plan, meant also to secure a convenient supply for the planners, was held in abeyance while Rainer worked on the script, though something very like it began to take effect right away. Rainer would always close one eye to such machinations, sometimes secretly enjoying them, and he never had any illusions that his drug-runners were consistently altruistic. In any case Fengler, as his partner in business, was rapidly falling out of his favor. To protect his interests, Rainer summoned Peter Berling from Rome, insisting over Fengler's objections that Mutti be hired as executive producer. Not since the making of *Whity* and *Holy Whore* in 1970 had Berling been called on to oversee a film for Rainer, so perhaps he can be forgiven for having forgotten the lessons learned then, and the Fassbinder he speaks of now was quite different from that of old:

> I wasn't as happy about Rainer's offer as he imagined I would be. I'd grown wider and lazier than I had been when we were creating anecdotes in Almería and Sorrento, and I disliked leaving my sunny terrace in Trastevere for a year of cold and ugly Germany. Besides, I was working with another German "mad genius," Werner Schroeter, who was directing a film being shot in Naples. But Rainer wouldn't let up, and when he said he'd wait until I finished with Schroeter, I caved in.
>
> I finally got to Munich in January 1978, and Harry and I went to work on what I thought was an inhuman fifty-one-week shooting schedule. The minute Rainer heard that the start date had been set for June and that he had a good five months ahead of him, he declared that in the meantime he'd shoot another film, a "cheap quickie" that had been hanging around in his head for a couple of years. He called it *The Marriage of Maria Braun*.
>
> I was energetically against Rainer squeezing in another film before *Alexanderplatz*, trying with Harry's support to convince him that the months ahead would be packed full of grueling

preparations for what was to be the biggest and most expensive (fifteen million marks) project ever undertaken by German television. Of course the bulk of all this groundwork was my job, not his, but what I really was aiming at was to give him a chance to recover physically for the tough shooting schedule ahead. The truth was that Rainer was a wreck, his body bloated and gutted by drugs. His skin, which was never something you'd want to feature in a soap commercial, now looked like the rind of a sweating Swiss Emmenthal cheese. It had been a while, more than a year, since I'd worked with him on a day-to-day basis (a film project in Rome that fell through), so I suppose I was more keenly aware than the others of how his drug habit was taking its toll. But Rainer didn't listen to a word I said, and Fengler and his backers were so eager to churn out another Fassbinder movie in the interim that they agreed to all the conditions he imposed—a colossal mistake that only encouraged more and more outrageous ones every single day.

The making of *Maria Braun,* which ended up to be by far his most successful and perhaps his finest film, was one of the decisive self-destructive episodes in Rainer's life, and I was among those who had the sorry labor of watching it in silence from the front row of his captive audience.

What had attracted the producers in the first place was the idea of bringing Rainer together with Romy Schneider, Germany's most famous actress at the time. Courted for one or another project for years, she had finally accepted the title role in *Maria Braun,* but Rainer, after a meeting with her in Paris, publicly described her as a "dumb cow," whereupon Romy issued a press release declaring that she would never work with a "beast" named Fassbinder. Sheeplike were the producers, who went along with Rainer's surprising and uncommercial choice for the part—all-but-forgotten Hanna Schygulla. Since her banishment from the Fassbinder "team" almost five years earlier, Hanna had hardly worked. She'd made a few films for talentless directors, appearing in every one of them about as sexy as a sack of potatoes. By now she was convinced that only Rainer could redeem her, so her thrill at receiving the call was quite thorough.

The filming began in Coburg, not far from the Thuringian Forest, near the East German border. Harry and I, setting up *Alexanderplatz*, shuttled back and forth between Munich and Berlin, stopping regularly at Coburg—to see the boss—so much so that I ended up saddled with an acting chore in *Maria Braun*, no pay, of course ("Pay? You're getting paid for *Alexanderplatz*, aren't you?" said Rainer).

Money, or the lack of it, was one of the big troubles with *Maria Braun*. The idea had been to make it low-budget, for no more than the million marks Fengler already had. But when Rainer disappeared and didn't show up once in the first week of shooting, Fengler, who found him locked inside his apartment, unwilling or unable to open the door, knew he'd been hopelessly naïve. On the set at last, Rainer worked as hard and as sure-handedly as ever, directing Hanna, for example, down to the tiniest movements of her fingers. Whatever combination of drugs he'd concocted, it certainly stimulated output, though once he couldn't move or be moved for two days. When he wasn't directing, he sat in his trailer, writing the script for an entirely independent cinema version of *Alexanderplatz* he planned to make with a whole new cast after the television commitment.*

To keep the engine going, Fengler hired three assistants who did nothing but fly all over Europe to get stuff for Rainer, but his thirst for cocaine alone seemed unquenchable. It grew to seven or eight grams a day, and Coburg turned into a nightmare for all.

"It was the first time he screamed at me," says Juliane, who was ordered by Rainer to Coburg for an editing job. She had become his most ardent admirer, worshiping him as the kindest and most gentle man she'd ever known in all her twenty-one years. They had recently spent a night together alone, "the most wonderful night of my life," Rainer told Armin when he came to fetch them in the morning. They had been in an editing room, making the final cut of *Despair,* and

*The film was never made, but Rainer's cast list survives: Gerard Depardieu (as Franz Biberkopf), Isabelle Adjani (Mieze), Charles Aznavour, Jeanne Moreau, Andrea Ferréol, and Martin Balsam. The part of Reinhold was to have been played by himself.

Juliane, watching and servicing the master at work all night long, would remember the experience as being "like flying, like fucking." But now, setting out by car for Coburg, she was terrified, so much so that she lost her way.

I didn't get there until four o'clock in the morning, and Coburg was deserted. I knew where I was supposed to stay, a small hotel, where Rainer and the others were living. But the door was locked and nobody answered. I went looking for a place that was open. Suddenly, a taxi pulled up alongside me, and somebody jumped out. It was Rainer. He was very drunk. It was the first time I'd seen him that way.

He staggered up to me and stared. "Who are you?" he asked. "You're a white angel. Go away."

"Please, Rainer," I said, trembling, "I just got here and I don't have a key to the hotel. I have no place to go."

"Go away," he said. "I hate you." He went off, leaving me alone. I couldn't imagine why he wanted to hurt me. He was always so considerate. I knew he was having troubles with Fengler and with Armin, but I thought I had done something terribly wrong. I started back toward the hotel, but I got lost again. When I finally got there, he was standing at the door, swaying this way and that way, dangling something in his hand. "You need the key, don't you?" he said. "Here's the key." I'd thought he'd forgotten all about me, but there he was, so very drunk, but I knew everything was okay again.

But it wasn't. In the days ahead, he got "ugly," says Juliane, and he screamed at her until she ran out of tears.

Berling's account continues:

He was thrown out of his hotel, then out of another and another. He was so riddled with coke, and God knows what else, that he'd become incontinent and there were feces all over his rooms, walls included. Blood, too, because his mucous membranes were ulcerated and he continually bled from the nose. One of the hotels sent photos of Rainer's room to Fengler, who destroyed them immediately and paid whatever was asked.

Fengler shopped all over Germany for money to finish the film, which he knew would cost more than twice the original budget. He more or less succeeded, but he had to sign away 85 percent of the rights, which he shared fifty-fifty with Rainer. In other words, he'd sold 135 percent of the film, or at least that's the way it was interpreted by Rainer. He went into a rage of rages and refused to give up an iota of his 50 percent. He called Fengler a gangster, and that was when the great feud between them really got going.

"I tried to explain to him," Fengler says, "that yes, he owned half, but like me, only of the part remaining. His answer was blackmail." Fengler adds:

He did things like this: "I stop shooting tomorrow," he'd say, "unless I get thirty thousand marks in cash first thing in the morning. Figure out what it will cost you if I don't shoot for only two days. It costs more, believe me." Of course I knew he was right. So I showed up with the cash. But when he did it again, then again, I threatened to punch his face in. "Do it," he said. "See how much *that* costs you."

That was how he managed to extort a hundred thousand marks over his salary, and he needed every pfennig for his drugs. He kept at it even after the shooting. In order for me to get one of the final payments from the backers so that we could edit and complete the film, he had to show them a rough cut of the stuff he'd shot. When he had it ready—a day or so before the screening—he called me from Cologne, where he'd been cutting. "Bad news," he said. "The copy has been stolen. But there's a chance, a slight possibility, that I can get it back from the people who robbed it. But it's going to cost. They want twenty thousand marks."

"Rainer," I screamed, "no! This is too much! I'm coming to Cologne and I'll . . . I'm going to kill you!" I think I really meant it, but after I'd slammed down the phone, I realized I'd get nowhere, and to redo the cutting would cost more than he asked. So I sent him the twenty thousand.

"Rainer treated Fengler like a street dog," says Berling, continuing:

> One bitter-cold night that winter, the two of them and I were driving through a snowscape in the countryside looking for a place to eat. They came to loggerheads over that 50 percent business, and Rainer, who was at the wheel, stopped the car in the middle of nowhere and shouted at Fengler to get out. Fengler didn't even have a coat on, but he was too mad to notice, so he left the car, slammed the door behind him, and trudged off in the snow as Rainer sped away.
>
> "Rainer," I said. "Are you crazy? He'll freeze to death in an hour!"
>
> "I sure hope so," said Rainer.
>
> I argued with him until I got him to turn back and pick up Fengler, who by now had also changed his mind, but now I was a "traitor" because "friends of gangsters are gangsters." Later, however, when Fengler wasn't around, I discovered what was really on his mind. "Leave those gangsters, Mutti," he said, "and we'll do *Alexanderplatz* without them. You'll be executive producer for all of my films from now on. Think that over carefully, Mutti." All I needed was one thought of what *that* might be like, however, and I preferred to side with the "gangsters." I reminded him that Fengler owned the rights to *Alexanderplatz.* He sneered. "He'll give them up," he declared. "I have the power to force him."

About which Fengler says:

> He came to me and put it to me this way: "You think you had troubles with *Maria Braun,*" he said. "That was nothing. If you want to go on to *Alexanderplatz,* I'll destroy you!" I believed him.

Fengler sold out at a loss. He took his revenge by refusing in perpetuity to relinquish the rights to the separate cinema version, which was the aspect of the project that was dearest to Rainer. *Berlin Alexanderplatz,* postponed for one year, went to Bavaria Studios, and Mutti, the "traitor," was unemployed. Fengler claims now that Rainer drove him out to collect a half-million-mark bribe from Bavaria. His source for this unsavory piece of news, he says, was Armin, who related the circumstances of the alleged payoff two days before his suicide. According to Fengler, Armin wanted him to know how truly "nasty" Rainer had been. Considering the story of Armin's death, which it is now time to recount, there is hardly a reason to doubt it.

23

O N or about May 31, 1978—no one will ever know the date for certain—Armin, sitting alone in the celebrated Reichenbachstrasse kitchen, swallowed the contents of four bottles of sleeping pills, washing them down with alcohol. His decomposing body was found by Rainer's mother one week later.

Mother Fassbinder tried to put across the notion that Armin had died of stomach ulcers. Juliane insists to this day that the death was accidental ("Armin didn't want to die"), and others, mainly the dead man's friends at the Deutsche Eiche, accusing Rainer, called it murder.

Two months earlier, the couple had sailed to New York on the *Queen Elizabeth,* trying to mend their clashing ways. Rainer had just completed *Maria Braun.* Armin had played a feature part in a film produced by Rainer and portentously titled *Loser's Game.* They were accompanied on their voyage by another couple, Daniel Schmid and his friend Raul Jimenez.

Daniel recalls:

> For the first two days we were all in heaven, and Rainer was even higher. But then he suddenly discovered that his supply of coke was gone, and heaven became a hell. He accused me of having stolen the cocaine to keep it from him. Of course he'd used it all up, but he managed to get Armin to believe him, so I let them search my cabin. When this yielded nothing, Rainer turned on Armin. One night, in a fit, he threw him out of his cabin. I'd heard the fight, and when I went on deck to see what happened to Armin, I found him just about ready to jump into the ocean.

Terra firma was no better. Rainer took up with a sporty New Yorker. Armin, racked with jealousy, flew back to Munich, and Rainer literally wrote him off. Sitting in his room at the Algonquin, he composed a long goodbye on paper, a letter of many pages, saying that he would never again return to the Reichenbachstrasse, though he would continue to pay the rent and provide Armin with a daily allowance of fifty marks. He dispatched an ample sum of money to the Deutsche Eiche with instructions to mete it out to Armin day by day.

In the lobby of the same hotel, and all over America, was the edition of *Time* magazine in which the newsweekly, "discovering" the New German Cinema, named Rainer as one of the "two young visionaries" leading the movement, the other being Werner Herzog. *Time* found nothing but glamor in the German "film tribe," but when it described Rainer, it somehow came very close to getting it right. *Time* wrote:

> It is hard to imagine Fassbinder . . . very far from the pavements of a modern city, whether it be Munich, Berlin or New York, his favorite place. Though he dresses in dirty jeans and a leather jacket, and looks like a Hell's Angel, Fassbinder is rigidly disciplined. Since he finished his first film in 1969, he has turned out, on average, one full-length movie every three months. "I want to build a house with my films," he says. "Some of them are the cellar, some are the walls, and some are the windows. But I hope in the end there will be a house."
>
> Fassbinder is a homosexual. . . . however, his concern is not really homosexuality, but power, its uses and abuses. His movies assert that in any relationship, personal or political, there will be the oppressor and the oppressed. But the worst tyrant of all is love. Says he: "Love is the best, most insidious, most effective instrument of social repression."

He had spent all of April in New York, and in May, traveling now with his new American friend, whose name nobody remembers, he went directly to Cannes for the premiere of *Despair.*

Despair, heartbreak, and disorientation were what Armin expressed when he received the letter from Rainer, and unable to fully comprehend it, he began to wander in and out of the Eiche searching for someone to interpret its "hidden" meanings. One of the many to whom he showed it told Kurt sometime afterward that it was written "very complicatedly but it was also very beautiful and a clear farewell." The clear part of the message, at least, finally got through. Armin took to straying around the city, abandoning himself to drinking and drugs, a habit he had continually sought to conceal from Rainer, who when it came to Armin strongly disapproved. He told everyone he saw that he was going to fly to Cannes to join Rainer, and though he appeared to be in no condition to travel, when he stopped showing up at the Eiche, his friends thought that Cannes was where he was.

At the film festival, Rainer sulked. *Time* had touted *Despair* as a movie to watch for, and the press conference that preceded the formal opening was packed with more Fassbinder-watchers than ever, but Rainer brooded alone in his suite at the Martinez. He had sent Peter Chatel as his stand-in, and in the end the film was poorly received.* Neither this nor anything else helped to lighten his mood, until he had the idea of flying-in brand-new *Maria Braun* and showing it at a private screening, where it received a standing ovation and a huge offer from Hollywood for U.S. distribution rights. The word of mouth at Cannes was that *Maria Braun* was going to be an enormous international success, which of course it was, and this sent a long line of producers to Rainer, proffering projects, Havana cigars, and champagne. He was utterly delighted.

Rainer left Cannes with a juicy contract to film the novel *Cocaine.* Feeling free at last of Armin, he was heading for Paris, where he planned to live for a while in the small house he maintained in the Rue Cocteau. On May 31, he celebrated his thirty-third birthday there in particularly festive spirits. That was the very day and very moment, people hurt by Rainer apparently derive some sort of pleasure in insisting, that Armin did himself in.

Truth to tell, it was not until June 6 that the concierge of Rainer's

*Chatel knew nothing about the film other than what he'd learned from having seen it. "Before going to the press conference," he says, "I asked Rainer some questions that were likely to come up, like why there were so many Nazis seen at the beginning and none later on. Rainer said: 'I forgot to shoot that.' Was that what I was supposed to say? 'No,' said Rainer, 'you tell them that the Nazis are in the beginning because in 1933 people were much more aware of them, but then they got used to their presence and they weren't noticed anymore.'"

building in the Reichenbachstrasse ventured into the Eiche to report a foul odor emanating from the apartment. Mother Fassbinder was called. She had a key, and when she opened the door she saw on the floor an arm reaching out of the kitchen. The authorities were unable to determine either the cause or the time of death, but the empty bottles and the condition of the corpse allowed for the various pet theories of this or that person, depending on what he or she thought of Rainer.

Having infinitely more enemies than friends, Rainer went underground on hearing the news. He was sheltered by the few while the many posted threats of violence, warning him never to return to Munich, much less to the Deutsche Eiche. Mother Fassbinder, who had nothing but contempt for her son's male lovers, buried Armin without tears. Wisely, Rainer stayed away from the funeral, but his mourning was complete enough.

"I felt the only thing for me to do was kill myself, too," he later told Juliane, "but I couldn't bring myself to do it." He locked himself in a room of Volker Spengler's apartment in Frankfurt and didn't come out for days. Word reached Munich that he had broken down and was "rolling on the floor," overcome with guilt. But the more cynical among the group were betting that he'd turn his latest grief into a film. He did, comforting the cynics all the more by seeming not to miss a beat from his customary pace. Writing a screenplay in three or four days, he was behind the camera again in July, filming his story of the last five days, capped by suicide, in the pitiful life of a transsexual he named Elvira.

"Naturally, it was the simplest and most logical thing to do in my case," Rainer said two years later. "What was important was for me to make a film that did not merely record my feelings about [Armin's] suicide,* pain and sadness, that is . . . but to go much beyond that, to say much more than I could say about Armin."

The film is titled *In a Year with 13 Moons,* and there are two aspects of it that distinguish it from all the others. One is that Rainer assumed more control over the finished product than ever before; not

---

*In the same breath he said that he no longer thought Armin's death was an intentional suicide, adding: "But if it was, and I believed it was at the time, I wouldn't be lacking in feelings of guilt, thinking of how I had lived three years with someone, unable to provide the minimum amount of happiness one needs to survive."

only did he write, direct, and edit but he also served as his own cameraman and production designer. The second is that he deviates for the only time from his otherwise consistently rational point of view, assuming the supernatural as his point of departure. He describes it:

> Every seventh year is a Year of the Moon. Certain people, whose existence is predominantly determined by their feelings, are afflicted by unusually severe depressions in these Moon Years, comparable with those they suffer in years with thirteen new moons, albeit less intense. And if a Moon Year coincides with a year of thirteen new moons, they can often suffer major personal disasters. In the twentieth century, there are six years when this dangerous conjunction occurs: one of them is 1978. Previous ones have been 1908, 1929, 1943, and 1957. After 1978, the year 1992 will again jeopardize the existence of many a human being.

True, the years of coincidence certainly weren't happy, but there have been worse, and though forewarning is more useful than hindsight, one probably needn't view the approach of 1992 with exceptional alarm. In any event *13 Moons,* the movie, returns in the end to the conventional Fassbinder outlook, that the trouble with society is located not in the sky but right down here on earth.

Rainer put it this way:

> *In a Year with 13 Moons* describes a person's encounters during the last five days of his life, and attempts to determine —through these encounters—whether this one person's decision not to carry on beyond this last day, the fifth, should be rejected, at least understood, or maybe even found acceptable.
>
> The film is set in Frankfurt, a place whose particular structure virtually provokes biographies like this one—or at least doesn't make them seem particularly unusual. Frankfurt is not a haven of friendly mediocrity, not a place where opposites are squared off against each other, not peaceful, not fashionable or nice; on the contrary, Frankfurt is a town where you run into all the general contradictions of society at every street corner, incessantly.

Almost always ranked among Rainer's more memorable films, *13 Moons* tells the story of the former butcher boy Erwin (Volker Spengler), who has been surgically rendered Elvira, one of the most pathetic female film characters ever created anywhere. Critic Wilhelm Roth, who has reviewed every Fassbinder film, found much of it new and audacious, in particular the relationships between image and sound. He captured the essence of the Armin-like story: "If all the people whom Elvira meets in the last five days of her life are unable to help her, it is not that they intend to do her wrong. They are too occupied with their own problems, and in a certain sense they are as much without hope as she is. As in a train-station drama, they cross paths with Elvira, either recounting their own lives or listening to hers, but in the decisive moment they leave her in the lurch."

The film has no dedication, but the next film, *The Third Generation*, shot at the end of that same moon year, bears the following dedication: "To a true lover—and hence, probably, to nobody?" The question mark is Rainer's heart bleeding.

24

THE fateful letter to Armin is lost, but before that moon year passed—during the December filming of *Third Generation*—Rainer wrote another intricately constructed farewell to love. The recipient was someone who adored him so exaltedly that the specter of suicide loomed once more, or so it had seemed to the sender. This missive survives.

The could-be victim, who in any case at the time of the writing was in a state of psychic collapse and under medical supervision, was Isolde Barth, enchanted Isolde of the tristful eyes.

Her Roman-candle rise and fall had begun at Cannes the previous May. Having played a small acting part in *Despair,* she had been a member of Rainer's entourage, ensconced in the Martinez with nothing to do. Here is how Isolde tells it:

> We got very close at Cannes and had lots of fun. Since I had plenty of free time, I went around getting him invited to everything and picking up news and gossip. He enjoyed all that and he suddenly had the idea that I was a good organizer and that I ought to be in production. When Armin died and he decided to make *13 Moons* with a small cast and crew of close friends, I was given the job of producer, without knowing a thing about how to go about it.
>
> I worked day and night, exhausting my nerves and my body, but I drove myself. Rainer was in such a bad way after what had happened to Armin that there were times I thought he would kill himself, and I felt so sorry for him. But the more I was with him, the more I became like him. It was a new experience for me to be able to live out my emotions. I had always kept everything inside me, and here I was suddenly, like him, capable

of laughing, crying, and letting off steam all in the same breath. For me, it was psychotherapy. But at the same time it wore me out and got me into trouble because I was naïve about the power games, not to speak of the rules, that were going on among those who knew Rainer longer and better than I did. The film got done, though, and Rainer was so satisfied that he wanted to make me his permanent production manager, melting my fear and reluctance by offering me major acting parts in his upcoming films.

So I started working on *Third Generation,* the next film, which we were going to shoot in Berlin. I rented a large apartment there, in the Niebuhrstrasse, where we were all going to live together like one big happy family. But the moment Rainer and the others arrived, I sensed that something had changed between Rainer and me. It may have been because Harry, who'd been away since *Maria Braun,* had rejoined the production team and Rainer didn't want him to know that he liked me. It was something strange like that. Or maybe it was because I had a love affair in Berlin, my first in the five months I'd been so close to Rainer, and when somebody told him, he got jealous, hiding that from the others and putting more distance between him and me.

He began picking on me, screaming at me for everything that went wrong, blaming me most of all for not having found the money to finance the film. I couldn't understand how he could have placed so much confidence in me and then withdraw it so abruptly. All this took place in front of everybody in that apartment, day after day. It was late November, always dark and dreary, and I couldn't stand it. Then Rainer's mother, who took care of the books, accused me of taking money and writing false receipts. Rainer believed or wanted to believe her, and we fought constantly. He said I was killing him, and twice I packed my things to go back to Munich, but my heart wouldn't let me leave him.

I got so ugly. I couldn't sleep. I was swollen with alcohol. I lost my strength and my soul. I couldn't work. I went into depressions, crying jags one moment, euphoric the next, then tumbling lower than ever.

143

Finally, we had the big fight, just before Christmas, on a day when not only did I have to organize the shooting but also act my part in the film. The tension was unbearable for everyone by then. We couldn't shoot that morning because Rainer was displeased with the location I'd found, and I had to go looking for another. When I got back to the apartment, he began yelling at me, smashing up the kitchen, calling me terrible names.

Back on the set that evening, I couldn't concentrate on my acting, and I asked for a few minutes to study the script. So he stopped the shooting, humiliating me in front of the others, saying, "Madame Barth doesn't know her lines." I hated him. When I was ready, the lights blew, and it took a few hours to get going again. At last, we shot, but he didn't like what I did, and he cried, "You're stupid!"—blaming me, again in front of everyone, for having made him lose a day's shooting. That was my breaking point. I ran off the set in tears. I locked the three doors to my room in the apartment and didn't come out the next morning. People knocked on my door and the phone wouldn't stop ringing, but I didn't answer. Finally, Rainer tried to break in to the room, shrieking anger. "I'm sick," I said. "I can't go on."

When everyone left I went to a doctor because I was sure I was having a nervous breakdown. He said I should move out at once to a hotel and sleep for a couple of days. He gave me a lot of pills and called Rainer's office, leaving word that I was in no condition to work. For Rainer, my not showing up on the set was the worst thing of all. It was high treason. That's when he wrote me the letter.

Even Juliane, who was present (still on the sidelines) and admits to no fondness for Isolde at the time, says that Rainer treated her unfairly and that she was the unwitting victim of the backbiting old-timers. Juliane is probably near the mark in her belief that thin-of-skin Isolde was the last person in the world one would send out into the cold to secure the financing and production of a feature film. What the episode shows is the warp in Rainer's judgment, brought on no doubt by the loss of Armin, as well as his continuing use of heavy drugs. Nevertheless, the three-page single-spaced letter, saved all these years by Isolde, reveals another dimension to the story. He was the smith of two million words, but almost always they were more or less carefully fashioned for public consumption, and his private correspondence borders on the nonexistent. Thus, in the letter to Isolde, written in the formal second person, we are given a rare "live" and above all unedited perspective of Rainer's mind churning.

Tango Film
Rainer Werner Fassbinder
Niebuhrstrasse 78
1000 Berlin 12

Berlin, 27.12.78

My dear Miss Barth,

Since you continue to disturb my friends and even my mother with odd versions (to say the least) of your connection with me, versions that in no way correspond to the actual circumstances, and since these disturbances are now and then laced with sinister demands, I feel constrained to put our verbal agreements in writing, hoping to give effective emphasis to my plea to you to spare my friends, my mother, and myself from further persecution.

Confronted as I am by your ceaseless threats, among them some very depressing ones, such as your intimations that you will do something unspeakable to yourself if I fail to behave according to your wishes, desires, and dreams, you will understand why finally I feel obliged to bring to a conclusion, herewith in writing, a relationship that has been perceived by you in a completely different way from me, a relationship of friendship, perhaps, which may account for most of the misunderstandings (to use a friendly term) that have arisen. However, there are times in one's life when even a robust comprehension that certain mistakes were made out of uninhibited desperation does not allow one to tolerate those very mistakes.

And so I refuse to accept any responsibility for decisions

made by you concerning your existence. You may feel that I am the guilty party, and perhaps you will succeed in convincing others of my guilt, whoever they may be, but in the depth of your soul you know as well as I do that all this is nothing more than squalid intrigue. What counts in the end is what you and I know and not what others believe. People always believe what they want to believe in order to reinforce their fantasies, however odd and alien they may be, with a semblance of reality.

In the sad event that this letter ends up being aired in public, I shall begin by stating a verifiable fact: In one unhappy moment for both of us, during the making of *In a Year with 13 Moons,* the idea arose of founding a production company in Berlin, independent of Tango Film–Munich but with the same name, Tango Film–Berlin. This was brought a step further by the intention of filming the then extremely vague idea for *The Third Generation* in Berlin.

By now, we had completed a production together, namely *In a Year with 13 Moons,* and you had assured me of its positive outcome, by which I mean that you told me we had kept all expenses within the budget. As it turned out later, this was a lie on your part, although as far as I'm concerned you can go on calling it a miscalculation.

At that point in time, however, it was an extremely welcome "fact" for me, and I was further swayed by your very credibly presented fears for your future, manifested in what looked like serious depressions (and here I may be mistaken), in the event that your life were not to remain in some way linked to mine. As this appeared to me to be not a threat but merely your way of pressing the issue of my taking some sort of responsibility for your well-being as a person, I suggested that we go ahead with this enterprise, Tango Film–Berlin, together.

You will surely remember your spontaneous enthusiasm for the project, while at the same time, it was only natural for both of us to be left feeling uncertain about how this partnership would fare, an uncertainty that, considering its vast implications, could be neither easily nor quickly reflected upon nor decisively discussed. I well remember the problem you had about whether you wanted to be an associate or only an employee of this company, as well as my own not-so-groundless fear of giving you all my confidence and frankly putting myself in your hands.

That was why the project seemed to both of us as fascinating and as fortunate as it appeared frightening and worrisome. All this was understandable then, but the result of our work on *The Third Generation,* ending in the catastrophes that drove everyone connected with the production, but especially me as a person, to the edge of a precipice, appears to be almost a logical progression and, by hindsight, terrifyingly predictable.

Nevertheless, we decided to try it out, and to reduce our feelings of insecurity, we put off making the decisions that ought to have been taken at the outset. In practice, however, it became clearer with each passing day that I had to shoulder all of the responsibilities. You tried out the organizational mechanics of being an associate of the company, but, as I said, made me responsible for absolutely everything.

Since this was all so new to you, we didn't want your tryout as a producer to become a superhuman task, so we formed a kind of production team consisting of V. Spengler, who took on the job of production design and looking for locations, and Harry Baer and me, both of us in charge of the shooting schedule and other planning, while you had the task of finding the financing and concluding contracts with outside parties, including the actors' commitments regarding the schedules drawn up by Harry Baer and me.

Concerning your first task, that of the financing, you played a most unusual game, resulting in serious consequences. You conveyed the impression to the entire production group, including me personally, that there were no financial problems, by giving us false, misleading, and inexact information. This went on for so long that the cancellation of the production would have been just as costly as its completion. You gave no thought at all to the tremendous disaster this will probably, and as the matter stands at the moment, almost certainly, signify for me. You therefore abused my trust in you in a most evil and monstrous way.

You carried out your other tasks more or less in the same

manner. Contrary to what you constantly assured me, many things were imprecisely or falsely concluded with outside parties.

It may be that your excessive consumption of alcohol is your excuse. But no excuse can alter the costly and catastrophic consequences that have in fact occurred.

As to the question of your compensation, one of your complaints concerns your being discharged from playing the role of "Hilde" in the film. As you know very well, as many acting roles as possible are given to people who are already working with the group in other capacities, in order to cut costs. In view of your self-dismissal from the tryout production team of *The Third Generation,* your playing "Hilde" is simply out of the question, so there is no need to mention that your first day of shooting had to be canceled because of your difficulties with your lines. Finally, there is your claim of having put a certain sum of money, the amount of which changes day to day, in the production account. I'll leave that figure for you to sort out.

Clearing up these problems, you understand, will take some time, and since the papers you left behind were in an unheard-of state of disarray, it will take even longer to go through them. Furthermore, among the vouchers you handed in, there are some that one could at least call dubious. Whether they are worse than that remains to be checked out. But you can be sure that you will be informed as soon as possible.

In spite of everything, I wish you luck in your further search for success.

With friendly regards,
RWF

One could peck at the kernels of truth Rainer's letter contained, but there's probably no one who would. It was pure overkill, to which there cannot be a response. "It was sad," says Isolde, "because I loved him. I dreamed of him every night." She, too. But the story is not all sad. It has a happy ending. That comes later.

Isolde and her financial "sources" were gone, and the rest of the group making *Third Generation* milled about during the New Year's holiday, waiting for money to somehow materialize so that Rainer could complete the film. With Hanna back in the fold and two brand-new resurrections—Margit Carstensen and Günther Kaufmann—it seemed as if little had changed from the time when it all began ten years before, except for cocaine. In the meantime, another head was put to the chopping block. It belonged to Peter Chatel. He had a contract for sixty thousand marks to play a leading role, but when he showed up he was told that the money had run out, and Rainer offered him a take-it-or-leave-it proposition to work on a percentage basis, with a promise of a paying part in the next film, *Berlin Alexanderplatz.* He took it and joined the bunch in the Niebuhrstrasse apartment.

> The atmosphere was absolutely mad [says Chatel]. On a wall of one room in the apartment there was the whole shooting plan for *Berlin Alexanderplatz,* which was well funded, and for *Third Generation* there was no money at all. So to keep everybody in a good mood, Rainer changed the cast of *Alexanderplatz* daily, rubbing out names with an eraser and giving us bigger and better parts. So there was always this compulsion to pass through the room to see what point you were at now. Rainer had the room adjoining this one, and his was always dark because he never stopped watching television, but the room with the plan was brightly lit by overhead fluorescent bulbs so he could always see, without being seen, who was looking at the cast list. It was his way of being reassured of our dependence on him.
>
> When this was exhausted and the money situation got desperate, he phoned me up one day and said, "I need the five thousand dollars you owe me and I need it immediately." I knew that I didn't owe him anything, and that he was in debt to me from films I'd never gotten paid for, but he went on and on about this five thousand dollars, and I suddenly remembered what he was talking about. On one of our trips to New York, I'd come across a black boy with whom I had an enormous sexual affair. He was actually one of the few outsiders Rainer ever accepted; he usually didn't talk to anybody but his friends. But this American boy was always with us, and out of the blue he suggested that I take him back with me to Paris, where I was

living with a lover whom Rainer couldn't stand. I said it was too complicated and too much of a responsibility and also too expensive. "Don't worry about a thing," said Rainer. "I'll pay for everything. I'll give you five thousand dollars." I said thanks but no thanks at the time, but now he was insisting that he'd given me the money. "We don't have enough money to go on with the film," he shouted over the phone, "and if you don't give me my five thousand dollars by tomorrow morning, I'll come over and destroy your apartment!" After that fight, I was out of both *Third Generation* and *Alexanderplatz* and he didn't talk to me for two years. Even when we got together again, our relationship was officially altered. I was no longer his second-best girlfriend; I was from now to the end his second-best enemy.

The main reason why there was none of the usual TV and government-subsidy money for *The Third Generation*—and in the end Rainer had to pay for it out of his own pocket—was the film's subject matter: terrorism, at the time a taboo in Germany for anyone who could not be counted upon to repeat the shibboleths formulated by the terrorized state.

The movie may not be among Rainer's best, but it certainly is one of the most independent and courageous of them all. When it was finally completed, early in 1979, and he had a chance to choose his words, he called it "a comedy in six parts, about party games, full of suspense, excitement and logic, horror and madness, just like the fairy stories they tell children to make life which ends in death more endurable."

Played as a political farce, it articulates an early, if not original, insight into the true nature of contemporary European terrorism. By "third generation," Rainer means the terrorists who arose, phoenix-like, from the ashes of those, like Baader and Meinhof, whose mixture of idealism and, according to Rainer, "almost pathological despair at their own impotence within the system finally drove them virtually insane." The second generation, which fared no better, was a natural offspring of the first, but the third, said, Rainer, "has less in common with its predecessors than it has with this society and the power that it wields."

He had become convinced that these third-generation terrorists "do not know what they are doing, that the only sense that can be found in their actions lies in the act itself, the pseudoadventure of taking on the system." Speaking specifically of West Germany's fragile, received democracy, he viewed his country as using the threat of terrorism as a pretext for becoming just a little more totalitarian with each passing day by placing more and more restrictions on freedom. "What a godsend this terrorism must be to the state in its present stage of development," he declared. "If these terrorists did not exist, the state would have to invent them. Perhaps it even has?"

Bearing this politically scalding statement, the film was released in May 1979 and immediately provoked violent controversy. In Hamburg, a movie projectionist was beaten unconscious and copies of the film were destroyed. A movie theater in Frankfurt was attacked by youths hurling acid. In Hamburg, the assault had come from the neo-Nazis and in Frankfurt from the "third generation" itself. The extreme right accused Rainer of glorifying the extreme left and the self-proclaimed heirs of Baader-Meinhof saw the "glory" betrayed. Rainer took an exotic vacation.

25

JULIANE was leading the sweet life in which everything that happens, happens for the first time, and now, for the first time, she was sitting alone with Rainer in an outdoor café on the Kurfürstendamm. The Kurfürstendamm, or the Ku-damm to initiates, is the closest thing in Europe to the Sunset Strip in Los Angeles. It was a beautiful day at the beginning of June, rare everywhere, rarest of all in Berlin.

They had gone to inspect the sets for *Berlin Alexanderplatz,* the shooting of which was set to start at last on June 18. All systems were go. Even gutted Rainer's. He had been stung by his failure to win the Golden Bear for *The Marriage of Maria Braun* at the Berlin Film Festival in March, and that had smarted for a while, but he was in high spirits today.

He had just celebrated his thirty-fourth birthday. He had taken on the dowdy-snowman look he would have until the end. Gone forever was the trim, drug-free body of Fox in *Fox and His Friends.* Since making *Maria Braun* a year earlier, when he was already pudgy, he had put on about twenty pounds, and he had begun to pop buttons on the part of his shirt covering the paunch that hung over his belt. He had also stopped shaving, and a sparse beard had grown out as much as it ever would. The leather jacket and boots, the pummeled fedora, the dark glasses, the shawl, the key ring hanging from his jeans, and the lit cigarette between his chubby fingers had become the fixtures of a German film institution known nationwide as RWF.

Although the more he ate, the fatter he got, and the more he corrupted his lungs, heart, and bloodstream, the more he rotted on the inside, he had convinced everyone around him that his body was not accountable to the laws of nature. Whether he believed that himself is in doubt; Rainer, the son of an ill-reputed doctor, had an aversion that was nothing less than phobic to physicians in general and anything that smacked of preventive or therapeutic medicine. In any case, on that June day on the Ku-damm with twenty-two-year-old Juliane, he was of a mind to rejuvenate.

Juliane remembers it this way:

The café was right in front of the production office for *Alexanderplatz,* and we were sitting together drinking beer, eating ice cream, and laughing, about what I don't recall, when the production manager saw us and came up to Rainer. He had a big smile on his face and he said, "Well, Mr. Fassbinder, what are you going to do for the next two weeks until the film starts?" Rainer looked around and then his eyes fell on me, and he answered, "I'm going on holiday with Juliane." This seemed natural enough to the production manager, but since I never dreamed such a thing was even remotely possible, I thought Rainer was simply putting him on. But after he'd gone, Rainer turned to me and said, "Where do you want to go? Athens? Rome? Oslo? Or Tangiers?" My jaw dropped. I'd never been to any of those places, and not a word came out of my mouth. "Yes," he said, "let's go to Tangiers." I was terrified. In my mind, Tangiers was someplace completely exotic and frightening. My only comfort was that I was still pretty sure he was kidding. Now that I look back at it, I realize that he never said anything he didn't mean, and I wonder why I never saw that and was always so skeptical. Strange, isn't it? I also understand that what he really wanted to do was to get away somewhere and stop taking drugs. He wanted to go through the year's shooting of *Alexanderplatz* without drugs. It was psychological. A challenge. He was making the film that was closest to his heart, the film he'd been dreaming of all his life.

Anyway, the next thing I knew he was putting a wad of money in my hands, telling me to make all the arrangements and buy us both some clothes. "I want to fly tomorrow afternoon at one o'clock," he said. I went to a travel agent, and sure enough there was a flight at one. I booked it, but even after I told him I'd done so and he said he'd be ready, I didn't believe I was actually going until an hour before departure when I went to fetch him at the Niebuhrstrasse apartment, and there he was waiting alone on the sidewalk with a suitcase between his legs. I burst out laughing with joy, and we flew off for ten days. I didn't believe this was happening to me. I thought: Who am I? Why does he want to be with me?

In Tangiers we stayed at a marvelous hotel, the most expensive in Morocco. It was an old monastery in the middle of the Casbah. This was the beginning of our close relationship. We had a magnificent suite with two bedrooms. The first thing he did was tell me that he'd decided not to take any cocaine, and I discovered a man, who, yes, I already knew fairly well, but somebody who had so much tenderness, somebody so lonely, incapable for all his brilliance of looking after his own good. What I remember most is that we were always eating, talking about our lives, strolling through the Casbah hand in hand like two people falling in love.

We went to the beach every day, even though Rainer always hated being in the sun. So we swam a lot. Most of the other people on the beach were men, because in Morocco women aren't allowed on the beach alone. One day, I was wearing this scanty black bikini that Rainer liked very much, and by then I was pretty well tanned, and with my hair blonder than ever from the sun, I suppose I didn't look too bad. At least the men on the beach seemed to think so. Well, I was in the water alone, and when I'd had enough, I came out and joined Rainer, who was under an umbrella reading. I threw myself onto a deck chair, and somehow my movement made my bra strap snap and my top flipped off, attracting the attention of some of my admirers. My God, you should have seen Rainer. He leaped to retrieve it and tried to get it back on me. "Put it on! Put it on!" he said frantically, and it didn't go on because I couldn't stop giggling. When it was all over, at one point he looked up from his reading and said very quietly, "You have such beautiful breasts." His voice was like a lover's.

That night we had a wonderful candlelit dinner, and at a certain moment he leaned very close to me and said, "Now you're going to stop taking the pill. We're going to make a baby."

I was speechless. I didn't want him to be like that. Maybe I should have said, yes, come on, let's go. That might have been the clever thing to do, and later his mother reproached me for having resisted him, because having a baby might have changed his life. Sure, I was attracted to him sexually, but I wanted our relationship to be something much more than that. I was utopian. My experience with men, which wasn't a lot, had always been that the minute we went to bed, afterward nothing was ever the same again, and I didn't want that to happen with Rainer. Also, I had a sense that he wasn't that interested in me as a woman. The truth was, I later found out, that he was afraid of fucking women. He did it, sure, but he was never satisfied with himself. I know that doing it was just his way of showing that he was a man, but he always thought he failed. Maybe, in my case he thought it would be easier with somebody as young and inexperienced as I was. Anyway, I felt that he liked the idea of me being too shy to say yes. So we had a wonderful time in Tangiers, but we didn't fuck then.

Rainer's resolve to purge himself of some of his worst habits and get through *Alexanderplatz* cleanly was more or less realized. Veterans of the marathon shooting generally remember the experience as one of no-nonsense professionalism. His superdisciplined, high-speed performance was a source of continual amazement to those on the set, and a delight to the producers, since he trimmed the 200-day shooting schedule down to 154, saving them millions of marks. Cameraman Xaver Schwarzenberger, who in *Alexanderplatz* was working with Rainer for the first time, recalls that "Fassbinder took pleasure in going at it like an Olympic athlete going after a gold medal." Schwarzenberger had never met Rainer until shortly before the filming began. The young Austrian cinematographer had of course been chosen because Rainer liked his work but also because he was known to work fast. "I couldn't keep up with him," says Schwarzenberger, echoing words spoken by his predecessor Michael Ballhaus ten years earlier, "but after the first three weeks, he slowed down to my fastest pace, and I realized that the opening burst had been a test that I guess I passed."

Except for provocative treatment of Günther Lamprecht, who

played Rainer's beloved Franz Biberkopf, the mood he created on the set for the sixty-man crew and the cast of ninety-seven plus six thousand extras was like an improbable amalgamation of an ashram and a resort hotel in the Catskills. The first part of the film was shot in Berlin, but most of the group was from Munich, so Rainer, to keep everyone entertained, offered extracurricular activities after each day's work. There was bowling on Mondays, soccer on Tuesdays, movies on Wednesdays, social events on Thursdays, and on Fridays, Rainer, shooting fastest of all, never failed to end the workday early to lengthen the weekend. Many of the weekends were programmed, too, with sightseeing trips to Paris, Amsterdam, and elsewhere. Rainer took part in almost all of the events and was a fierce competitor in bowling and soccer. His favorite was soccer. He formed a team and called it FC Alexanderplatz, the FC meaning Football Club. Naturally, he was the captain. Tarred lungs and flab notwithstanding, he displayed an incredible reserve of energy on the field, and the Alexanderplatz eleven got to play a big-league team, though they were thrashed eleven to one.* Later into the shooting, he even tried to go on a diet, but the complimentary steaming pot of this wurst and that wurst and the unlimited beer ever present on the *Alexanderplatz* set proved to be a temptation as irresistible as cocaine.

Film commentator Daniel Selznick visited the set in Munich in October 1979 and reported his impressions in the *International Herald Tribune*. The article was headlined "Fassbinder: The Brain Won't Stop," and part of it remains of interest as an indicator not only of the atmosphere but also of Rainer's continuing inroads into the English-speaking world:

> *Munich*—On a hushed sound stage at Bavaria Film Studios, a verdant, modern complex on the outskirts of Munich, two actors stand in a perfectly recreated Berlin apartment of the late 1920s. A medium-sized figure in dark glasses, a short leather jacket, with an old shirt hanging outside tattered jeans, flicks

*Rainer's passion for soccer, and particularly for the Bavarian world-class team FC Bayern, was fanatical. Nothing but foreign travel could keep him from watching the weekly game on television, and even when abroad, he would telephone Germany for the results. The soccer-crazy Fassbinder anecdotes are numerous, but none is so bizarre as the one told by Harry, who says that Rainer somehow acquired and collected the sweatshirts of famous players and "guarded them like relics."

open his cigarette lighter to light yet another cigarette and asks the two actors to put more bite into the reading of their lines. They try. . . . Finally, the director is satisfied. "Danke," he says bluntly.

At the age of 33 [sic], Rainer Werner Fassbinder has finally arrived at the moment where he is more than just the bright new hope of the contemporary German cinema. His recent film *The Marriage of Maria Braun* has made more money in Germany than any other film of German origin in 34 years of postwar distribution, something that Fassbinder's earlier films, celebrated by the critics of Paris, New York and Tokyo, never managed to accomplish. *The Bitter Tears of Petra von Kant,* the play he wrote (now playing in Paris) and filmed years ago, is taught to film history students at Harvard University, alongside Eisenstein and Fellini. *Effi Briest, Fear Eats the Soul,* and *Beware of a Holy Whore* already play return engagements at small cinemas in European and American cities that previously shunned any product from West or East Germany. But just at the moment, Fassbinder is nursing a bad cold. "No one is allowed to get ill," he says belligerently, as if he refuses to accept the vulnerability of his own system. "These 200 days are exactly scheduled." . . .

On the set, Fassbinder consults his black leatherbound script. The small, sketched boxes in the margin indicate notes for picture composition, arrows for intended camera movement. [He] decides to film the continuation of the scene before the "second breakfast break," the daily ritual at which a member of the crew traditionally contributes a sausage or something from home (this morning, it's Sachertorte). The atmosphere is that of a repertory company: Most of the actors have worked with Fassbinder before and know what he will demand.

"He is one of us," Hanna Schygulla, star of many Fassbinder films, notably *Maria Braun,* says softly. She means that Fassbinder has been and continues to be an actor. He not only appears frequently in his own films (sometimes in a leading role), he also performs the various roles on the set, repeating the difficult period Berlin dialect and slang with the proper emphasis and timing. Evenings or weekends, the company gets together and plays the director's favorite game, soccer. Two weeks ago, the entire crew took a paid weekend in the Italian-Austrian Alps. . . .

Fassbinder himself feels the most important part of his new film lies in the development of the relationship between Franz and Reinhold. "It is an erotic but not a sexual relationship," he explains with painstaking care. . . .

The issue of sexuality is a sensitive one in Fassbinder's life. Married to Antitheater actress Ingrid Caven in 1970 and since divorced, he has publicly acknowledged having homosexual relationships, while recently confiding to friends that he intends to settle down soon, marry and raise a family. (The key word here is clearly "family.")

The truth is that like Ingmar Bergman, Fassbinder is obsessed with the ways in which man's complex nature—and the conventions of society—keep him from being completely understood by man or woman. The cool tone of his films deliberately betrays a sense of outrage not far below the surface, inviting the audience to share the Muenchener's vision of an intolerant, corrupt and deceitful society.

The notion that Rainer was going "to settle down soon, marry and raise a family" sounds like a refrain from Rainer's mother. Since the ascendency of Juliane, Lilo had come to regard her as someone who might succeed in keeping her son out of trouble, meaning away from the boys and "their" profligate ways. The source of this gossip, however, was undoubtedly Harry, who also was interviewed by Selznick. But Harry, as wary of Juliane as he was of any other potential territorial encroachment, was only being catty, creating good copy for the press. Nobody but Lilo ever dreamed of Rainer's mellowing out and going straight. It was therefore doubly surprising when shortly after the newspaper report Rainer eloped with Juliane.

Like the groom, the sole witness to Rainer's marriage to Juliane in Fort Lauderdale, Florida, on December 31, 1979, is dead. The marriage certificate is destroyed, and Juliane never pretended in Rainer's lifetime to be the second Mrs. Fassbinder, but there is not the slightest reason to doubt the story she tells for the first time now.

In Morocco that June, Rainer had declared that from then on they would be a couple, and back in Berlin she was entrusted with his personal affairs and began at once to handle them in an old-fashioned housewifey way. She had not yet moved into his apartment, but they had already had their first domestic spat (over another woman). Now, at the start of the six-week Christmas and New Year's shooting break for *Alexanderplatz,* they flew to Fort Lauderdale. Rainer had been there before with Armin, and continuing his quest for some sort of rebirth, he wanted to return, he told Juliane, "to exorcise my nightmare." Instead, Fort Lauderdale became Juliane's very own inferno.

They checked into separate bedrooms at the Marlin Beach, "a big gay hotel," to hear Juliane describe it, hardly a honeymoon retreat. She had already heard Rainer, speaking of his first wife, tell an interviewer, "Ingrid Caven is a terrific person but not when you're married to her," and she had taken that as fair warning. "I was afraid the same thing would happen to me," says Juliane. "He had made all those films about bad marriages, and I couldn't understand how he could be so inconsistent. My mother had failed with two husbands; one of them, my father, I'd never even seen. I was afraid of marriage." But not Rainer. Juliane continues:

I was in very bad shape when we got to Florida. I had some kind of skin ailment, sores all over me, and I got so many headaches that Rainer was convinced I had a brain tumor. He wouldn't let me go swimming, because he said that with my skin the way it was, I would end up with pockmarks. That was what had happened to him, he said. We were always quarreling. And then I had to eat with him without stopping. I couldn't stand it. So he decided to send for his latest gay lover, who had a bit part in *Alexanderplatz.* Werner—that was his name—had an enormous appetite. He would eat everything in sight. After he died, we found out that he had had stomach cancer and eating somehow eased his pain, but he never said anything then. I was happy for a while that Werner was coming because our living room was always filled with these horrible American gays, and now he would want to be alone with Werner.

That didn't last very long, and he began harping on us getting married. He gave all the reasons no girl would want to hear, including that he'd be able to pay less in taxes. At one point I shouted out a flat no, but when I saw the look in his eyes, I got scared that I'd gone too far. I picked up the phone book, went into my room, and called a justice of the peace, just as Rainer had been telling me to. The justice of the peace said all we'd need is our passports and a blood test, and when I told this to Rainer, he said, "I'm not taking any blood test, but let's go there anyway."

So the three of us, Rainer, his friend Werner, and I went off, but of course the first thing that went wrong was that the justice of the peace wouldn't marry us without the blood test and he insisted that nobody else would. Rainer got furious. He started shouting at him in perfect English that you don't need a blood test in Las Vegas. Then I saw a roll of bills change hands, and the justice, mumbling something about us having to confirm the marriage when we got back to Germany, quietly performed the ceremony. We all signed the certificate and he gave it to me and we left him happy to be rid of us.

That night, it was New Year's Eve, we got dressed up, Rainer in a black suit, and we all went out to celebrate in a gay place called the Copa Bar. I drank a lot and smoked a lot, and I got very stoned. I drank more than I ever did in my life, about twenty Black Russians—coffee liqueur, whisky, and cream— horrible stuff—and then, at twelve o'clock came the champagne and a terrible, terrible fight with Rainer.

There was this go-go boy, a transvestite, who to start off the new year, I suppose, lifted up his skirt and exposed himself. I made a remark that made Rainer explode. I said, "Oh, look, he has a nice little one." Rainer screamed. 'What? What did you say? Oh, my God, I married somebody who says things like that! Ingrid would never have said that! Now, I'm stuck with this woman on my back!"

I couldn't believe he was reacting that way. How could I have known what a problem he had, and I guess a lot of gays have, about whether it's thick, or long, or whatever? He wouldn't let up on me. I couldn't stop crying. I was so drunk, and I began vomiting violently, all over his black suit. I really believed I was all to blame, that I'd hurt him deeply. He grew calm and began to clean up both of us, trying to soothe me, but only upsetting me more by asking me questions about my invisible father and my stepfather's father, my so-called grandfather, who had molested me sexually when I was five years old. I felt I was in hell. This strange marriage. This strange reaction to a word. This Freudian session in the middle of a pool of vomit.

I wanted to drive my car to the hotel, but he wouldn't let me go behind the wheel. He took me in a taxi. He put me to bed, and about two hours later, it must have been four in the morning, he came into my room. He asked if I was all right, and when I said yes, we went out again, everything forgotten, to finish off New Year's Eve.

The next day, though, he started picking on me again, calling me a whore for having spent a night with an electrician from the *Alexanderplatz* crew. How he found out, I'll never know, but he didn't speak to me for the next two days. All he did was read the newspapers, and look away from my gaze. So, on the second day, I took out the marriage certificate, and ripped it up in front of his eyes. He smirked and went back to his reading.

The strangely married couple moved into a small hotel on their return to Munich. Juliane, when she wasn't in the cutting room, doing everything wrong, according to Rainer, catered to his every whim, though some whims brought out the battle-ax in her. She wasn't *that* easy. The new life continued, but Rainer's past had one overriding account that needed settling in Munich. One day that *Alexanderplatz* winter, he shored up his courage, and with Juliane on his arm, he went to the Deutsche Eiche. Shortly after Armin died, Rainer had received a written death threat from some of the departed's friends, warning him never again to set foot in the Eiche, and he hardly doubted its authenticity. But when he walked in, shaking, says Juliane, no one at first seemed to notice. He took a small table in a corner far from "his" table in the center, and before long he was passed a paper napkin scrawled with a short message. It was from the owner, Sonja Neudorfer. "We still love you," she had written, and Rainer glowed as she came up to him and escorted him to the Fassbinder table of old. You can find Sonja in a bit part in *Alexanderplatz* and in two of the last five films that followed.

At peace with the gay covens of Munich, he sent Juliane shopping for a new apartment while he himself moved into a room at the Eiche. His homosexual life appears to have grown particularly complex now. Apart from his Florida gourmand companion, Werner, he had lately revived his boyhood friendship with Udo Kier (Dodo) and the ambiguous sadomasochistic relationship he'd established with Peter Braetz as a threesome with Armin. He also populated the *Alexanderplatz* cast with such old boys as Daniel's lover Raul Jiminez, Günther Kaufmann, and even Peer Raben, though his connection with Willi had long ago turned strictly professional.

Juliane's apartment-hunting was rendered superfluous by an extremely generous gift from a rich producer, Horst Wendlandt, who was courting Rainer's favor. Wendlandt said that he couldn't bear the thought of the world-famous director all but homeless in his cramped quarters above the Eiche. Rainer saw his point and relocated without further appeal to Wendlandt's penthouse on the fourth floor of a mansion on the Clemensstrasse in the heart of Schwabing. Bright and airy, and tastefully furnished, it had nothing in common with the velvet-lined dungeons of the Reichenbachstrasse except the well-appointed kitchen. For the first few months, Rainer lived with Udo Kier and Peter Braetz, Dodo running the kitchen. But that arrangement ended summarily with the bodily expulsion of both men in quick succession, and Rainer, a hygienic basket case, sent for Juliane.

Juliane, who resisted in Tangiers and Fort Lauderdale, can be trusted when she says she resisted crossing the threshold of the Clemensstrasse apartment.

"If nobody takes care of me," Rainer pleaded, "the rats will come and eat me."

Juliane gave in. "When I came to stay," she says, "he showed me to my bedroom and I was completely surprised to discover that he'd cleaned it up by himself. He treated me like a princess. There were flowers, and the next morning he brought me breakfast in bed. Very soon, it was the other way around."

And there they would stay, with some cataclysmic interruptions, until death would them part.

26

THE worldwide success of *The Marriage of Maria Braun* had partially answered Andrew Sarris's question of a few years back, raised in the title of one of his articles in the *Village Voice:* "Can Fassbinder Break the Box-Office Barrier?" The answer was inconclusive, because although *Maria Braun* was a highly profitable movie internationally—a rarity for a non-American product—it remained dwarfed by Hollywood standards. It did not, for example, make *Variety*'s list of All-Time Film-Rental Champs, which requires a minimum in the U.S. and Canadian markets of four million dollars. The list it did make, however, was the one found in the desk drawer of virtually every Hollywood producer, that of bankable directors. Rainer had already gained a small but loyal and trend-setting audience in America, including influential critics such as Sarris, Canby, David Denby, and Penelope Gilliatt, and now he had proved that he could make people rich, or at least produce bullish returns on investments. Thus, along with acclaim and glad hands in the States,* he now acquired a Hollywood agent, Steve Kenis, of the William Morris office in London.

Kenis plied him with offers from Los Angeles, the imperial capital of the film world, but as most offers in the movie business are contingent on one thing or another, including the vaticinations of producers' wives and the zodiac, it was easy enough for Rainer to play hard-to-get. By now, he had an exquisite sense of himself as being number one in the New German Cinema, though his justifiable self-assessment was temporarily deflated when in March 1980 Volker Schlöndorff's *The Tin Drum* won the Oscar for the best foreign film.

---

*Rainer and Hanna, given a carte blanche expense account, had gone on a promotion tour of America for *Maria Braun,* though he flew back to Europe almost at the outset, irritated that the media paid more attention to his photogenic star than to him.

In any case, as they say in the imperial capital, he was hot, and this was a season of wheeling and dealing in the fast lane.

Horst Wendlandt, of Rialto Films, was not the only producer lavishing kindnesses on Rainer. Wendlandt had him under contract to make two high-budget Hollywood-style productions, *Lili Marleen*, set to start in July 1980, and next, *Cocaine*. Wendlandt and his high-powered partner in these ventures, Luggi Waltleitner of Roxy Films, had joined those who had been convinced of Rainer's marketability by the success of *Maria Braun*. But the man who was still reaping the worldwide profits from that film was more eager than anyone else for Fassbinder product. His name was Hanns Eckelkamp, and he was an energetic producer, not in the same league as Wendlandt and Waltleitner but possessed with a flair for the *coup de scène* and the nerve for taking more than the usual high risks in making motion pictures. He had been a silent partner in earlier Fassbinder films, which had brought him nothing but grief and patchy results. But it had been Eckelkamp's Trio Film that had provided the financial wherewithal to rescue Fengler's bankrupt *Maria Braun* in mid-shooting, and Eckelkamp was the one who ended up with 85 percent of Rainer's most profitable film. At the same time, he, like Fengler, had been declared an incorrigible "gangster" by Rainer, who still clung to his untenable claim of owning 50 percent of the film. Even after Eckelkamp, making a peace gesture, voluntarily lowered his share by ten points, Rainer, who would never see a pfennig of the profits, continued to revile him as a man with whom he would not do business again.

But Eckelkamp was not dismayed. "Fassbinder had a sort of aura," Eckelkamp recalls, "and I wasn't sure enough of myself to confront him man to man. I feared his cynicism and his strong reactions. He was a human porcupine, and I kept getting stuck. But I still wanted to work with him, and I searched for a way."

As luck would have it, Rainer saw no sacrifice of principle in dealing with Eckelkamp through third parties, and Eckelkamp chose his third party with aplomb: Peter Berling. This was an astute decision because no matter what he did "wrong," Berling, being Mutti, occupied an inviolable space in Rainer's heart.

Mutti tells how Eckelkamp's choice was made:

164

I was talking privately to Rainer at the Martinez Beach Club in Cannes of seventy-nine. We were making up, that is, I was being forgiven for my "betrayal" in that nasty business with Fengler about the rights to *Alexanderplatz,* and after a while we got to talking about working together on future projects, big, international films, now that Rainer had really made it in America. He had another appointment, and everything was left up in the air for the moment, but the minute he was gone, Eckelkamp stepped out from behind one of the posts that hold up the pergola. He'd been only a few feet away and had overheard everything. He told me that I should accept any proposal whatsoever from Fassbinder and that I could count on his one-hundred-percent backing.

Eckelkamp had the hope that Rainer's animosity toward him would diminish in time, and he agreed when Berling insisted that they would get nowhere, at least for the time being, if they even breathed Eckelkamp's name. Their strategy worked, in a convoluted way. Berling even succeeded in bringing Rainer and Eckelkamp face to face for the very first time, though Rainer used the occasion to turn down Eckelkamp's pet project, a remake of George Orwell's *1984.*

Rainer, while remaining noncommittal, had allowed Berling and Eckelkamp to open negotiations with Orwell's widow to purchase the film rights to the novel. After her approval of the director, her only remaining stipulation was that he follow the original story as precisely as filmically possible. Rainer, though he had made himself incommunicado when he was supposed to have met with Mrs. Orwell, didn't pronounce his views on the project until his encounter with Eckelkamp. Nevertheless, a Fassbinder film, with a tortuous story, did come out of that meeting, and Mutti, ruing it to this day, remembers how it all began:

The meeting took place in Kay's, a plush gay restaurant in the Reichenbachstrasse. I showed up with Eckelkamp, whose uneasiness at coming to grips with Rainer was doubled by the thought of having to eat "homosexual" cuisine. Rainer, late of course, came with Juliane, Harry, and his latest scriptwriters,

Peter Märthesheimer and Pea Frölich, the couple who had written *Maria Braun.* Rainer declared himself almost at once. It was one of the most eloquent nos I'd ever heard, and I still find it enlightening.

"Technology," he said, "has so advanced since Orwell's times that the television surveillance he describes has been made ridiculous today. Now, we hunt our terrorists by grid-search done by computers. This is something invisible and not filmable. Furthermore, I detest the idea in the novel that the love between two persons can lead to salvation. All my life I have fought against this oppressive type of relationship. Instead, I believe in searching for a kind of love that somehow involves all of mankind, and my way of looking at *1984,* I'm quite sure, will not be acceptable to widow Orwell."

For a long while everybody was silent. I suppose it was because what could any of us say to an argument like that one, especially when pronounced so decisively by the man we had hoped would be the director. Finally the tension broke and he began to talk directly to Eckelkamp.

This is how Eckelkamp tells it:

He treated me very kindly. We spoke for nearly an hour, about what we could do together. We discussed three projects. One of them was *Bent,* the Broadway play about a homosexual relationship in a concentration camp. The second was *Future 2,* a novel about a utopian society. And the third was the idea of remaking *The Blue Angel.* Finally, I said, "Which would you like to do?" And he said, "We'll do all three. The question is which one first?"

Eckelkamp didn't hesitate: *The Blue Angel,* that haunting tale of Lola-Lola and beguiled Professor Unrath. The great director Josef von Sternberg had introduced Marlene Dietrich to everlasting glory in *The Blue Angel,* and now, Eckelkamp imagined, Rainer would do likewise for Hanna. So, with Rainer blessing Eckelkamp's fantasy, *Blue Angel* it was. Or rather wasn't.

In the first place, Hanna, shortly after that meeting, committed the

166

"sin" of no return. In all innocence, she, as the lead in *Maria Braun,* had outstarred Rainer in America, and this had pinched his vanity. Then, with good sense, she had agreed to play the title role in *Lili Marleen* only if Rainer would direct her, and this had pinched, too, because the producers had gone first to her and not to him. Finally, with neither innocence nor good sense, she had given a most premature interview to *Variety,* the pinching part of which read: "Hanna Schygulla will topline in Rainer Werner Fassbinder's upcoming remake of the 1930 classic *The Blue Angel.* Actress . . . will limn Lola-Lola role which catapulted Marlene Dietrich to international stardom and a Hollywood career."

"If this dumb broad thinks she can decide who plays the lead in my movies," Rainer was heard to exclaim on reading the trade-paper item, "I'll show her she's wrong!"

He showed her; he directed her lamely or hardly at all in *Lili Marleen,* and she was never again asked to play in a Fassbinder film.

Dashed then were Eckelkamp's hopes of parlaying the small fortune he'd spent on promoting Hanna in America, and dashed, too, was the dream of reviving the marketable nostalgia of the first *Blue Angel.* We have Rainer's words on that score:

> I thought it was an exciting idea. But my scriptwriters . . . didn't find the story particularly interesting. In the meantime I'd also come to the point where I said to myself that the period in which the novel plays (before the First World War) didn't interest me especially. I happen to be interested in the fifties. Especially because I had decided to do a complete history of West Germany after the war, from my point of view. So, we began to think about how the story would fit into the fifties.
>
> We soon noticed that if it played in the fifties it no longer worked. [In the end] we had a completely new story which had nothing to do with the novel or Josef von Sternberg's film version of it. It was an entirely new story of our own.

Trampling on Eckelkamp's fondest aspirations was what it was all about. Mutti knows it well:

Rainer said "Yes, Mr. Eckelkamp" to everything, but the minute Eckelkamp was out of earshot the broken record of how he'd been screwed on *Maria Braun* was played full volume. Of the three projects we'd talked about that evening, *The Blue Angel* became *Lola,* which was the only word left from the original; *Future 2* was simply forgotten; but as for *Bent,* we took it as a good sign when Rainer, as soon as he wrapped up *Alexanderplatz,* flew to Los Angeles to meet with Richard Gere, the actor. Rainer had seen him in the Martin Sherman play in New York and Gere owned the rights. We knew they'd gotten friendly. Gere was keen on having Rainer direct him in the film version, and he'd been the one who'd sought Rainer out. We were hoping for a German-American coproduction, but word soon got back to us that Rainer would only speak to him about playing the male lead in *Lili Marleen,* taking a wait-and-see stance for the future. Gere wasn't interested in the part, or at least not as enthusiastic as Rainer expected him to be, so that was the end of *Bent.*

We'd also heard that Wendlandt had paid for the Concorde flight for Rainer and his friends and that he'd put the villa he owned in Beverly Hills at Rainer's complete disposal. Eckelkamp trembled. He induced me to go to L.A. at once with a bunch of money to compete as best as I could with his more powerful rival's pursuit of Rainer's good graces. It was a losing game. When I got there I found Rainer, Dodo, and Peter Braetz living like Arab emirs, with Rainer boasting that Wendlandt had ordered in a dynamite crew to blast into the rocky slope behind the house; he was going to build a swimming pool just for Rainer. "All I did, Mutti, was ask, 'Where's the pool?' " Rainer said with a foxy smile.

We began to do as they do in Hollywood and "take meetings." The meeting point was the Eagle, a gay bar off Fairfax, the likes of which I'd never seen before. It seemed everyone wore leather trousers with flaps that opened front and back, and some of them were open. The door to the john was perforated as though it had been riddled by a submachine gun. The whole scene made me uneasy, which so delighted Rainer that he made it the only place he would see me. Against Wendlandt's no-contest largess, all I could do was pick up the tabs at the Eagle.

But Rainer was not someone who would sell *all* of himself to the highest bidder. He confided in me that Wendlandt was trying to sabotage Eckelkamp's *Lola* because he didn't want another Fassbinder film sandwiched between *Lili Marleen* and *Cocaine,* Wendlandt's and Waltleitner's biggest scheduled productions for eighty and eighty-one. It was a question of oversaturating the market.*

Lola had been projected as a high-budget film, too, and I had been in Los Angeles a month earlier negotiating with Ryan O'Neal, who was hot at the time, to star.

"If we make it a small, European film," Rainer said now, "I'll talk Wendlandt into backing off."

I knew Eckelkamp would settle for anything, so I flew back to Munich and drew up the agreements. On April twenty-ninth, while I sat in the Deutsche Eiche eating Debresciner sausages with sweet Bavarian mustard, Rainer signed and initialed the one hundred and fifty pages of the various contracts in his one-room flat above me. He wasn't "in the mood" to see me. I didn't mind; when Harry brought down the signed papers, I knew Eckelkamp finally had Rainer committed to an October twenty-seventh start date for *Lola,* and I had a huge piece of the action. How after all these years could I have been so naïve?

We went to Cannes ten days later, hoping to presell the distribution rights on the world market. Eckelkamp hired a PR firm. They came up with a striking logo: plump red lips on a pink background. Everywhere you went along the Croisette you saw the posters: the *Lola* logo and a line of type reading, "A New Film by Rainer Werner Fassbinder." *Variety* and all the other trade papers that come out with special editions at Cannes carried full-page ads. The *Lola* display in the lobby of the Carlton, which is the real hub of the commercial side of Cannes, flashed pink lights like a disco. Some people said it was beautiful; at least it was high kitsch. Within a couple of days, Eckelkamp, wearing a fixed grin, was being flooded with offers. It was

*Wendlandt offered Rainer a five-year contract at an annual salary of 360,000 marks on the condition that he make only one film per year. Rainer wasn't interested. "What would I do for the rest of the year?" was his answer.

Eckelkamp's finest hour. That was when Rainer pulled the plug.

He gave an interview to the most widely distributed daily bulletin at the festival, *Le Film Français,* which was running a front-page column in English that year featuring a breakfast chat with somebody big in the news.* "He is irritated with the pink ads for *Lola*," part of it read, going on to quote him directly: " 'Stinky pink. It is not my next film and I would never do a film so pink, I hope. If I do *Lola* at all, it will be after *Lili Marleen* and *Cocaine*.' "

"Do something!" Eckelkamp cried to me when word spread instantly along the Croisette that he was selling pie in the sky.

That evening I found Rainer in his usual spot on the Carlton terrace, a Côte d'Azur–style café looking out on the sea. It was the cocktail hour and as always [the terrace was] packed with everyone in the business. He was sitting with Dodo (his head shaved bald) and Peter Braetz. The first thing he said when I mentioned the interview was "Forget about *Lola.* I don't feel like making this movie."

I said, speaking softly so as not to be overheard, "Rainer, you can't do this. You signed the contracts, one hundred and fifty pages. You took money. You cashed the checks."

He raised the pitch of his voice to the whine that was as much his alone as his fingerprints. "Did you hear that?" he said to Dodo and Braetz. "This is Mutti Berling, the gangster! Now you see him in action! I never signed anything!"

Everyone around us looked up and stared our way in a dead silence. I turned white. You could suddenly hear the tiny waves of a calm Mediterranean washing the shore. I whispered, "But, Rainer, we have the papers, the canceled checks."

He shouted, "I can't believe this! You forged my signature!" He turned to the others. "You see what I mean? He forged my bloody signature!"

I looked at Dodo and Braetz. Their gaze shifted the other way. It was deadly embarrassing, and the only thing I could think of at that moment was to disappear fast. I got up and

---

*It began with what the interviewee had consumed for breakfast, and in Rainer's case it appeared as follows: "Breakfast with Rainer Werner Fassbinder. Menu: Shrimp, Asparagus, Bloody Mary, and one pack of Camels (filter-tipped) at 4 p.m."

walked away. I could feel every eye on the terrace watching the Iniquitous Forger slink away.

I went straight to Eckelkamp and told him that the situation was hopeless. His only chance of recovering his investment, I said, was to sell out to his archenemy Wendlandt, who I suspected was somehow using Rainer's implacable hatred of Eckelkamp to gain control of *Lola* and hence the timing of its release.

We all went back to Munich, and a day or so later, I received an unexpected invitation. It was a message from the Clemensstrasse, where Rainer had just moved into Wendlandt's penthouse. Would I come to dinner? I didn't want to go, fearing more fireworks, but Eckelkamp pleaded with me to accept, seeing it as a last chance.

I arrived to the smoky, appetite-whetting aromas of Bavarian cooking. Dodo, shaved head and apron, was in the kitchen making Krautwickel, Rainer's favorite meatballs; mine, too. Braetz was opening the champagne. Rainer appeared in a silk robe. He immediately switched on the replay of how Fengler and Eckelkamp had "robbed" him of all the money being made by *Maria Braun*. When, quite gingerly, I brought up *Lola* and his contractual obligations, there was not a word this time about forgery, but he said, "If Eckelkamp forces me to make this movie, Mutti, it will be the most expensive and the worst movie I've ever made!"

I couldn't help myself. I said, "You can't do that, Rainer Werner. You've already made *Despair.*"

His mouth opened. He leaped to his feet. He shrieked. "At last I know what kind of friend you are and what you think of my films. Please leave my house at once!" He turned and stormed out of the room, slamming three or four doors behind him.

Peter Braetz and Dodo, running out of the kitchen, were dumbfounded. "But I've worked all day cooking dinner," Dodo said. He may have been cutting onions, but there were tears in his eyes. Braetz tried to get Rainer back on the scene, but he'd locked himself in his bedroom and wouldn't respond. I excused myself and left. On the street, for the first time in a long time I felt free, but I sure was hungry.

Eckelkamp surrendered to Wendlandt, though he managed to keep a minority interest. As part of the terms of surrender, Berling was fired as executive producer (as he had been from *Alexanderplatz*), holding on, however, to a 12 percent share of the profits. Coming after *Lili Marleen, Lola,* the fortieth film in Rainer's life's work, was made, adding to everyone's misfortune. It was a commercial flop, returning little to the producers and nothing at all to Berling. Wendlandt, cutting his losses, shelved *Cocaine.* Rainer and Berling became friends all over again before very long, and Eckelkamp, the imperturbable whipping boy, began looking for new, more imaginative ways to back whatever Rainer cared to do.

27

BY the time he had completed *Berlin Alexander-platz,* Rainer said later, he had lost an "obsessive fear" that had accompanied him throughout his career thus far. "Every time I went on the set," he said, speaking of all his films until *Alexanderplatz,* "I was terrified of failing completely." He went on:

A week before the shooting [of *Alexanderplatz*] started, I wanted to commit suicide. I'm not kidding. I really thought about it seriously. I felt that I wouldn't make it. . . . But when the film ended, I was able to say to myself that now I could face anything. Yes, I'd needed all that time before I could honestly say, "Now I know my job, now I feel secure."

He also felt the need to return to drugs. Toward the end of the nine-month shooting his on-the-set intake of bourbon, which he drank out of a beer mug, rose steadily. Less visible was his use of cocaine. His assistant director, Renate Leiffer, "knew" he was back on drugs when he began getting restless and impatient with the actors. Schwarzenberger, the cameraman, was aware of such suspicions, but he did not observe any change in Rainer's behavior. "He was one of those people," says Schwarzenberger, "who convinced you that he had it under control, that nothing could happen to him because he knew when to stop."

Nevertheless, drugs there were, plenty of them, and now he would find no way back. With *Alexanderplatz,* he had made the film of his dreams. Indeed the final episode of the series, a so-called epilogue, is a filmic dream, which he entitled "My Dream of Franz Biberkopf's Dream." It is a phantasmagoria; in one of the more self-indulgent scenes Franz is crucified on an atomic mushroom cloud and as he

173

ascends, presumably to be tucked away in paradise, Janis Joplin on the soundtrack sings, "Freedom is just another word for nothing left to lose." This may be taken as Rainer's rendition of his own liberation. He had opened a gate to maturity, but what was there left to dream now?

Berlin Alexanderplatz, all fifteen and a half hours of it fresh from the laboratory, was first shown over a period of ten days at the 1980 Venice Festival. It was greeted by the motion-picture critics with eulogies, but when it was telecast in Germany over fourteen weeks that fall and winter, the TV critics rated it very low. It also precipitated a hostile reaction from the other mass media, aimed more at Rainer than at his film. The main complaint of the television reviewers was justifiable. Several long sequences shot in dimly lit interiors, while perfectly defined on a motion-picture screen, were little more than smudges when reduced to a TV tube. The press attacks, however, inspired by the right-wing Springer publishing chain, were politically motivated. Rainer had been one of the signers of a public statement denouncing the control of the media exercised by Springer's holdings. Playing on the public nuisance of the "unviewable" TV transmissions of *Alexanderplatz,* the Springer group now assailed Rainer's interpretation of the popular novel and his "misuse" of substantial government subsidies in making the film.

In character, Rainer simply went ahead and shot his next film, *Lili Marleen,* which was another unhappy experience. He had been enticed by a script not of his own creation, nor even to his liking, solely by the eleven-million-mark budget (then the highest ever in Germany) and the idea of making a Hollywood-like movie. The picture was commercially successful but a critical failure, and it brought him only regrets. *Lola* produced the opposite effect, but by now it had become clear that the Fassbinder films of the eighties had broken with those of the decade before. Rightly convinced of his artistic prowess, he had turned away from the autobiographical clay he had been molding and remolding until then. Unrevisited, though never forgotten, was the place in his heart where he wept the bitter tears of Petra von Kant for the recurring miscarriage of love. His projected "complete history" of modern Germany was meant to be an indictment of the culture itself. Thus *Lili Marleen* portrays the German people as perceiving Hitler as "something wonderful," to use Rainer's words, and *Lola,* set in Germany vanquished, shows them already recorrupted by the time of the economic boom of the fifties. Such were the themes on the last agenda, and the driving force behind them was the ravenous hunger for ever greater fame.

A timely reading of this desire was made by another German producer. Rainer had never ceased being an actor. In addition to his stage roles, he had appeared in twenty-seven films by now, though with few exceptions in minor parts. More than half of these were in his own productions, where, like Hitchcock, he made his face familiar, turning up somewhere along the way. His latest part was that of the barely seen leader of the anti-Nazi resistance in *Lili Marleen,* in which he acted out a minor fantasy as the only good guy in Germany.

Shortly after *Lili* came out, he received an offer to star in a film being planned by Regina Ziegler for her husband, director Wolf Gremm. Gremm, who had been among those admitted to the fledgling Berlin film school the same year that Rainer was rejected, had gone on to earn an unwarranted reputation. He held the record for winning more frequently than anyone else the German film critics' Sour Lemon, presented to but never accepted by the director of "the worst film of the year."

"I don't need a good director" was what Rainer told Juliane while contemplating Ziegler's proposal. "I will direct myself. And besides, who says a bad director can't make one good film."

The role he was being asked to play would have been hard for almost any actor to refuse. The movie was to be based on the novel *Murder on the Thirty-first Floor* by the late Per Wahloo, a Swedish detective-story writer with a sizable following in many countries, including the United States. Wahloo's detective is a lonely, brooding, emotionally drained figure named Jansen, who appears on every page of the novel, which meant that he would be in every scene of the movie. He never fails, of course, to get his man, but the third dimension of his character inevitably draws him into clashing with and unmasking the most insidious forces in the bourgeois Establishment. Hammett said it all first, but Wahloo was a man of the sixties, and the sixties, at least to some men and women of the sixties, seemed smarter.

Rainer, convinced that the film, directed by anyone, was bound to be a hit, accepted the part, but when Gremm's script arrived in the mail, he backed out in utter disappointment.

Undaunted, Regina Ziegler, a big woman who would have no trouble filling a sofa in a Goya painting but was about as hard to daunt as Mildred Pierce, knew exactly where to turn for assistance. Hanns Eckelkamp, as willing as ever to bet on any dice Rainer cared to roll, had already been encouraging Regina, and now he came up with the idea of hiring an American screenwriter to rewrite Gremm's script. Eckelkamp was hoping to broaden the film's appeal and tap the English-language market. Unfortunately, the writer, myself, reacted to the script the same way as Rainer had and thought little better of the filmic possibilities of the novel. It seemed hopelessly trapped in the sixties, which in the eighties no longer looked all that smart.

Attracted nonetheless by the chance to work with Fassbinder, as well as by Eckelkamp's appreciation of the difference in pay scale between Germany and America, I gambled on suggesting that the plot be projected into the near future, a gimmick voguish in Hollywood at the time. It worked.

Rainer, for insurance, packed the production with his regulars, both actors and crew. Juliane, picking up on his view of Lieutenant Jansen as an apocalyptic presence, conjured up the rather questionable title *Kamikaze* to substitute for Wahloo's original, and Gremm added an " '89" to connote the future. *Kamikaze '89* was shot mostly in Berlin in August and September of 1981, and while Rainer didn't quite direct himself, Gremm rarely restrained him from doing whatever he pleased.

Gremm later explained how the relationship worked:

> When I plan a film, I often think in terms of animal images for the characters. In conceiving *Kamikaze '89,* I always had Fassbinder in mind as a leopard, but I never told him this. At the first costume fitting I showed him fifteen possible futuristic detective and police costumes of very different styles. It happened like this: He came in. I was smoking a cigar. I offered him a Camel cigarette. He looked over the costumes. I smiled. Then

176

he looked at me and smiled too. He said, "You like this leopard one." And I said, "Don't you?" And he said, "Let me try it on." He looked at himself in the mirror and said, "I love me. Now I'm Lieutenant Jansen." From this point on, we never had to discuss the style of the film.

How did it all turn out? Rainer, according to both Gremm and Juliane, loved it, especially seeing himself in every scene. I was asked to start thinking about *Kamikaze-2* and *-3*. Eckelkamp did gain access to the American market, though far from cracking it, he barely scratched it. When the film opened at the Waverly Theater in New York, however, he had Vincent Canby on his side. Canby wrote in the *Times:*

> [Fassbinder] is the main reason to see Wolf Gremm's *Kamikaze '89*, in which he stars as Jansen, a taciturn, tough but humane police lieutenant in a futuristic Germany. The time is 1989, when Germany has become the richest of nations and all economic, social and political problems have been solved. To emphasize his own nonconformist tendencies, Jansen, from start to finish, wears a memorably awful simulated leopard-skin suit and a bright red shirt.
>
> You don't know your science-fiction very well if you don't immediately suspect that life is not great in this chilly paradise, a place that has prohibited the use of alcohol but is so boring that it drives its citizens to drink. . . .
>
> *Kamikaze '89* will be of far more interest to people fascinated by Fassbinder's extraordinary career than to casual filmgoers. It suggests a curious but not surprising blend of influences, including Fassbinder's films, Jean-Luc Godard's *Alphaville*, Fritz Lang's *Dr. Mabuse* and Louis Feuillade's virtually endless silent serial *Les Vampires*.
>
> Though puffily overweight, his eyes mere slits in folds of skin, Fassbinder remains an impressive, witty screen presence as he plays out this satiric charade. . . .
>
> The focal point of the film is Fassbinder's easy, neo-Wellesian control of every scene in which he appears—a control that has as much to do with wisdom as with weight. . . .
>
> It is weirdly handsome, having been beautifully photo-

graphed by Xaver Schwarzenberg . . . and it is punctuated by
good supporting performances. . . .

Kamikaze '89 is a footnote to film history.

That year Gremm failed to win the Sour Lemon, though the
German critics and the box office were hardly as appreciative as
Canby. Rainer, showing that his delight was constant, kept the
phony leopard-skin suit and wore it from time to time during the few
remaining months of his life.

28

ON October 20, 1981, Rainer's photo and his name
in headlines were on the front pages of all the
many tabloids in Germany. The previous day he had given testimony
as a witness subpoenaed by the prosecution in a sensational trial
involving people in entertainment and the traffic in cocaine. When
summoned to appear, Rainer quipped, "Cocaine? What's that?" and
on the witness stand the exchange between him and the judge went
like this:

> **RAINER:** I cannot understand what I have to do with this whole
> story.
> **JUDGE:** Really? Well, we have a check signed by you for twelve
> hundred marks, which was used to purchase cocaine.
> **RAINER:** Not by me. I gave that check to an actor, Mr. X. It
> must have been for his salary.
> **JUDGE:** Is it really true, as most of the accused have testified,
> that artists and actors take cocaine to increase their
> energy for their work?
> **RAINER:** I wouldn't know. I have enough energy without using
> cocaine.

Rainer, twiddling his thumbs on his belly, was imperturbable.
Among those in serious trouble, however, was the mysterious Mr. X,
accused of purchasing a substantial quantity of the drug with
Rainer's check. Mr. X was Harry, whose name can be revealed
because in the end he was identified and let off with a slap on the
wrist. Just how Harry, caught red-handed, managed to escape
sterner punishment has also been revealed, though it's one person's
word against another's and must be told without naming names.

The night before the verdict was handed down, a person of great influence, let us call him Mr. Y, found himself in an unusual situation. He had been among those who had wondered if show people took cocaine for professional reasons, and now, fate being fate, he was lying thigh to thigh in the same bed with one such person, Ms. Z. Invited to exhaust his curiosity, Mr. Y did so to his pleasure, and upon taking leave, he was beseeched by Ms. Z, an actress in several Fassbinder films (apparently unseen by Mr. Y), to use his good offices to obtain clemency for Mr. X. That would be the only way, she said, to avoid disclosure in the tabloids of a detailed report of their nocturnal encounter. The influential Mr. Y saw the wisdom in her appeal, and the following morning, Harry was somehow dismissed with a suspended sentence and a fine. Rainer paid the fine.

Cocaine, the film, had been definitively abandoned by now, but with Rainer and drugs so conspicuously in the public eye, producer Eckelkamp once again emerged from the shadows, brandishing a new drug-film proposal. With indomitable enterprise, he pulled a forgotten true story out of his hat, that of Sybille Schmitz, a film star under Hitler who died in obscurity in 1953 of her addiction to morphine. The subject matter sat well with Rainer's wish to interpret German history, as it turned out, through the vicissitudes of unusual women. He saw how he could insert his version of the episode chronologically between *Maria Braun* and *Lola.* Thus, Eckelkamp, money first, was allowed once again to return, albeit only through a contractual back door. Rainer renamed the fallen actress Veronika Voss, and that became the title of his penultimate film.

Had he died in his bed during the night after the premiere of *Veronika Voss,* instead of 112 nights later, he would have died in ecstasy, and the memories of him, at least those recorded on his death, surely would have been sweeter. The first showing of the film took place at the Berlin Film Festival on the evening of February 18, 1982, and afterward he was awarded the top prize, the Golden Bear, which he had coveted unrequitedly all the previous years of his career. It may have been the purest moment of happiness in his life, though a moment was all that it was. Juliane had *made* him a tuxedo to be worn if he were to win, but he had refused to be fitted, saying little-boy things like "I won't get it" and "I'll believe it when I see it." But she flew to Berlin a few days before the awards, and, why not, he let her pin and sew. That night he wore it, white tie and all, his beard clipped short and straggly with what must have been a dull scissors. When his name was called, he went up onto the stage, took the Golden Bear in his cigarette hand, and made a short, self-effacing speech just like a regular guy. Later, his hair matted with sweat, he stood for a hundred pictures, embracing this or that important person. Sheer joy beams back at you from those photos, and when, after the party, he came home the next day to Juliane in Munich, he had the prize in his fist and he looked like a little boy.

Veronika Voss, a tight little black-and-white movie with a bite that's hard to forget, would have been, if you had to die young, the film to exit on. Maria Braun tells you how she crawled out and stood up from the pandemic rot Hitler bequeathed to his nation; Lola speaks of the new rot eating away at whatever is new, but the plaintive tale of Veronika Voss says those things and more.

The melodramatic plot has B-picture simplicity. Veronika was a glamorous film star in Nazi Germany, but now it's the early fifties and she can't get a job. Her marriage has been destroyed by alcohol, followed by addiction to drugs. She has fallen into the clutches of a female physician, the personable but evil Dr. Katz, with whom she rooms as a patient, secretly but totally dependent upon her for her daily requirement of morphine. Into Katz's snakepit stumbles Robert, a well-meaning reporter who normally covers sports.

Meeting Veronika by chance, he is haunted by her lingering beauty and by the apparent mystery of her relationship with Katz. Probing, Robert discovers what lies behind the façade of Katz's medical practice. The ghoulish doctor is preying on lonely people suffering from depression and able to afford her costly therapy. Addicting them to drugs, she slowly takes possession of their will, and later, either before or after inducing death by "natural causes," she drains them of their wealth. Katz, Robert learns, is being supplied with drugs (at the time they were less accessible than today) by her partner in crime, an official of the city health department.

Foreshadowing the ineluctable ending is a subplot about another patient, a retired antiques dealer named Treibel. When Dr. Katz cuts off his drug supply, the antiquary and his aging wife die in a double suicide pact. In the meantime, the good reporter and his faithful companion, Henriette (unwavering in spite of her fear that Robert is falling in love with Veronika), set a trap to expose the cunningly fiendish pair and rescue Veronika from mortal danger. Their amateurish plan fails. Henriette is murdered, and though Robert cannot prove the doctor's guilt, Katz knows the heat is on. In characteristically diabolical fashion she abandons Veronika as a troublemaker. Withdrawn from her doctor's "care," Veronika is found dead a few days later, having succumbed to an overdose of sleeping pills. Like old man Treibel, she had been unable to go on living without narcotics. Robert knows this after the fact, as well as Katz did in premeditation, but he is impotent to pursue justice, and so he goes back to reporting the sports news.

How such a mediocre framework, rattling with plot holes, was dressed with such rich layers of meaning and transcendental beauty ought to be a film-school lesson in the merely relative significance of the story line, demonstrating why some directors direct rings around others. Part of the answer is the shining performance Rainer nursed from Rosel Zech in the title role. An actress untried until then by Rainer, she gave lift to a Fassbinder film that stands on the shoulders of most of the others.* Zech's Veronika is compelling not as an innocent victim of miscreants and social corruption but because she subsists on memories of past grandeur, and what she takes for grandeur is nothing but Nazi Germany. A democratic state has replaced the most repugnant totalitarian system ever known, but to some people living beyond the pale of justice it is uninhabitable. The tragedy of loneliness is made whole by the parallel story of the old couple. They are Jews, survivors of Treblinka. Under Hitler, Veronika flourished while the Treibels were wounded body and soul in a concentration camp, but the new Germany reserves the same fate for them all. In Robert we have the good intentions that pave the road to hell.

*Zech immediately added her name to the long list of actors who claim to have experienced mystical inspiration from Rainer's direction. "He was giving something away all the time," she told Hayman, "and that's very rare. You simply felt loved and cherished. He protected me." She performed with such selflessness that in the suicide scene, Harry remembers, she actually took thirty pills. They were made of sugar to be sure, but the excessive dose was sickening all the same.

Rainer knew that ambience well. At the Berlin festival that year, he was asked, in one of those courtly interviews that accompany film press kits, if he had a weakness for downtrodden characters. He replied, "I feel a lot of tenderness for them. I understand them and I understand where they went wrong. Maybe all that relates to me in some way. Sure, you say to yourself, 'Okay, but it can't happen to me, not that way.' But it can. I know people who can't wait for the day when I fall."

29

ARLY in 1982, German health authorities banned the sale of a pharmaceutical trade named Mandrax. Mandrax formed an integral part of Rainer's drug-consumption regimen. Without it, he could rarely fall asleep. In the best of circumstances, before retiring he would take two or three Valiums and one or two Mandrax tablets. When, as often, sleep wouldn't come, he would repeat the dose a half hour or so later, and repeat it again and again if need be until, as always, it worked.

The difference between the two drugs is that Valium, being a minor tranquilizer, does not necessarily induce sleep, whereas Mandrax, if enough of it is taken, cannot fail; classified as a hypnotic, it is also addictive. Because they are invariably effective, hypnotics are often taken with stimulants such as cocaine. This cocktail combines the euphoric effect of both drugs; the stimulant neutralizes the drowsiness normally produced by the hypnotic, and when the cocaine wears off, sleep comes on sweetly. Rainer had been taking the mix for years; it was called ups to sleep on.

Juliane, who by now had become the curator of the Clemensstrasse's state-of-the-art medicine cabinet, was never quite sure whether or not the responsibility demanded that she do battle with Rainer the way some mothers scold abusers of the cookie jar. When she tried it, this particular abuser would often throw a tantrum, invoking Nietzschean license to affirm his life in his own way. It was far less abrasive to treat Rainer "like an adult" and say a silent prayer that his essence had somehow been cast in bronze.

Thus, when Mandrax was taken off the market, it seemed a blessing. There would be fewer "cookies" to keep track of, and though, without Mandrax, Valium taken in any quantity failed to put Rainer to sleep, she saw a chance to reduce his dependence on hypnotics.

Rainer said he had to have *something* [Juliane recalls]. I don't want to sound like he was always on drugs, but the truth is that when something wasn't right with him, a headache or any ache whatever, the first thing he wanted was a pill to make him better. So I went to a doctor friend of mine, hoping he could suggest a milder remedy than Rainer had been taking. I explained the problem to the doctor, and he suggested two other kinds of pills, one of them called O-Hypnol, and the other, a stronger drug, named Vesperox. It was even more powerful than Mandrax, but the doctor put a strict limit of a dose no higher than half of one tablet. "If that doesn't make him sleep," the doctor told me, "he'll have to go to a hospital to lower the tolerance he's built up over the years."

First Rainer tried O-Hypnol. That didn't do a thing. Then Vesperox. That put him to sleep immediately and he slept soundly all night long, day after day. But about three weeks later, I woke up in the middle of the night to a noise and I found Rainer wandering aimlessly around the apartment, going from one room to another. He was wide awake mentally, but completely disoriented and physically numb. I discovered he'd been taking three whole Vesperox pills for days, and when I asked him why, he said his body had already gotten used to it.

I was furious and I cried and cried. "Don't worry," he said very calmly. "I know exactly what I'm doing. When I take something at a certain time, Juliane, you don't have to be afraid. I know what goes with what and what's really enough and what isn't." He spoke so confidently. It's hard to understand why, but I believed him. I imagined him like a racing-car driver or a sky diver. All of them know the dangers they face but they race and dive anyway. I didn't even notice, though he later told me that he did, that Vesperox, in the dose he was taking, had begun slurring his words.

Twelve days after taking the Golden Bear, Rainer, back in Berlin, began shooting his last film, *Querelle,* a story, he said at the time, of "a boy whose soul had changed into an alligator." In this, he was echoing Jean Genet, on whose novel *Querelle de Brest* the film is based, but he might as well have been speaking of what in the end he thought he himself had become. Querelle, a sea-going thief, dealer in opium, and murderer, is, the way Genet saw him, an incorrigibly narcissistic monster. He is also ineffably beautiful and desirable, his armored self deriving its majesty in the same monstrous way a princess derives hers, says Genet, "from the imperial train of lace, armorial bearings, battles and crimes."

"Is there something of you in him?" Rainer was asked in a filmed interview a few hours before his death.

"Yes, certainly."

The filming of *Querelle* was not a happy time. The mood is preserved in the film's refrain, sung repeatedly but not repetitiously by Jeanne Moreau:

> Each man kills the thing he loves
> Each man kills the thing he loves
> Some when young
> Some when old
> Some with passion
> Some with gold . . .
> Each man kills the thing he loves

Querelle de Brest had been the second great book of Rainer's life, but he approached and executed its film version with neither the trepidation nor the triumph that had accompanied the making of *Berlin Alexanderplatz*.

In *Querelle,* he made perhaps the most homosexually oriented film ever produced for a more-or-less general audience, with explicit gay sex scenes that would later cause censorship problems and scandal. Because of the subject matter, Genet's novel, written forty years earlier, had been considered unfilmable, or at least unfinanceable. The project had been in the hands of other directors, notably the man Rainer considered his artistic equal, Werner Schroeter, but only when Rainer put his name to it was the money forthcoming. He put his signature on promises to gloss over the more graphic homosexual contacts, such as anal intercourse, but he never once thought of keeping them, and though he earned Schroeter's eternal enmity for having "stolen" the film away from him, he united much of the German gay-film community behind and in front of the camera. But the whole experience, when he didn't find it irritating, left him cold. It bored him from beginning to end, and he raced through it faster than anyone else on the set could follow what he was doing.

Shot entirely on a sound stage in the tangerine light of a simulated sunset, it is the work of an eremite or a melancholy caveman painting his humanity on the underground walls of Lascaux. Rainer's loneliness, that unfillable hollow beneath his alligator hide, was in every sense complete now, even as he was being surrounded by more and more of those he had cast out of his life. Forgotten were the tormented reasons why Isolde had been driven away; she now had a part in *Querelle*. Forgiven for all his misdemeanors was Dieter Schidor, Kitty Babuffke once again, and producer of the film. Cleared of his five-thousand-dollar "debt" was Peter Chatel, who, given Rainer's good wishes and a promise to direct along with him, was putting together a stage production with Ingrid. Rainer's old-pal relationships with Günther and Willi, both at work on *Querelle*, were proving to be enduring. There was no more friction with Hanna, and Irm, mother of little Franz, had been cast with appreciation in minor roles in recent Fassbinder films. The "gangster" Fengler, with whom Rainer was on speaking terms again, had returned, too, as a financial partner in *Querelle*, and even Emma, Rainer's "greatest enemy," Kurt Raab, was coming back. The dedication for *Querelle* was written from the start: "To my friendship with El Hedi Ben Salem."

But Rainer no longer believed in friendship. It was better to have declared enemies than devoted friends; "at least you know where you stand," he told Isolde, summarizing a lifetime of observing his fellow man. Libido was percolating away from his pores, leached by the contaminated potion he continually mixed with his blood. And he no longer believed in love.

Yet he tried it one more time, an attempt as pathetic as it was ignoble. On the third day of shooting *Querelle*, he had a violent fight with Juliane. It was probably all pretext, considering his ulterior motive, but he struck her with his leather jacket and one of the zippers drew blood. They had been living in a block of furnished flats in Berlin. He kicked her out and barred her from the set, perhaps to hide his evident guilt. Alone, he began to actively court the affections of a pale New Zealander, Michael McLernon, his express intentions being "marriage." McLernon, renamed Mascha by Rainer, had been working with him as a production assistant since *Lola*. He had brought Rainer together again with Kitty, and that was the great complication. It had been Mascha with whom Kitty had eloped to Africa, abandoning the set of *Satan's Brew* and earning Rainer's crustaceous animosity. Mascha and Kitty—Mike and Dieter to each other—were by now longtime lovers living together in Munich, and Rainer, during the filming of *Querelle*, grew close to both men. But when in April Kitty went off to Los Angeles on business, Rainer proposed his love to Mascha, inviting him to move in permanently to his Clemensstrasse home. The feelings were not quite mutual. Rainer persisted, pleading with an around-the-clock fervor that wore them both down. Kitty returned. Mascha, appearing on the verge of nervous collapse, confessed. Kitty put him on the next flight to Munich. He told him to lock himself in their apartment and answer neither the door nor the phone. Rainer followed. His calls were received by a machine only. The tapes of his voice breaking, begging for "just one beer" to ease his loneliness, were more than Kitty and Mascha could bear. But the tapes fell silent.

The force that remained, the current that kept the pump pumping in a broken heart, came from the mechanical desire to accomplish his "hat trick"—after taking the Golden Bear in Berlin, to win gold at Cannes, to win gold in Venice, to win gold plate in Hollywood and be ugly on the cover of *Time*.

As always, he kept no secrets. During the making of *Querelle*, Schidor produced and directed an 83-minute documentary film of Rainer at work. It is titled *The Wizard of Babylon*. Apart from providing candid-camera views of the wizard backstage, it contains the interview made on the last afternoon of Rainer's life. But what really distinguishes it is the startlingly frank narration, composed by a writer Rainer himself requested, Wolf Wondratschek. Better than anything seen on the screen, it conjures lasting images of what it was to be Rainer Werner Fassbinder at the nadir of his discontent.

Some of Wondratschek, reaching somehow into Rainer's head, has been quoted above in the first chapter. Here is more:

> The wizard of Babylon: excesses of abasement, shit on the walls, monumental erections, chartered planes loaded with nothing but coke, scandals of dismay and derision, jealousy and

anarchy, intimacy swept away like a corrupt, decaying regime. Possessed when sober, possessed when not. Ups to sleep on, betrayal to survive.

Like Querelle—to do evil with the heart of a fighter, to be gentle with ferocity, to be torn by one's feelings, cruel, mean, and proud beyond all taboos.

What you wanted to be, to be praised by those who follow you. You no longer have to make sense to the living. . . .

The garden of your loneliness: the greedy life of New York gay bars where men are as indifferent to one another as they are to ecstasy and murder.

And at times, when your loneliness was darkest, you hoped one of them would pull a knife.

But even the murderers loved your films and they only pulled out their ballpoint pens for an autograph.

You are famous. America reveres your name. Hollywood waits, still the confident seductress. But instead of making films there, you are here, trapped in this voracious life.

You stick your cock in a boy's mouth. But the boy, innocent and indifferent, just stares at you. His hesitation could drive you to murder. The boy proves it to you again: You are famous.

It's no use, not even the sailors of the waterfront flesh markets are hot for you now.

And as the boy kneels there staring at you, he can only think of the autograph he will ask you for later. . . .

You want to go to New York, to live a little, finally, to write a novel—to disappear.

You want to go to the desert, somewhere, to do something— to disappear.

You want to stay here in Germany, shoot another hundred films, and then, before you disappear, leave all Hollywoods behind you.

Now that everyone calls you a genius, it annoys you. Soon even that will be boring. Even life. And the desire to disappear.

Death was on his mind. He had always, in moments of hysteria, depression, or plain old crankiness, threatened suicide. But lately, when alone with Juliane, he'd be taken with an impulse and propose

189

a death pact, and when she would say, "Okay, I can't wait to do it," they would laugh.

"I'm going to kill myself," he told Peter Chatel, for no clear reason, when they were in New York that April. He had summoned him from his room below at the Pierre. "In that case," said Chatel, "let me go back to my room, then jump out the window, so when you pass mine, we can wave our last goodbye."

"So, I'm gonna die," he said to Juliane on Christopher Street when she informed him of an insignificant change in his schedule. And when, hoping to allay his despair about having to cut *Querelle* solely to appease his American distributors, she said that perhaps the time had really come for them to marry and raise a family, he laughed at her bitterly. It was "too late," he said. His body was too poisoned by drugs to father children.

He began to lavish gifts on his friends—a full-length ermine coat for Juliane, a Gianni Versace jacket for Harry, Missoni sweaters for Kitty, silver shoes for Isolde, a hundred white roses for Jeanne Moreau. At dinner one night in Cannes that May, he offered Mutti eighty thousand marks and a Rolls-Royce as a wedding gift if he and the young woman he was living with would marry. Again at Cannes, he offered Peter Chatel a permanent job with his Tango Film at a salary of ten thousand marks a month.

"What do I have to do?" asked Chatel.

"Just be stimulating," said Rainer.

On still another occasion at Cannes, he spoke of a last will and testament to Chatel and Harry.

> It was very strange in its precision [says Chatel]. We were talking about something far removed from the subject when all of a sudden, Rainer said, "Well, anyway, in my will, there are [the rights to] two films for you, Harry." They were *Third Generation* and, I think, *Wildwechsel,* in which Harry had played the lead. For me, he said, there was *Fox and His Friends,* where I costar with Rainer, plus a Gianni Versace jacket. He pulled out the jacket and gave it to me on the spot.*

*No will was ever found, but in one impetuous moment in 1977, Rainer made what can only be called an extravagant gift of his rights to seventeen of his films to Fengler.

Was Rainer feeling the approach of death? Perceptions lie and play a cheating game. The last leg was not a journey straight down. "The books were full for the next five years," says Harry, speaking of the upcoming film projects after *Querelle,* and Rainer worked on them harder than anyone else every single day, vaunting a desire to become really rich in the eighties. Friends who were with him in New York and Cannes are, before or after they dispose of the omens of what was to come, unanimous in remembering what a good time was had by all. None of them is more ebullient on this score than Dieter Schidor. The intimacy between Rainer and him continued to wax in spite of the episode with Mascha, and in Cannes they spent nearly all their time together. Full of tension and apprehensiveness, Kitty discovered in Rainer a depth he'd never known before. He speaks here of that spring interlude on the Côte d'Azur:

It's easy to talk about Rainer's monstrosities, which were always present, but much more difficult to explain what made you love him anyway and want so badly to be with him. When you had him all to yourself, an evening with Rainer was the most wonderful thing in the world. He would be so tender, so gentle and understanding that you would sit there and have the feeling that nobody in your life had ever understood you as well as he had. He would know your innermost thoughts and wishes even before you were aware of them yourself.

It sounds contradictory, but though he himself was totally amoral, he was like a moral institution. If you had a problem —in my case, say, with Mike, or my parents, or anybody—you could go to him and speak about it in the most personal way, and for that moment, while he was trying to find a solution, you would feel that that was the most important thing in his life, and you knew you could place all your trust in his advice. That he would use whatever you'd confided against you like a knife in your back the very next morning was another story. Yes, he would do that, but then you would realize that it didn't matter at all. That was the great thing I learned about him. I'd been given a glimpse of the thing, or part of the thing, that made him freer than anybody else I knew. So what if your secrets, some you may have hidden all your life, come out in the open. You were suddenly that much unburdened. Oh, you would feel so comfortable and secure with him afterward.

Then, there were the childish adventures, which you knew would go on into old age. One day, when the news was all about trouble in Poland, he said, "Let's get into the car and go there. We can stay in Wajda's house* and organize the revolution. If *I* do it, it'll work." You didn't, you couldn't, doubt that he meant it. If you didn't actually go to Poland, it was only because something more adventurous came up, just as spontaneously. Every day was the first day of a new life. Money was meant to be spent or even thrown away. You could go places suddenly and stay there until the fun, or the money, ran out. Nothing you had learned before was important anymore. All your prisons crumbled.

But it was too late to become his friend. With a friend you can sit and do nothing, watch television or go out for a beer. Rainer demanded your fullest concentration, and if his motor couldn't stop, which is what he said, neither could yours. He'd crossed the line where friendships are made, but he'd got so frightened of being alone he'd go with you to the bathroom and want to sleep in your bed.

Being famous—this was his ersatz reasoning—he didn't need the love of one person anymore. That was how totally lonely he'd become. We'd be walking up and down the Croisette (he loved that) and he'd say to me, "Kitty, fall back a few steps behind me and watch what happens when people pass me, how they turn around for a second look. You can't see it when you walk alongside me." At Cannes, this being-famous thing really got out of hand. He made me call all over the world to find out if he could win the Oscar, not for best foreign film but as best director. "I'm really famous now," he'd say. "Aren't I?"

Rainer spent twenty thousand marks for cocaine in Cannes, and in exchange for a guaranteed supply of the same drug he dealt away part of the distribution rights of what was to be his next film. It would have been titled *I'm the Happiness of This World.*

*The reference is to the Polish filmmaker Andrzej Wajda.

192

30

"So now you want to know about the last days," says Juliane. She has already revealed to you more than she'd ever imagined she would have; she has wrestled with and overcome a hundred distressing hesitations that began with a sigh or a whispered "I mustn't talk about that" or "I'm not sure I should say this" and so on. But now you've arrived at the Gordian knot of it all. She begins with a pleasant memory:

> When Rainer got back from Cannes, he was in a wonderful mood. He was relaxed, and he seemed to me in very good shape emotionally. He'd brought me a beautiful gift, aquamarine-colored shoes with gold straps. His birthday was coming up, and he said, "I want a party that lasts two days." We took over the Deutsche Eiche for the evening of May thirty-first, and invited friends from all over the world. The party would go on for a smaller group of friends at the Clemensstrasse through the night and the next day, and I got busy at once, making his favorite dishes, Krautwickel and Kartoffelnsalat.

By now, Rainer's annual birthday party had become a social ritual in the German film world. Possession of an invitation—there were often more than a hundred—was a measure of status. It was the envy of outsiders, a certification for new arrivals, but not always cherished by those in the true inner circle. "Rainer's birthday parties," says Peter Chatel, "always ended unpleasantly, either in a hysterical gay mood or in a drunken stupor. But if you tried to avoid them, you found yourself being blackmailed."

Juliane continues:

On the day of his birthday, he changed. Very much. He took a lot of sleeping pills that day and I couldn't tell what was on his mind. We'd said we would arrive at the Eiche around ten o'clock, but he wouldn't move. I had to dress him. I put him in his white suit. He was sweating heavily. I wore the blue silk dress he'd given me during *Querelle,* after we'd made up, and while I was putting on my makeup, he just sat there and kept mumbling, "I don't wanna go, I don't wanna go." And I said, "Everybody's waiting for you, Rainer. You know how they love you." He was in such a strange mood.

Anyway, we got to the Eiche. It was packed, and he cheered up the minute we walked in when a producer came up and handed him a packet of money, a first payment for a stage play he'd signed to do, *A Streetcar Named Desire.* But he was silent most of the time, wearing his hat and his dark glasses all through the evening.

The guests celebrated on ten thousand marks' worth of lobster, caviar with new potatoes, and bubbly. Juliane recalls Rainer being pleased to see his "greatest enemy," Kurt Raab, and treating him especially nicely. Kurt, who would never cease to rankle when it came to Rainer, had just come out with a quibbling anti-Fassbinder article in a popular magazine, and even before receiving a surprise invitation to the party, he'd begun to regret its publication. He remembers Rainer's friendly reception, too:

His birthday was celebrated with pomp and many people, as it had [been] the years before. I, contrary to expectation, was also invited, and went, as always, with a pounding heart. Everyone was wanton and happy. Fassbinder came late; he was tired and silent. The congratulatory reception began at midnight. I too, bound by duty, stood in the long line of hand-shakers and well-wishers. He, to my surprise, suddenly pulled me down on him, pressed me to him, and kissed my whole face. I wiped the moisture away with pleased confusion and wondered, as I went back to my place, what this surprising display of affection could mean. Was this perhaps meant to be, could it even be, a new beginning?

Juliane says Kurt was "totally drunk," and he himself admits to having imbibed more than enough, but he was not beyond taking notice of a black handkerchief in the pocket of Rainer's white jacket, which he interpreted as a sign of mourning in memory of the fourth anniversary of Armin's death. Armin was also on someone else's mind; Juliane continues:

Around two or three in the morning, we went home in a smaller group of about twenty or thirty to go on with the party. Lilo, Rainer's mother, and a few others got into one of the taxis and when they arrived at the Clemensstrasse, she was crying terribly. I asked Regina [Ziegler], who'd been in the same cab, what had happened, and she told me that while they were getting out and paying, the taxi driver turned to Lilo, saying, "Best wishes from Armin Meier."

Then Rainer came up to me and said, "Why is my mother crying?" I didn't want to tell him, but he insisted and I did. He just turned around and went out of the room.

The rest of the night was very weird. Rainer suddenly showed up again, wanting everyone to stop what they were doing. He called it "a moment of truth," and divided the group into who had to watch *Querelle* and who *Kamikaze,* neither of which had come out yet. He put *Querelle* on the video machine in my room and *Kamikaze* on the one in his. But that didn't work out very well either. Fights began to break out, mostly started by Ingrid, who was upset with Rainer and in a horrible mood. At one point, he handed her a huge plastic cock, which had been part of the set decoration for *Querelle,* saying that that ought to keep her amused for a while. Then he went out on the balcony to watch the sun coming up. People began to leave; some slept over. Crazy Y Sa Lo wanted to sleep with me in my bed, so that I could wake her up in a few hours to catch a morning flight to Berlin. When I did get her up, she played *I Ching,* and said it had changed her mind; she couldn't go. After Rainer died, she said that his death had been decided that morning.

The second day of the party saw the arrival of new guests and the return of old, but it took place without Rainer, who made no appearance and kept to himself in his room.

The filming of *I'm the Happiness of This World,* to be produced by Dieter Schidor, was set to start on June 21, so the days between the second and the tenth, Rainer's last, were filled in the usual way with a heavy schedule of work. He had finished the script, about three men who become rock stars after failing as private detectives. Harry and Günther were to star, along with Hanno Pöschl, who had played a feature role in *Querelle.* There was a daily meeting with Kitty, and the group went scouting for locations, in search of a suitable disco or cabaret to hire for the shooting.

Rainer was depressed, but since Armin's death, he was always down this time of year, and everyone expected it to pass. To ease the way, they catered more than usually to his fancies. On the second or third of June, they were in the Eiche when Juliane saw someone slip Rainer a small plastic container, the kind normally used to hold a single roll of 35-mm still-camera film. Its contents cost him seventy-five hundred marks. He gave it to Juliane for safekeeping. It was filled to the brim with cocaine, about thirty grams. He'd paid for it with the money he'd received from the producer of *A Streetcar Named Desire,* and consumed it within a week.

Juliane went off to Paris to rerecord a few sentences on the soundtrack of *Querelle* spoken by Jeanne Moreau. Rainer kept busy not only with his upcoming film, but also making script notes for the Rosa Luxemburg story, *Rosa L.,* and working with Thomas Schüly, the young producer of *Veronika Voss,* he began planning the remake of *Possessed,* and a film based on the George Batailles novel *The Blue of Noon.*

One evening that week, Rainer went out with Isolde and some other friends to the opening of an art exhibition in a Munich gallery. The artist was Ursula Straetz, in whose remodeled movie theater in the Müllerstrasse the whole saga had begun. He was photographed there for the last time. He is standing slightly behind Ursula, whose joy is evident although she is completely out of focus. The lens sharpens on Rainer. He appears disheveled in his trademark outfit. He is trying to smile, but his gaze is empty. He seems covered with a thin slick of moisture. He looks like a clothed seal.

Juliane returned from Paris. Rainer and Harry picked her up at the airport. "He just started talking about what's going to happen when he dies," Harry said to Juliane, "who gets what film and who gets another." By now, this had become a recurring topic, and it was dropped as easily as it arose.

Early in the hot afternoon of Wednesday, June 9, Wolf Gremm, puffing and chewing on a Havana cigar, arrived at the Clemensstrasse in his gold-colored Mercedes. Gremm, who had directed *Kamikaze '89,* had driven down from Berlin to film an interview with Rainer for the documentary *The Wizard of Babylon.* Rainer had shied away from earlier requests but had suddenly changed his mind. Juliane was scheduled to go to Berlin the next day to complete postproduction work on *Querelle,* and Rainer, dreading the thought of being alone, had invited Wolf to stay with him. He had in the short time since they'd gotten together for *Kamikaze* developed a bigbrotherly fondness for Wolf, whose easily ignited childlike enthusiasm was sunshine in Rainer's leaden sky.

While Wolf set up his 16-mm camera, Juliane was getting ready to go shopping. She wanted to leave the two men with enough food for the time she would be away, and she also had to arrange for a housekeeper to look after them. With them in the apartment was Dieter Schidor, who would pose the questions in the interview, and Mascha and Thomas Schüly.

Rainer was in his room. He had one other appointment that afternoon, with a sculptress named Karin Mai, whom he had never met before. Mai had been commissioned by Hanns Eckelkamp many months earlier to do a portrait of Rainer in bronze. It was to be the first of a series to immortalize the leading directors of the New German Cinema. The idea had been Mutti's, and Rainer thought it a good one, though he had repeatedly postponed the required sittings.

Shortly before two in the afternoon, Rainer came out for the interview. He was dressed in a black caftan. Juliane noticed that he was under a heavy dose of Vesperox, probably mixed with cocaine, but knew better than to comment. She was feeling uneasy about having to go away. His birthday-time depression had not yet showed any sign of subsiding.

When Juliane went out to do her errands, the men rehearsed the interview, laughing over the question of whether or not Schidor should address Rainer on-camera in the formal second-person mode of speech. "If you do, Kitty, I'll giggle," said Rainer. That issue settled, Rainer asked what the others thought of his caftan. Schüly didn't like it, so Rainer changed into his leather, a pink shirt, dark glasses, and his battered gray fedora.

The doorbell rang. Rainer opened the door. It was Karin Mai, a tall, slender woman, her beauty worn but not diminished by middle age. Rainer was quietly charming. He invited her to watch the interview, and she did so willingly, using the time to study the face she had been hired to render in clay.

You can see in the film what she saw: That face and every other part of him are grotesquely waterlogged. He is submerged in a corner of a leather sofa. His eyes, veiled but not hidden by his glasses, are barely opened frog eyes. A meaty hand moves like a pendulum, flicking cigarette ashes into a tray on one swing, carrying smoke to his lungs on the other.

The questions are tiresome. His answers are keen, but the words are sluggish, slurred. There is tension and calculation in the questions; there is neither guile nor hesitation in the answers. You are witnessing the exact opposite of brain death; a sound mind imprisoned in a corpse.

SCHIDOR: When the novel [*Querelle de Brest*] was banned, it was because it was said to be pornographic. . . . What's your opinion?

RAINER: Everything that reaches the social boundaries, or crosses it, must necessarily be pornographic in this society.

SCHIDOR: How would you say that homosexuality is depicted in films?

RAINER: Always wrongly. You can't do justice to any group. You can't do justice to homosexuals, not to heterosexuals either. You can just keep doing everything wrong. Homosexuality isn't a theme anyway. The theme is the identity of an individual and how he obtains it.

After about a quarter of an hour of this kind of exchange, the battery on Wolf's camera went dead. There was a discussion about whether to replace it, but Rainer didn't care to go on. He asked Karin Mai how she wanted to proceed with the portrait. She said she would need six sittings. Rainer in a good-natured way complained that he had agreed to sit only twice, but he asked the sculptress to begin anyway on the following day at two in the afternoon. She agreed and left. There were a few laughs about how nervous Kitty had been in the interview. They also spoke of the imminent German elections. Rainer went on pessimistically about there being no longer anything to vote for. He seemed to be on the same "black trip," to use Schidor's phrase, as he was in New York, when he said to Kitty, "If you want a new society, maybe you have to destroy the old one completely; maybe you have to go that far."

Sometime before five that evening, a man called Mick showed up at the front door. He had a reputation of being the best drug-dealer in town. He always gave you a little extra for your money. He brought Rainer another 35-mm-film tube of cocaine and told him that he could also get him some of the banned Mandrax pills, the hypnotic that caused no apparent side effects in Rainer. Rainer put in his order.

When Juliane came home shortly afterward, all the visitors except Wolf were gone, and Rainer was back in his room.

"Juliane," Wolf said, "Rainer was very bad in the interview. He's acting very strange."

"Why didn't you stop it?"

Wolf had no ready answer. Juliane went into Rainer's room and asked him how the interview went.

"Can't you see?" he said. "I can't form my words anymore." He looked thoroughly exhausted. He said, "I have no more sleeping pills. Please, you have to bring me some."

"I'm sorry, Rainer. You took them all today. I can't. I can't."

"But Mick found some old Mandrax. I swear to you, I'm going to stop with all these things. But now I have to sleep. I'm so tired."

"So sleep. You don't need any more."

"Oh, God," he said, "why do I always have to beg for this?"

Juliane couldn't bear his agony. She said she was going out to have dinner with a friend. She would go to Mick during the evening, and be back around eleven.

"Why do you have to eat first?" Rainer asked. "I can't wait that long."

Juliane agreed to get the pills and come back without delay. She found Mick in the Eiche. The Mandrax hadn't arrived yet. She settled for Vesperox. She returned to the Clemensstrasse, went to Rainer's room, and threw the pills at him in anger.

He looked up at her. "Thank you," he said.

"Do me one favor," said Juliane. "Don't take any more today."

"I just wanted to have them. Just in case. I'm so tired. I have to sleep."

Juliane went off to dinner at the Romagna Antica, an Italian restaurant in Schwabing that drew the film crowd.

At nine o'clock, Kitty called Rainer on his private bedside line, a red telephone with a number known only to five persons. He was not asleep. They spoke about an offer from Gaumont to coproduce *I'm the Happiness of This World.* Rainer was still bitter over the French production house's role in forcing him to cut *Querelle,* but he was willing to accept its money for the next film. They made a lunch date to eat outside the next day, weather permitting, at the Chinese Tower in the English Gardens.

Juliane returned again. It was midnight. She found Wolf sitting in the kitchen. She saw that the door to Rainer's room was closed, and asked Wolf if they'd spoken.

"No," said Wolf. "He closed the door and I didn't want to disturb him."

She didn't care to either, knowing that when he shut his door it meant that he wanted seclusion. Through the door, she heard the speaker on his television set and the distinct switching sounds of the video recorder being operated manually. She now had to pick up the film materials she would need to take with her to Berlin. She was planning to leave at seven in the morning. She went out once more, to her cutting room at Bavaria Studios.

At one in the morning, Harry dialed the number on Rainer's private phone. When the call was answered, Harry blurted out triumphantly, "I found it! The Song Parnass." That was the name of a local discotheque, and Harry saw it as the location for *I'm the*

Happiness of This World they had been hunting for all these days. "We can shoot everything there," he went on, describing its attributes. "And the price is okay, too!"

"Great," said Rainer. He told him to make a deal. "Anything else?"

"Everything's just fine. How are you doing?"

"I'm watching television, video. In between my reading. I have a few more things to do."

They hung up.

At around the same time, Ingrid called from Paris. She didn't know the red-phone number, and she got Wolf on the other line. She wanted to speak to Rainer. She would often call him this late or even later, and it was not unusual for them to chat, argue, or commiserate with each other for as much as an hour. The telephone relationship between the ex–married couple was, as it is wont to be with many people in similar circumstances, far better than their relationship at striking distance. But Wolf didn't know either of them well enough to make that judgment. He had been present at the birthday party when Ingrid and Rainer were clearly angry at one another. He now took it upon himself to say that Rainer wasn't home.

The sun was rising when Juliane finally returned home. It was around four-thirty in the morning, June 10, 1982. She had stopped off at Kitty's place for a while, and again at an all-night bakery to pick up some hot rolls. She and Rainer had planned to have breakfast together before her departure for Berlin, so she went directly to his room to see if he was asleep. Rainer was curled up like a baby. The room was growing light. The television set was still on, transmitting nothing but a gray hiss. She started to go out, but she saw a half-consumed line of cocaine by his bedside. Deciding to use the situation to advantage, she gathered up the powder and spirited it out of the room, feeling that she had done a small good deed by making it disappear.

She went to the bathroom and fixed herself up. Standing in front of the mirror, it suddenly struck her that Rainer, an inveterate snorer, had been soundless. She strained her ears, expecting to hear sooner or later a breath-catching snore. Silence. She returned to his bedroom. She shut off the TV set, an abruptness that never failed to rouse him. He didn't wake up. Juliane relives that moment:

I looked at his face. There was nothing going on. I saw a tiny blue point on his eyelid. And there was a little bit of blood coming out of his nose. I got scared. I shook him. He never covered himself but he was warm. I shook him again. He didn't react. I started to scream at him, "Rainer, I'm going! I'm leaving! Wake up." I stared at him. He was lying on some notes he'd been making about Rosa Luxemburg. There was a cigarette in his right hand, burned down but with the ashes gone.

I thought maybe he'd had a heart attack. I ran into Wolf's room, but I couldn't wake him either at first. "Help me!" I cried. "Help me!" Finally we went together to Rainer's room and tried to get him up. I listened for his heartbeat and his pulse. There was nothing going on. Wolf said, "He's dead." I didn't believe him.

I called an ambulance. The moment I did that, my next thought was that the apartment would soon be filled with strangers. I knew they would say bad things about Rainer. So I got all the drugs together, and I flushed them away. That was the right thing to do.

Rainer was examined by one of the ambulance attendants. "This man is dead," he said. He turned to Juliane. "Is he Fassbinder?"

She was in a state of hysteria, but whatever she replied was confirmation enough. The police were summoned. They arrived quickly, and began at once to make sure that nothing in the apartment was moved.

The first person Juliane called was Daniel Schmid in Paris. He was one of Rainer's oldest friends, and she wanted him to break the news to his mother. Daniel heard only incoherent grief on his end of the line, but he sensed the truth. He called Willi back in Munich and asked him to find out what had actually happened. His friend Raul Jiminez called Udo Kier. Dodo called Isolde. She went numb, reflecting that Rainer had died on the day of the Rolling Stones concert in Munich. In the meantime, Daniel had walked across the hall to where Ingrid lived, on the same floor as he. He found her in a wrecked apartment. After she had failed to get through to Rainer, she'd had a fight with her lover and had smashed everything in sight. They sat in the kitchen over coffee. At six o'clock in the morning *Time* and *Newsweek* called her for a statement. Ingrid said nothing. Daniel said, "It can't be true. He's playing a trick on us. He lies every time he opens his mouth except when he's eating."

Wolf's first call was to Schidor. When he heard the phone ringing, Kitty imagined it could only be Rainer. Wanting to sleep, he covered the phone with pillows, but at last he answered. He didn't react. He woke up Mascha; neither did he. Kitty put on the Missoni sweater Rainer had given him as a gift, and he went to the Clemensstrasse. By the time he got there, the body had already been taken away for a coroner's autopsy*

Kitty found people already on the street downstairs and Juliane, Wolf, and Thomas Schüly in the apartment. Calls began to arrive from the press, seeking confirmation that Rainer and another person had died in an orgy. Kitty broke into fits of laughter. Willi called to ask Juliane if he should tell Rainer's mother, but she took on that responsibility and went to her, hoping to arrive before the rumors. The police sealed the apartment, forcing everyone to leave.

The rest of the day was marked by confusion and recriminations under a scorching sun. Most of the Fassbinder people, past and present, got the news like everyone else, on the morning radio or in later editions of the newspapers. The prevailing response was an absence of surprise. It was only much later that some individuals who had been close to the dead man began to assess what he had meant to them. At the time, almost all of them had something to say to the press, something very middle-class, spoken with a wagging finger, about reaping as ye sow. Only Harry, laconic Harry, who had the good sense to get drunk at the Eiche in the morning of that day, had something enduring to say: "Fucking cocaine!"

*The only conclusion reached was that Rainer had died of what in medical terms is called a "cerebrovascular accident," a stroke.

KARIN Mai speaks:

I arrived at the Clemensstrasse right on time for the two o'clock appointment. I'd come by bike, carrying a bucket of clay. It was terribly hot and I was sweating. I rang the bell downstairs on the street. I rang it again and again, but nobody answered. I thought: Some appointment! What a rotten thing to do! Finally, a woman came out of the building. She looked at me oddly. I asked if she knew Fassbinder, and she said, "Haven't you heard? He died this morning."

How could it be? I was with him only yesterday. Here I am with all my things, and he's dead.

I pedaled back to the friends where I was staying, not very far away. I needed to think. I needed to take a walk.

The next day, I called Juliane Lorenz to pay my respects. She asked me if it would be possible for me to make a death mask. I said okay. After a lot of telephoning, Mr. Schüly got the permission. The body was autopsied and then transferred to a morgue alongside a cemetery. I had to go there the following day.

I was there at eight o'clock that morning. The body was rolled in on a cart, and laid out on a marble slab. I was left alone. Very alone. I lowered the covering sheet. Fassbinder was dressed in a nightshirt tied loosely at the neck in a bloodstained bow. I untied the bow. I could see the autopsy wounds in his torso and on the back of his head. They'd removed his brain. There was more dried blood.

I'd made a death mask only once before, of a child. But that was seventeen years ago, and now it was as if it were the first time. I couldn't get used to his being dead. His face had changed color, because all the liquid in his body had been drained. There was a faint but a bad smell. I needed a whole hour to get to myself. Every now and then, workmen came into the room, grave diggers. They were joking about him. One of them said, "No more orgies for Mr. Fassbinder, right?" But somebody else saw the trouble I was having, and he gave me some cognac and a Coca-Cola to give me a lift.

As soon as I was alone again, I began. But the first thing I had to do was the worst thing, applying cold cream to his face to isolate it from the plaster. Otherwise, when the plaster would set it would stick to his skin. It was a terrifying sensation. His skin was colder than the cold cream.

Then I mixed the plaster and put it on his face, slowly, gently, so as not to distort his features. It was a very good face. Really good forms. You could see the ambition.

When I'd finished, it dried in about half an hour. I had an awful time removing it. The hairs of his beard, in spite of the cream and the little pieces of paper I'd put there as separation, had stuck in the plaster. I tried my best, but I couldn't help pulling some away. I cut them from inside the mold with a scissors. I felt horrible.

I went back to my friends and I made the positive right away from the plaster impression. When it was done, I called Juliane. She asked to see it. We met in the apartment of Fassbinder's mother. I showed the mask. The reaction was strangely reserved. Juliane said it was okay. Fassbinder's mother asked me if I'd like to see a story he had written when he was nine years old. She called it his first theater sketch. I read it. It was very beautiful, very sweet, a story about flowers that fall in love. Even as a child, she said, he knew that he was different, not like the others of his own generation. He wanted a family, but he couldn't have a real family because, his mother told me, "he had a very, very heavy childhood." So he created one by always having people with him.

Then she turned on the videorecorder. She darkened the room, and Juliane, Fassbinder's mother, and I watched *Querelle,* his original version. They wanted me to see how it was before he had to cut it.

APPENDIX I

The Making of *Whity*
by Peter Berling

THE telephone rang. Seldom in my life could I resist this sound. I rolled over in my bed in the Tel Aviv Hilton Hotel. I was sweating and angry. I had just come back from looking for locations at the Dead Sea. The prospect of having to spend the next three months in a rocky wilderness was hardly exciting, not even the thought that the salt lake would support my three hundred pounds without my splashing. People were giving me trouble, and I was in a mood to quit.

The telephone rang again. "Who is disturbing me?" I shouted into the mouthpiece.

It was Ulli Lommel. "Listen," he said, "I'm making a western and you have to produce it for me."

At the word "western" I became weaker than when tempted with Lindt Edelbitter chocolate. "Do you have the money?"

"I'll be at the airport with the check."

I quit. I flew to Munich. The check didn't bounce. In front of the bank, I asked for the details. "Who's the director?"

"Rainer Werner Fassbinder. And the whole Antitheater group. Hanna, too."

Hanna had left me two years before. She had called me a capitalist, and had ridden off on her bicycle, the way she had come. "Rainer and Hanna will refuse me," I said now. "They all will."

"I don't believe it," said Ulli.

"Well, find out for yourself."

In the afternoon, Ulli came back from his confrontation with the group. "You're right," he told me. "They don't want to make a movie with you. But I said, 'No film without Berling!' So they accepted you, but they won't speak to you."

"This could be fun!"

Lommel and I flew to Madrid on the night plane to meet the Spanish coproducer. Early the next morning, under my interrogation, he turned out to be a crook. Give up the project? "No," I said, "off to Almería!"

Almería, a provincial port in southern Andalusia, had become one of the favorite "backlots" of Europe in the sixties. The stable good weather guaranteed uninterrupted shooting. The landscape was varied, sometimes bizarre, and it included a real desert (see *Lawrence of Arabia*). There were often more productions on the go there than in the film capitals of the Continent. The Los Angeles Hotel was on the road to Almería's airport, which was used only twice weekly when a Convair from Barcelona arrived and departed. It had the advantage of keeping the cast and crew together, making after-hours excursions difficult. In addition, I managed to push the price down to the level of a youth hostel, and since the only capital at the moment was Ulli's Diners Club card, I also convinced the Los Angeles to join the club.

Within five days everything was organized. A "village" left over from a spaghetti western was rented on the cheap, and horses, stuntmen, and an American B-picture movie star were engaged, if not always on the Diners Club, then on promises of good fortune in the wind. Finally, when Ulli found a raw-film supplier who would take plastic, the green light was given to Munich and the entire Antitheater rolled across Europe, Rainer and Günther in the maestro's 230 SL and the others on lesser wheels. Hanna flew.

On arrival, Rainer said he had come only to announce that he had no intention of making the film and that he would leave immediately, and he stormed off, which is when Harry said that Rainer was merely unhappy with his room, that he was eager to make a western, and that there was nothing to worry about. "You just have to get used to him."

I had resolved not to let Fassbinder get to me. The more provocative and unexpected his demands, the more I would let them bounce off my belly, so to speak. I would take all difficulties in my stride, soothe whatever grated, and none of the director's desires would remain unfulfilled.

But the tension didn't subside, it grew. Harry, the go-between, went between Fassbinder and me at shorter and shorter intervals.

Fassbinder would start the day demanding ten Cuba libres—rum and Coca-Cola. He would drink nine and throw the tenth at the cameraman. I proceeded stubbornly according to the shooting plan. Fassbinder did, too.

The explosion came on the third day.

A crowd scene had been planned, activity in front of the saloon. I sat on the steps in the sun, observing the arrangements approvingly. Extras, directed by Harry and outfitted by Kurt, strolled over the sandy square. Wagons rolled. The sheriff rocked on the porch. Horses reared. Chickens and pigs abounded.

The only one missing was Fassbinder. Harry brought the news. Rainer has changed his mind. He refuses to shoot the scene and he wants to leave again.

I raised my voice: "Tell him I said he's shitting in his pants because there are more than three people in the scene."

Harry smarted but was delighted to report the insubordination. I sat on the porch, not knowing what to expect when Fassbinder came growling around the corner.

"I'm going to bash your fucking face in!" he shouted, coming at me like an angry bull. I had no time to get to my feet, but I used one of them, inserting it between his legs and sending him diving into the dust. He gathered himself together and charged again, but I was standing now and I literally let him bounce off my belly, adding a swift karate chop to the back of his neck. This time, flying over the steps, he landed on the porch. He got up with difficulty, lowered his head, and attacked once more. Feeling a lot more sure of myself now, I let him come, but he threw his arms around my neck and whispered in my ear: "I love you! Now I know I can finish this film!" Dropping his voice still more, he added, "Ulli doesn't have a pfennig, you know, only the credit card!"

I was both touched and not a little piqued, touched by the flood of emotion and piqued because Rainer had realized that there was no money to finish the movie before I had.

I got Ulli to lay his cards on the table, and the first thing I learned was that the Diners was no longer among them, the club having ousted him in the meantime. While the search for new credit went on, we kept to the shooting schedule. The staging of the film gave Rainer ample opportunity to vent his implacable rage, particularly at Ulli. There was a character in the script who was a nymphomaniac not averse to beating her grown, mentally retarded stepson. So Rainer cast Ulli's wife, Katrin, as the nympho-sadist and Ulli as the half-wit, and in one scene Rainer made her strike Ulli so many times that they both dropped to the ground weeping for mercy.

Even Hanna fell into disfavor, though her punishment wore kid gloves. The female lead, she played a chattel barmaid at the beck and call of the sexual fancies of a big landowner, our American B-picture star, Ron Randall, and when she began to double in the same role off-camera, Rainer, who viewed her as his creation—an immaculate conception—went bananas. He costumed her as whorishly as his fertile mind could imagine, turned the part into a saloon hooker who sings for her supper, and when the shooting called for a barroom rowdy to louse up her act, Rainer played the bit himself, sporting a whip.

Harry and Kurti, who had had the leads in the last two pictures respectively, were, on general principles, I suppose, demoted drastically. Kurt played a pianist, Harry another idiot stepson, and much to his surprise and humiliation—since Rainer had him made-up blindfolded—he played it as an albino.

But Rainer reserved the most poisonous arrows of his ire for Günther. Günther played "Whity," a half-caste who works as the dastardly Nicholson family's personal nigger. "Hanna"—played by Hanna—the sexually exploited barmaid, raises Whity's conscious- ness and incites him to murder his white masters. But just as Whity in the script is somehow unable to bring himself to act, Günther had the same problem in playing the part. Rainer was merciless. Günther was indifferent. There was a wicked game of dominance going on, ill-defined in my mind back then, but no one, myself included, was immune.

The example that springs to my recall sounds funny today, but at the time blood boiled, particularly my own. In one of the night scenes, which had required meticulous and costly arrangements, Whity has to climb a long rope ladder into Hanna's room on the top floor of the saloon. Günther rehearsed one climb, but not all the way to the top. He was saving his courage, such as it was, for the actual scene, which called for him to swing over the ledge at the top and make for a doorway, through which he was to disappear. End of take.

When everything was ready and Rainer signaled for action, Günther set off intrepidly, clambering upward, and sailing almost gracefully over the ledge toward the doorway. But when he got there, much as he struggled with the handle, the door wouldn't open.

Rainer had a fit. He screamed for Kurti, who was doubling as propman. Kurti declared that there was absolutely nothing wrong with the handle. The trouble lay with the "door." It was painted on the wall. Rainer had a second fit. I suggested, to save time and money, that the scene be shifted to an adjoining room that had a real door. Rainer said that the door had to be where he wanted it to be, and he demanded a carpenter. I had a fit. I started to walk off the set, but Rainer said that if I took one more step he would quit. Kurti brought him a tray of Cuba libres, and while the painted door was sawn away to make room for a real one, Rainer drank, I fumed, and Günther was indifferent.

Now it was my turn for punishment. Rainer, who, if he was great, it was because he had a thousand eyes, had evidently noticed that I had more than a business relationship with my secretary, Barbara. She was a beautiful young widow of an American Formula-One racing-car driver. I had put her in the room next to mine, but the territory, I suspected, was not my domain alone. I professed to be free of all jealousy, which was chic in those days, but I suppose I protested too much, and Rainer must have seen that.

In any case, late one night the phone by my bedside rang, and Barbara was on the other end of the line.

"I'm lying here in bed with Rainer," she said, "and we're naked and making love."

Rainer got on the phone. "Are you hurt?"

Sure, I was hurt. But I pretended to be more hurt than I really was, or thought I was, and that was pleasure enough for him to throw her out of his room. I understood, or imagined, that Barbara had been merely used, sacrificed on the altar of my auto-da-fé. I could bounce him off my belly any day, but he was the Force.

By now I felt I had paid my dues, but the same group that had refused to speak to me had lately gone on to protest against having to "take orders" from me, a nonmember. I had tried to impose traditional film-production discipline, but we were living in the Age of Communes, and Rainer, Great Democrat that he was, summoned everyone together for a hearing.

"This Mr. Berling," I heard anticapitalist Hanna say, "treats us as though we are the underlings in his privately owned company."

No one dissented, and finally Rainer with Solomonic wisdom passed judgment. He dubbed me Group Mother—Mutti in German.

"Listen, everybody," he said. "What Mutti says, will be done."

How clever he was to characterize me in that time and circumstance not as a boss but as an all-caring mother, and it worked. "Mutti," I was shortly to hear again and again from then on, "what time do we have to get up tomorrow?" "Mutti, can I go to the john?" "Mutti, can I have some money?" Although my answer to the last question was almost always no, the name has stuck with me through all these years.

The production money dried up completely. Salaries had already been frozen, and now the per diem allowances were cut off. We became prisoners of the Los Angeles Hotel, which was suddenly the only place within a thousand miles any of us could still sleep with a roof over his head and get a meal, and only because the owner was too far in the red to throw us out. Now everybody *but* Rainer was threatening to quit. Ulli was constantly on the phone to Germany, selling percentage points in the film by the hundreds for financing that never arrived. Suddenly, Rainer learned that he had won a huge State cash prize for a previous film, but when ever-faithful Irm Hermann arrived from Munich with the cash, it was only a small first installment, the rest to be paid out over a period that was too long to do us any good.

Rainer unleashed his fury not at the State but at Irm. He slapped her in front of us all. "Where's my money?" he wailed. "Everyone's betraying me. They're sucking my blood!"

Irm burst into tears. "You promised to marry me," were the words that came out of her mouth. "You promised to have children with me. Why don't you marry me?"

She was supposed to have played a part in the film, but Rainer banned her from the set and sent her home. The situation turned desperate when we began to run out of raw stock. The cameraman and I were the only ones who knew, and we kept it secret from Rainer. At first he was astonished and then he began to grow suspicious because the cameraman, Michael Ballhaus, didn't complain when he shot scenes in one take. Normally, a cameraman doesn't feel covered without at least a second take for insurance.

Then the day came when Ballhaus's assistant trudged into the production office and announced that there was no more film for the next day's shooting. I looked at Ulli. Ulli looked at the floor. But my own assistant said he had a possible solution. We all looked at him the way you sometimes look at heaven. All he could do, however, was hem and haw, and he even blushed, until I sensed what it might be. I left the room for his sake, but more so for mine. The truth was that my secretary, Barbara, the apple of my eye, was having an affair with one of the camera-crew members on an American production making a Jack Palance film nearby. They of course were loaded, staying at the luxury hotel Aguadulce, and Barbara's paramour had the key to where they kept their film supply.

Rainer throughout had expressed a desire to meet Palance, whom he had admired in *Panic in the Streets* and *Shane,* so late one night, a whole group of us set off for the Aguadulce. Rainer was annoyed and perhaps a little embarrassed by the size of the entourage, but he was not privy to the caper. We came in several cars and with our prettiest girls, including, of course, my peripatetic secretary, Barbara.

The great encounter between Palance and Fassbinder took place in the otherwise empty lobby of the hotel while the girls fanned out and disappeared. Palance, looking like a fugitive from a Beverly Hills men's shop window, seemed lonely and drunk. Rainer, who after a recent press conference had been described by a journalist as "almost idiotically inarticulate," was just that. We all sat in a half-light. Rainer in leather was lost in the leather upholstery. I remember the dialogue well enough, but what I remember most were the interminable skin-crawling pauses between each exchange. It went something like this:

"You're from Germany?"

"Yeah, from Bavaria."

A long silence.

"East or west?"

A long silence.

"It's west, but more east." A long silence. "Your family is from Russia?"

"No. Kiev." Silence. "You want a drink?"

"Vodka?"

"Whisky."

A long silence.

"I like Cuba libre."

"What's that?"

"Fidel Castro."

"Fucking communist."

"No, rum and Coke."

"And you drink that shit?"

Silence.

"Yeah, a lot."

"If there's not a lot of whisky, I drink vodka, a lot."

Silence.

"I see."

This took one hour. I know because the girls suddenly showed up and they had drunk a lot of something, about an hour's worth of steady drinking whatever it was. We gathered ourselves together.

"It was a pleasure to meet you, Mr. Palance," said Rainer, in one of the longest English sentences I would ever hear him utter.

"Same to you," said Palance. "What's your business?"

"Making movies."

"Oh, I see. Well, have a good time."

"Same to you."

Back at the Los Angeles, when Rainer was serenely tucked in bed with Günther, we opened the trunks of our cars. They were filled to the rubber seal with shiny metal cans of 35-mm Kodak movie film. What a great day!

The shooting schedule was twenty days long, which was a third of what it should have been, but that was part of the Fassbinder phenomenon, and I was as dogged as he was in wanting to keep it to the day. But in the last week the pressure became enormous and it began to take its toll. We were filming fourteen, fifteen, sometimes even eighteen hours a day, and we would get back to the hotel at three or four in the morning, too worked up to go to bed. A stereo system had been set up in the lobby and at that hour it would be going full volume, bouncing the hotel owner off his mattress and driving him clinically mad. In vain would he try in his pajamas to impose a legal prohibition against serving drinks after hours, pulling fuses and padlocking the liquor cabinet, and when it was more than once broken open, he threatened us with the police. But in the end he simply cowered night after night behind the bar, serving Cuba libres on the cuff and standing witness to alcoholic orgies that grew wilder with each passing day.

We were his only guests, all others having long since departed, and when occasionally unsuspecting tourists wandered in, they invariably left no later than the next morning, weary and cursing under, or more often over, their breath. Even without the intimidated owner's complaint, the police appeared more and more frequently. Rainer had fired the interpreter (the last vestige of the Spanish coproduction) and she had taken her revenge by giving fanciful and not so fanciful descriptions to the authorities of the troupe's drinking and unconventional sex life. Moreover, Günther had run his Lamborghini into a store window, and though we had settled the matter with the shopkeeper, we were unable to pay the settlement, and he too had gone to the police. The local extras filed complaints about being scandalously underpaid, which was true, and some members of the crew were continually brawling at the airport bar, expressing in fisticuffs what we were all feeling mentally: being fed up with one another and the Great Democrat's tsarist rule.

Violence broke out on our own territory, on the terrace of the Los Angeles. Rainer, drunk and stood-up by Günther, kicked the script-girl in the shins for no better reason. Two hefty stuntmen seized the moment and him as well and beat him to the ground. Luckily I wasn't present, so I didn't have to take a stand, but most of the rest of the troupe were, and nobody lifted a finger to come to his rescue. Rainer got up and slinked away in silence, and the incident was never spoken of again.

Emotional violence, too, the kind that ends in bleeding hearts and tears, erupted more and more, and one reason was that Rainer suspected that Günther was being unfaithful in the biblical sense. His suspicion was confirmed when either his spies or the view from his bedroom window revealed that Günther at dawn was taking long walks on the beach with Kurti. That was proof enough for Rainer, who knew how to put two and two together better than anybody else I ever knew, but Kurti, who had a sievelike capacity for keeping a secret, eventually told all, the following being the words of his own published confession: "I felt the sweet feeling of revenge when I took a walk a couple of times with Kaufmann on the beach at dawn. That was wonderful in itself, but the best thing was the secret now in my possession. I had only to think about Fassbinder waiting longingly for Kaufmann while he was giving a few moments of priority to me, and I couldn't ask for anything more!"

When the "secret" got out, one of the few scenes left to be shot called for Whity to be flogged naked by his master in rage. Everyone was convinced that Günther's marvelously muscular back would be thrashed to shreds, and mischievous Harry, as assistant director, acquired a cat-o'-nine-tails and a tarred towline from a boat for Rainer to choose from. Kurti, as propman, however, had been given other instructions from Rainer, and though the whip as seen in the film looks like a cat-o'-nine-tails, the knotted cords are made of the softest woolen yarn Kurti could find. The scene is not very effective, but some things for Rainer, such as his Bavarian Negro's flesh, had built-in immunity.

Thus, with Whity and Hanna dancing into a metaphorical sunset —the very last scene shortly afterward safe in the can—the shooting of *Whity* ended (on schedule) almost Christianly, though the long aftermath was more of the same. Some of the bunch went back to Munich. Rainer and Günther crashed the Mercedes in Alicante. Harry followed Juan Carlos to Madrid. Ulli and his wife, Katrin, were held hostage by the Los Angeles until the bills were paid, following which his company went bankrupt. *Whity* premiered at the Berlin Film Festival the following year. It received mixed reviews, but I did fine; I got a call from a friend in the middle of the night telling me that the film opens with the words "To Peter Berling." Coming from Rainer, this made me feel as if I'd won an Oscar. Of course he wielded it like a battle-ax over my head in the years to come. That's the way he was.

APPENDIX II

Where Are They Now?

MOTHER FASSBINDER

Involved in litigation over ownership of the rights to RWF's films, including suits against Michael Fengler, Peer Raben, Dieter Schidor, Hanns Eckelkamp, and Father Fassbinder.

FATHER FASSBINDER

Involved in separate, but the same sort of, litigation as above.

UDO KIER

Acting.

MICHAEL FENGLER

Sold his share of *Querelle* to Dieter Schidor; in litigation with Hanns Eckelkamp regarding profits from *Maria Braun,* and with Mother Fassbinder over rights to RWF's films

CHRISTOPH ROSER

Untraceable.

HANNA SCHYGULLA

A 1985 *Time* cover-person, she continues to shine, having made films for such internationally renowned directors as Jean-Luc Godard, Carlos Saura, Margarethe von Trotta, Andrzej Wajda, and Ettore Scola.

IRM HERMANN

Continues to work in films and theater.

DANIEL SCHMID

Continues to direct.

KURT RAAB

Author of an RWF biography; acting.

PEER RABEN

Continues to compose music.

URSULA STRAETZ

Wrote unproduced screenplay about the life of RWF.

ULLI LOMMEL

Lives in Los Angeles, where he produces and directs low-budget films, such as *Cocaine Cowboy.*

PETER CHATEL

After continuing his career as a stage director in Munich and Paris, he died in Hamburg on August 25, 1986, at the age of forty-two.

INGRID CAVEN

Has given concerts in Rome and Berlin.

HARRY BAER

Author of an RWF biography; directed a TV series, acts in TV and film.

GÜNTHER KAUFFMANN

Has made recordings of Peer Raben's songs.

DIETER SCHIDOR

Bankrupted by *Querelle* and a subsequent flop, he, too, is burdened with RWF-related litigation. His longtime companion, Michael McLernon (courted so desperately by RWF as "Mascha"), died in Munich on November 27, 1986, at the age of forty-one.

ISOLDE BARTH

Continues to act.

JULIANE LORENZ

Continues to edit films.

ACKNOWLEDGMENTS

For one set of reasons or another, but mostly because I have been the beneficiary of the painful soul-searching of others, I owe a great debt of thanks to the following people: Harry Baer, Isolde Barth, Hanns Eckelkamp, Michael Fengler, Irm Hermann, Wolfgang Limmer, Juliane Lorenz, Karin Mai, Peer Raben, Daniel Schmid, and Dieter Schidor. Appreciation is also due Ingrid Caven, Costa-Gavras, Wolf Gremm, Steve Kenis, Franco Nero, Kurt Raab, Werner Schroeter, Xaver Schwarzenberger, Robert von Ackeren, Regina Ziegler, Eva Zwerenz.

On the American side, mostly for putting up with me, I thank Rob Cowley, Erroll McDonald, and Peter Matson, and, finally, on the Tuscan side, especially for putting up with me, Beverly Katz.

FILMOGRAPHY

Abbreviations:

d	director
s	screenplay
ph	director of photography
m	music
ed	editor
a	principal actors
p	producer
f	format: mm = millimeters; bw = black and white; c = color; min = minutes
fs	date and place where first shown

1965 THE CITY TRAMP (DER STADTSTREICHER)
ds: RWF. ph: Josef Jung. a: Christoph Roser, Susanne Schimkus, Michael Fengler, Irm Hermann, RWF. p: Roser Film. f: 16 mm, bw, 10 min.

A man finds a gun in an alley and tries to get rid of it.

1966 A LITTLE CHAOS (DAS KLEINE CHAOS)
dsed: RWF. ph: Michael Fengler. a: Marite Greiselis, Christoph Roser, RWF, Lilo Pempeit. p: Roser Film. f: 35 mm, bw, 9 min.

Three youths selling magazines get into a woman's apartment and rob her.

1969 LOVE IS COLDER THAN DEATH (LIEBE IST KÄLTER ALS DER TOD)
ds: RWF. ph: Dietrich Lohmann. m: Peer Raben, Holger Münzer. ed: Franz Walsch. a: Ulli Lommel, Hanna Schygulla, RWF, Hans Hirshmüller, Katrin Schaake. p: Antitheater-X Film. f: 35 mm, bw, 88 min. fs: 6/26/69, Berlin Film Festival.

A young thief, recently let out of prison, tries to be independent from the mob.

Dedication: "To Claude Chabrol, Eric Rohmer, Jean-Marie Straub, Lino and Cuncho"

KATZELMACHER
ds: RWF, from play by RWF. ph: Dietrich Lohmann. m: Peer Raben. ed: Franz Walsch. a: Hanna Schygulla, Lilith Ungerer, Elga Sorbas, Doris Mattes, RWF, Harry Baer, Irm Hermann. p: Antitheater-X Film. f: 35 mm, bw, 88 min. fs: 10/8/69, Mannheim Film Festival.

A foreigner ruffles the middle-class prejudices of young couples living in a bleak suburbia.

Dedication: "To Marie Luise Fleisser"

GODS OF THE PLAGUE (GÖTTER DER PEST)
ds: RWF. ph: Dietrich Lohmann. m: Peer Raben. ed: Franz Walsch. a: Harry Baer, Hanna Schygulla, Margarethe von Trotta, Günther Kaufmann, Ingrid Caven, RWF. p: Antitheater-X Film. f: 35 mm, bw, 91 min. fs: 4/4/70, Vienna.

Released from prison, a convict works his way back into the Munich underworld.

WHY DOES HERR R. RUN AMOK? (WARUM LÄUFT HERR R. AMOK?)
ds: Michael Fengler and RWF. ph: Dietrich Lohmann. m: Peer Raben. ed: Franz Walsch. a: Kurt Raab, Lilith Ungerer, Amadeus Fengler, Harry Baer, Lilo Pempeit, Hanna Schygulla. p: Antitheater-X Film. f: 16 mm blown up to 35 mm, c, 88 min. fs: 6/28/70, Berlin Film Festival.

An ordinary man suddenly kills his wife, son, and neighbor, and commits suicide.

1970 RIO DAS MORTES
ds: RWF, from an idea by Volker Schlöndorff. ph: Dietrich Lohmann. m: Peer Raben. ed: Thea Eymèsz. a: Hanna Schygulla, Michael König, Günther Kaufmann, Lilo Pempeit, Harry Baer. p: Antitheater-X Film. f: 16 mm, c, 84 min. fs: 2/15/70, German television.

A war veteran teams up with an old school friend to live out a childhood dream—the search for a treasure in Peru.

THE COFFEE HOUSE (DAS KAFFEEHAUS)
ds: RWF, from play by Carlo Goldoni. ph: Dietbert Schmidt, Manfred Förster. m: Peer Raben. a: Margit Carstensen, Ingrid Caven, Hanna Schygulla, Kurt Raab, Harry Baer. p: Westdeutscher Rundfunk. f: videotape, bw, 105 min. fs: 5/18/70, German television.

TV adaptation of RWF's stage adaptation of the Goldoni play.

WHITY
ds: RWF. ph: Michael Ballhaus. m: Peer Raben. ed: Franz Walsch, Thea Eymèsz. a: Günther Kaufmann, Hanna Schygulla, Ulli Lommel, Harry Baer, Katrin Schaake, RWF. p: Antitheater-X Film. f: 35 mm, c, 95 min. fs: 7/2/70, Berlin Film Festival.

Half-black Whity is overworked by the Nicholson family and is incited to free himself by murder.

Dedication: "To Peter Berling"

THE NIKLASHAUSEN JOURNEY (DIE NIKLASHAUSER FAHRT)
ds: RWF and Michael Fengler. ph: Dietrich Lohmann. m: Peer Raben, Amon Düül II. ed: Thea Eymèsz, Franz Walsch. a: Michael König, Michael Gordon, RWF, Hanna Schygulla, Walter Sedlmayr, Margit Carstensen, Kurt Raab. p: Janus Film. f: 16 mm, c, 86 min. fs: 10/26/70, German television.

A sixteenth-century religious reformer fights alongside a twentieth-century revolutionary.

THE AMERICAN SOLDIER (DER AMERIKANISCHE SOLDAT)
ds: RWF. ph: Dietrich Lohmann. m: Peer Raben (song "So Much Tenderness" by RWF). ed: Thea Eymèsz. a: Karl Scheydt, Elga Sorbas, Jan George, Margarethe von Trotta, RWF, Hark Bohm, Ingrid Caven, Kurt Raab. p: Antitheater-X Film. f: 35 mm, bw, 80 min. fs: 10/9/70, Mannheim Film Festival.

After serving in Vietnam, a German-American goes to Munich and is hired to commit a string of murders.

BEWARE OF A HOLY WHORE (WARNUNG VOR EINER HEILIGEN NUTTE)
ds: RWF. ph: Michael Ballhaus. m: Peer Raben. ed: Franz Walsch, Thea Eymèsz. a: Lou Castel, Eddie Constantine, Hanna Schygulla, Marquand Bohm, RWF. p: Antitheater-X Film. f: 35 mm, c, 103 min. fs: 8/28/71, Venice Film Festival.

A film troupe awaits the arrival of the director in an old hotel. He arrives to find nothing but chaos and struggles against all odds to get the film going.

RECRUITS IN INGOLSTADT (PIONIERE IN INGOLSTADT)
ds: RWF, from play by Marie Luise Fleisser. ph: Dietrich Lohmann. m: Peer Raben. ed: Thea Eymèsz. a: Hanna Schygulla, Harry Baer, Irm Hermann, Rudolf Waldemar Brem, Walter Sedlmayer, RWF. p: Antitheater-X Film, Janus Film. f: 35 mm, c, 83 min. fs: 5/19/71, German television.

The transient love affairs of soldiers stationed in Ingolstadt with the locals.

1971 THE MERCHANT OF FOUR SEASONS (DER HÄNDLER DER VIER JAHRESZEITEN)
ds: RWF. ph: Dietrich Lohmann. m: "Buona Notte" by Rocco Granata. ed: Thea Eymèsz. a: Hans Hirschmüller, Irm Hermann, Hanna Schygulla, Kurt Raab, Klaus Löwitsch, Ingrid Caven, Lilo Pempeit, Peter Chatel, El Hedi Ben Salem, RWF. p: Tango Film. f: 35 mm, c, 89 min. fs: 2/10/72, Paris.

Dominated by his mother and rejected by his one "great love," a fruit-and-vegetable peddler enters a loveless marriage and finally drinks himself to death.

1972 THE BITTER TEARS OF PETRA VON KANT (DIE BITTEREN TRÄNEN DER PETRA VON KANT)
ds: RWF, from play by RWF. ph: Michael Ballhaus. m: the Platters, the Walker Brothers. ed: Thea Eymèsz. a: Margit Carstensen, Hanna Schygulla, Irm Hermann, Eva Mattes, Katrin Schaake. p: Tango Film. f: 35 mm, c, 124 min. fs: 6/25/72, Berlin Film Festival.

A fashion designer lives with her secretary and searches for love in a lesbian affair with a promiscuous ingenue.

Dedication: "To the one who became Marlene"

WILDWECHSEL
ds: RWF, from play by Franz Xaver Kroetz. ph: Dietrich Lohmann. m: Ludwig van Beethoven. ed: Thea Eymèsz. a: Jörg von Liebenfels, Ruth Drexel, Eva Mattes, Harry Baer, Rudolf Waldemar Brem, Hanna Schygulla. p: Intertel. f: 35 mm, c, 102 min. fs: 12/30/72, Munich.

A tortuous teenage love affair that ends in pregnancy, imprisonment, and murder.

EIGHT HOURS ARE NOT A DAY (ACHT STUNDEN SIND KEIN TAG)
ds: RWF. ph: Dietrich Lohmann. m: Jean Gepoint. ed: Marie Anne Gerhardt. a: Gottfried John, Hanna Schygulla, Luise Ulrich, Werner Finck, Anita Bucher. p: Westdeutscher Rundfunk. f: 16 mm, c, 570 min (five-part TV series). fs: October 1972–March 1973, German television.

Days in the life of the Kröger family, at home, in the factory—romance, troubles, and all that schmaltz. A miniseries about the silent majority.

BREMEN FREEDOM (BREMER FREIHEIT)
d: RWF and Dietrich Lohmann. s: RWF, from play by RWF. ph: Dietrich Lohmann, Hans Schugg, Peter Weyrich. ed: Friedrich Niquet, Monika Solzbacher. a: Margit Carstensen, Ulli Lommel, Wolfgang Schenck, Walter Sedlmayr, Hanna Schygulla, Kurt Raab, RWF. p: Telefilm Saar. f: videotape, c, 87 min. fs: 12/27/72, German television.

The story of Geesche, a woman who murdered fifteen persons.

1973 WORLD ON A WIRE (WELT AM DRAHT)
d: RWF. s: Fritz Müller Scherz and RWF, from novel *Simulacron III* by Daniel Galouye. ph: Michael Ballhaus. m: Gottfried Hüngsberg. ed: Marie Anne Gerhardt. a: Klaus Löwitsch, Mascha Rabben, Adrian Hoven, Ivan Desny, Barbara Valentin. p: Westdeutscher Rundfunk. f: 16 mm, c, 205 min (two-part TV series). fs: 10/14/73 and 10/16/73.

A computer expert commits suicide in a world where computer projections have replaced reality.

NORA HELMER
ds: RWF, from play *House of Dolls* by Henrik Ibsen. ph: Willi Raber. ed: Anne-Marie Bornheimer, Friedrich Niquet. a: Margit Carstensen, Joachim Hansen, Barbara Valentin, Ulli Lommel, Klaus Löwitsch. p: Telefilm Saar. f: videotape, c, 101 min. fs: 2/3/74, German television.

Nora Helmer saves her family from financial ruin, but that's when her troubles begin.

FEAR EATS THE SOUL (ANGST ESSEN SEELE AUF)
ds: RWF. ph: Jürgen Jürges. ed: Thea Eymèsz. a: Brigitte Mira, El Hedi Ben Salem, Barbara Valentin, Irm Hermann, RWF. p: Tango Film. f: 35 mm, c, 93 min. fs: 3/5/74, Munich.

The love and marriage of a German housekeeper and a Moroccan immigrant laborer a generation younger than she, a union unappreciated by their friends and neighbors.

MARTHA
ds: RWF. ph: Michael Ballhaus. ed: Liesgret Schmitt-Klink. a: Margit Carstensen, Karlheinz Böhm, Gisela Fackeldey, Adrian Hoven, Barbara Valentin, Ingrid Caven. p: Westdeutscher Rundfunk. f: 16 mm, c, III min. fs: 5/28/74, German television.

Martha marries a sadist who tries to convince her she's crazy.

1974 EFFI BRIEST (FONTANE EFFI BRIEST)
ds: RWF, from novel by Theodor Fontane. ph: Dietrich Lohmann, Jürgen Jürges. m: Camille Saint-Saëns. ed: Thea Eymèsz. a: Hanna Schygulla, Wolfgang Schenck, Karlheinz Böhm, Irm Hermann, Lilo Pempeit, Ulli Lommel. p: Tango Film. f: 35 mm, bw, 141 min. fs: 6/28/74, Berlin Film Festival.

Young Effi is compelled by her parents to marry an older baron, which brings loneliness and tragedy into her short life. RWF narrates.

FOX AND HIS FRIENDS (FAUSTRECHT DER FREIHEIT)
d: RWF. s: RWF and Christian Hohoff. ph: Michael Ballhaus. m: Peer Raben. ed: Thea Eymèsz. a: RWF, Peter Chatel, Karlheinz Böhm, Rudolf Lenz, Karl Scheydt, Harry Baer, Kurt Raab. p: Tango Film, City Film. f: 35 mm, c, 123 min. fs: 5/30/75.

Fox, an unemployed carnival worker, is picked up in a public toilet by an antiques dealer, who introduces him into a homosexual milieu, where he is exploited and driven to suicide.

Dedication: "To Armin and all the others"

LIKE A BIRD ON THE WIRE (WIE EIN VOGEL AUF DEM DRAHT)
d: RWF. s: RWF and Christian Hohoff. ph: Erhard Spandel. m: Kurt Edelhagen. ed: Helga Egelhofer. a: Brigitte Mira, Evelyn Künnecke. p: Westdeutscher Rundfunk. f: videotape, c, 44 min. fs: 5/5/75, German television.

Musical performance by Brigitte Mira.

226

1975 MOTHER KÜSTERS'S TRIP TO HEAVEN (MUTTER KÜSTERS FAHRT
ZUM HIMMEL)
ds: RWF. ph: Michael Ballhaus. m: Peer Raben. ed: Thea Eymèsz.
a: Brigitte Mira, Ingrid Caven, Karlheinz Böhm, Margit Carstensen,
Irm Hermann. p: Tango Film. f: 35 mm, c, 120 min. fs: 7/7/75, Berlin
Film Festival.

*Mother Küsters's husband kills his boss and commits suicide. She turns
to the Communists to help clear his name, but the party uses the issue
for its own lowdown purposes.*

FEAR OF FEAR (ANGST VOR DER ANGST)
ds: RWF, from an idea by Asta Scheib. ph: Jürgen Jürges, Ulrich
Prinz. m: Peer Raben. ed: Liesgret Schmitt-Klink, Beate Fischer-
Weiskirch. a: Margit Carstensen, Ulrich Faulhaber, Brigitte Mira,
Irm Hermann, Armin Meier. p: Westdeutscher Rundfunk. f: 16 mm,
c, 88 min. fs: 7/8/75, German television.

*A housewife sinks into a depression during pregnancy. Drugs and
alcohol lead to a breakdown. Recovery is not much better.*

1976 I ONLY WANT YOU TO LOVE ME (ICH WILL DOCH NUR, DAS IHR
MICH LIEBT)
ds: RWF, from book *Lebenslänglich* by Klaus Antes and Christiane
Ehrhardt. ph: Michael Ballhaus. m: Peer Raben. ed: Liesgret
Schmitt-Klink. a: Vitus Zeplichal, Elke Aberle, Alexander Allerson,
Ernie Mangold. p: Bavaria Atelier. f: 16 mm, c, 104 min. fs: 3/23/76,
German television.

*A young man who wants only to please his wife and child turns to
violence for lack of love.*

SATAN'S BREW (SATANSBRATEN)
ds: RWF. ph: Jürgen Jürges, Michael Ballhaus. m: Peer Raben. ed:
Thea Eymèsz, Gabi Eichel. a: Kurt Raab, Margit Carstensen, Helen
Vita, Volker Spengler, Ingrid Caven, Ulli Lommel, Y Sa Lo. p:
Albatross Film, Trio Film. f: 35 mm, c, 112 min. fs: 10/7/76, Mann-
heim Film Festival.

*The "poet of the revolution," now suffering writer's block, begins to
plagiarize Stefan George. He "becomes" George, and when he is beaten
up by a pimp, he discovers that he enjoys pain.*

CHINESE ROULETTE (CHINESISCHES ROULETTE)
ds: RWF. ph: Michael Ballhaus. m: Peer Raben. ed: Ila von Hasperg,
Juliane Lorenz. a: Margit Carstensen, Andrea Schober, Ulli Lommel,

Anna Karina, Macha Meril, Volker Spengler, Brigitte Mira. p: Albatross Film, Les Film du Losange. f: 35 mm, c, 86 min. fs: 11/16/76, Paris Film Festival.

An executive and his wife are tricked by their handicapped daughter into going to their country house with their lovers on the same weekend. Then the child shows up, too, for a game of Chinese Roulette.

1977 BOLWIESER (aka THE STATIONMASTER'S WIFE)
    ds: RWF, from novel by Oskar Maria Graf. ph: Michael Ballhaus. m: Peer Raben. ed: Ila von Hasperg, Juliane Lorenz. a: Kurt Raab, Elisabeth Trissenaar, Bernhard Helfrich, Udo Kier, Volker Spengler, Armin Meier. p: Bavaria Atelier. f: 16 mm, c, 200 min (two-part TV series, later reduced to 112 min for theatrical release). fs: 7/31/77, German television.

Stationmaster Bolwieser is unjustly suspected by his wife of infidelity. She has an affair, known to everybody in town but Bolwieser. When he perjures himself to protect her, he ends up in jail, and she divorces him to marry her hairdresser.

WOMEN IN NEW YORK (FRAUEN IN NEW YORK)
ds: RWF, from play by Clare Boothe. ph: Michael Ballhaus. ed: Wolfgang Kerhutt. a: Christa Berndl, Margit Carstensen, Anne-Marie Kuster, Eva Mattes, Angela Schmid. p: NDR. f: 16 mm, c, 111 min. fs: 6/21/77, German television.

Forty New York socialites in search of love and beauty.

DESPAIR (EINE REISE INS LICHT-DESPAIR)
d: RWF. s: Tom Stoppard, from novel by Vladimir Nabokov. ph: Michael Ballhaus. m: Peer Raben. ed: Reginald Beck, Juliane Lorenz. a: Dirk Bogarde, Andrea Ferréol, Volker Spengler, Klaus Löwitsch, Alexander Allerson, Bernhard Wicki. p: Bavaria Atelier. f: 35 mm, c, 119 min. fs: 5/19/78, Cannes Film Festival.

A Russian emigré chocolate manufacturer, bored with his life, exchanges identities with a drifter he believes is his double, whom he promptly kills.

Dedication: "To Antonin Artaud, Vincent Van Gogh, Unica Zürn"

GERMANY IN AUTUMN (DEUTSCHLAND IM HERBST)
ds: RWF. ph: Michael Ballhaus. ed: Juliane Lorenz. a: RWF,

Armin Meier, Lilo Pempeit. p: Filmverlag der Autoren. f: 35 mm, c, 26 min. fs: 3/3/78, Berlin Film Festival.

RWF's is one of eight episodes in a film about life in West Germany under the threat of political terrorism.

1978   THE MARRIAGE OF MARIA BRAUN (DIE EHE DER MARIA BRAUN)
d: RWF. s: Peter Märthesheimer and Pea Frölich, from an idea by RWF. ph: Michael Ballhaus. m: Peer Raben. ed: Juliane Lorenz, Franz Walsch. a: Hanna Schygulla, Klaus Löwitsch, Ivan Desny, Gottfried John, Gisela Uhlen, Günter Lamprecht, Elisabeth Trissenaar, Isolde Barth, Peter Berling. p: Albatross Film, Trio Film. f: 35 mm, c, 120 min. fs: 2/20/79, Berlin Film Festival.

During the American occupation, Maria Braun kills a GI. Her husband takes the blame and goes to prison. Maria rises in the postwar world and inherits wealth. Her husband returns, but the love between them is gone.

Dedication: "To Peter Zadek"

IN A YEAR WITH 13 MOONS (IN EINEM JAHR MIT 13 MONDEN)
dsph: RWF. m: Peer Raben. ed: RWF, Juliane Lorenz. a: Volker Spengler, Ingrid Caven, Gottfried John, Elisabeth Trissenaar, Eva Mattes, Günther Kaufmann, Lilo Pempeit. p: Tango Film. f: 35 mm, c, 124 min. fs: 11/8/78, Montreal Film Festival.

The last five days in the life of a transsexual rejected by lovers and friends.

1979   THE THIRD GENERATION (DIE DRITTE GENERATION)
dsph: RWF. m: Peer Raben. ed: Juliane Lorenz. a: Volker Spengler, Bulle Ogier, Hanna Schygulla, Harry Baer, Vitus Zeplichal, Udo Kier. p: Tango Film. f: 35 mm, c, 110 min. fs: 5/13/79, Cannes Film Festival.

A political farce about self-styled terrorists with nothing better to do.
Dedication: "To a true lover—and hence, probably, to nobody?"

1980   BERLIN ALEXANDERPLATZ
ds: RWF, from novel by Alfred Döblin. ph: Xaver Schwarzenberger. m: Peer Raben. ed: Juliane Lorenz. a: Günter Lamprecht, Hanna Schygulla, Barbara Sukowa, Gottfried John, Franz Buchrieser, Elisabeth Trissenaar, Brigitte Mira. p: Bavaria Atelier. f: 16 mm, c, 933 min (14-part TV series). fs: 8/28/80–9/8/80, Venice Film Festival.

Ex-convict Franz Biberkopf tries to go straight, but his relationship with his lifelong friend Reinhold spells trouble.

LILI MARLEEN

d: RWF. s: Manfred Purzer and RWF, from autobiography *Der Himmel hat viele Farben* by Lale Andersen. ph: Xaver Schwarzenberger. m: Peer Raben. ed: Juliane Lorenz, Franz Walsch. a: Hanna Schygulla, Giancarlo Giannini, Mel Ferrer, Karl-Heinz von Hassel, Christine Kaufmann, Hark Bohm, RWF. p: Roxy Film, Rialto Film. f: 35 mm, c, 121 min. fs: 1/15/81, Berlin.

Wilkie, singing "Lili Marleen," becomes a Nazi-era superstar, but she loves a Jew.

1981 LOLA

d: RWF. s: Peter Märthesheimer, Pea Frölich, RWF. ph: Xaver Schwarzenberger. m: Peer Raben. ed: Juliane Lorenz, Franz Walsch. a: Barbara Sukowa, Armin Müller-Stahl, Mario Adorf, Matthias Fuchs, Helga Feddersen. p: Rialto Film, Trio Film. f: 35 mm, c, 113 min. fs: 8/20/81.

A newly arrived building commissioner is at odds with local real-estate speculators. But then he falls for Lola, a brothel songstress, and everybody gets what he wants at the price of integrity.

THEATER IN TRANCE

ds: RWF. ph: Werner Lüring. ed: Franz Walsch, Juliane Lorenz. p: Laura Film. f: 16 mm, c, 91 min. fs: 10/8/81, Mannheim Film Festival.

RWF's only documentary, filmed at a theater festival in Cologne in 1981. RWF narrates.

Dedication: "To Ivan Nagel"

VERONIKA VOSS (DIE SEHNSUCHT DER VERONIKA VOSS)

d: RWF. s: Peter Märthesheimer, Pea Frölich, RWF, from an idea by RWF. ph: Xaver Schwarzenberger. m: Peer Raben. ed: Juliane Lorenz. a: Rosel Zech, Hilmar Thate, Annemarie Düringer, Doris Schade, Cornelia Froboess, RWF. p: Laura Film, Tango Film, Rialto Film, Trio Film. f: 35 mm, bw, 104 min. fs: 2/18/82, Berlin Film Festival.

A journalist sets a trap for a craven doctor preying on lonely people, but the plan backfires tragically.

Dedication: "To Gerhard Zwerenz"

1982   QUERELLE

d: RWF. s: RWF and Burkhard Driest, from novel *Querelle de Brest* by Jean Genet. ph: Xaver Schwarzenberger. m: Peer Raben. ed: Franz Walsch, Juliane Lorenz. a: Brad Davis, Jeanne Moreau, Franco Nero, Laurent Malet, Burkhard Driest, Günther Kaufmann, Hanno Pöschl. p: Planet Film, Albatross Film, Gaumont. f: 35 mm, c, 107 min. fs: 8/30/82, Venice Film Festival.

A handsome, unscrupulous sailor is the idol of the waterfront.

Dedication: "To my friendship with El Hedi Ben Salem"

BIBLIOGRAPHICAL NOTES

By far the most complete RWF bibliography appears in the revised edition (1983) of *Rainer Werner Fassbinder,* of the Reihe Film book series published by Carl Hanser Verlag in Munich. It contains a packed forty-page listing of practically everything worth mentioning ever written by and about its subject in German, French, English, and other languages. The categories of material included are illustrative: everything published by RWF, books about him, interviews with him, articles, obituaries, a film-by-film listing of major reviews, and a separate bibliography on the controversy over *The Garbage, the City, and Death* (see above, pp. 94–95).

Apart from a large number of articles generated in 1985 by a revival of the same controversy (collected in *Die Fassbinder-Kontroverse oder das Ende der Schonzeit,* Königstein: Athenäum Verlag, 1986), there is little to add. In 1984, a slim volume of RWF's "essays and work-notes," some of them previously unpublished (including a fragment he was working on the night he died), was issued under the title *Filme befreien den Kopf,* Frankfurt: Veröffentlicht im Fischer Taschenbuch Verlag.

The following is a list of books I found especially useful:

Baer, H. *Schlafen kann ich, wenn ich tot bin.* Cologne, 1982.

Eckhardt, B. *RWF in 17 Jahren 42 Filme.* Munich, 1982.

Fassbinder, R. *Der Film "Berlin Alexanderplatz."* Frankfurt, 1980.

Fischer, R., and Hembus, J. *Der Neue Deutsche Film 1960–1980.* Munich, 1981.

Hanna Schygulla, Bilder aus Filmen von RWF. Munich, 1981.

Hayman, R. *Fassbinder: Film Maker.* New York, 1984.

Limmer, W. *RWF Filmemacher.* Hamburg, 1982.

Magrelli, E., and Spagnoletti, G., eds. *Tutti i film di Fassbinder.* Milan, 1983.

Pflaum, H., and Fassbinder, R. *Das Bisschen Realität, das ich brauche.* Munich, 1976.

Raab, K., and Peters, K. *Die Sehnsucht des RWF.* Munich, 1982.
Rayns, T., ed., *Fassbinder.* Rev. ed. London, 1980.
Schatten der Engel. Frankfurt, 1976.
Schidor, D. *RWF dreht "Querelle."* Munich, 1982.
Zwerenz, G. *Der langsame Tod des RWF.* Munich, 1982.

Finally, any record of English-language materials would probably include the following articles: "The Brilliant, Brooding Films of Rainer Fassbinder," by David Denby, *New York Times,* February 1, 1976; "Fassbinder," by Penelope Gilliatt, *New Yorker,* June 14, 1976; "Can Fassbinder Break the Box-Office Barrier," by Andrew Sarris, *Village Voice,* November 22, 1976; "Rainer Fassbinder: The Most Original Talent Since Godard," by Vincent Canby, *New York Times,* March 6, 1977; "The Savage World of Rainer Werner Fassbinder," by Ralph Tyler, *New York Times,* March 27, 1977; "Fassbinder and the Politics of Everyday Life," by Ruth McCormic, *Cineaste,* Autumn, 1977; "Fassbinder and Sirk," by Andrew Sarris, *Village Voice,* September 3, 1980.

INDEX

ROBERT KATZ is the author of several books, three of which have been the bases for films, including *Death in Rome,* which the *Chicago Tribune* called "a masterpiece of literature [and] a masterpiece of historical scholarship." Both the book and the film became an international *cause célèbre.* Katz was indicted in Italy to stand trial in a freedom-of-speech case involving the Vatican that was to last ten years. His book on the kidnapping and murder of Italian prime minister Aldo Moro, *Days of Wrath,* was nominated for a Pulitzer Prize, and the film version will soon be released in the United States. As a screenwriter, Katz has worked with Fassbinder and many other internationally known directors. A Fellow of the John Simon Guggenheim Foundation, he lives with his wife in Tuscany. He is currently Visiting Professor of Investigative Journalism at the University of California at Santa Cruz.